$\overline{x}$, $\sqrt{6}$

ROWE
BOOKKEEPING and ACCOUNTING
PRACTICE

Business Executives Depend On Accounting Records to Chart Plans for the Future.

ROWE

BOOKKEEPING and ACCOUNTING
PRACTICE

Revised by

J. W. ALEXANDER, C. P. A.

President, Professional School of Accounting
and Finance, Cleveland, Ohio

THE H. M. ROWE COMPANY
BALTIMORE   CHICAGO

•

List No. 100

Manufactured in the United States of America

What This Book Means To You

WHEN you study bookkeeping and accounting, you are on the ground floor of business. You are dealing with facts and figures on which decisions of far-reaching importance are made.

Without proper records it would be impossible to transact business. Every business man appreciates the value of the work performed by the trained bookkeeper and the professional accountant. He is dependent on them for the *figure information* which will enable him to conduct his business intelligently and successfully.

The old-time bookkeeper with his green eye shade and his high stool has faded out of the picture, along with the stage coach and the pony express. In his place, business today employs thousands of keen, alert, *trained* young men and women who know the principles and practices of modern-day accounting.

You should understand that accounting is very much more than keeping a record of what people owe the business man and what he owes to other people. Its real function is to furnish information for the future guidance and direction of business operations.

The course which is given in this book is built on this broad view of accounting in modern business. From it you will get not merely a knowledge of how entries are made in books of account, but you will also learn how to prepare and interpret the kinds of statements on which the business man bases his business policies.

You will begin your work by a study of Purchase transactions. You will examine and analyze an invoice, which is the evidence of a purchase. Next, you will be shown how purchases are recorded by the bookkeeper in a Purchases Book. The third step is an investigation, or analysis, of all the entries on a part of a page from a Purchases Book shown in the text. Finally, you will apply your acquired knowledge by recording a list of purchases.

You will continue your work by the same sort of study and practice applied to Sales transactions. Then you will learn how a business keeps records of money which it takes in and pays out. Such transactions are called Cash transactions.

When you have studied these three kinds of transactions—Purchases, Sales, and Cash—you will be given a series of unclassified transactions as they occurred in the business of a wholesale dealer in sporting goods. You will be asked to classify those transactions—to determine which are purchase transactions, which are sales transactions, and which are transactions that involve the receipt or payment of cash. When you have made that analysis, you will study the recording of each transaction as shown in the text.

These three books are called books of original entry because in them is made the first record of every transaction which falls into one of the three groups you have thus far studied. The next step is to transfer—or "post"—the entries in the three books to the Ledger, which is called the book of final entry. You will be shown just how this posting is done for all the transactions that have been recorded in the Purchases, Sales, and Cash books. Then you will learn how to take a Trial Balance from the Ledger, and how to prepare a Statement of Income and a Balance Sheet. Here you have, in miniature, the complete bookkeeping and accounting cycle.

In this step-by-step procedure you will find nothing difficult—nothing that careful study of the text and attention to your instructor's explanations will not enable you to master quickly. You will find that the language of the book is simple, to the point, and easily understood. The script illustrations will provide you with excellent models for your own work. In the Introduction, those illustrations are shown with blue and red rulings, just as in the books actually used in business.

What you are really doing in this text, therefore, is familiarizing yourself with the "Story of the Books." You will find that story an interesting and fascinating one. Resolve to learn the story as it is unfolded in this book. When you have done so, you will have obtained a fund of skill and knowledge which is a passport to a position and a foundation for progress and promotion.

The Publishers

CONTENTS

INTRODUCTION

PART ONE

ELEMENTARY ACCOUNTING

PART TWO

PARTNERSHIP ACCOUNTING

A Few Practical Suggestions

YOU want to make rapid progress and get worthwhile results from your study. To do so, you need to keep certain things in mind.

▼

1. NEATNESS. Your work is a picture of yourself. Anyone can determine some of the characteristics of a person by simply looking at that person's written work. *You* want to be known as a neat and careful worker.

▼

2. ACCURACY. Strive for 100% accuracy. The business man doesn't want a 95 per center or an 85 per center. He wants a 100 per center. One mistake in accounting may prove extremely costly, both to the employer and the employee.

▼

3. THOROUGHNESS. Be thorough. Don't be satisfied until you have finished the work assigned. Read and study thoughtfully. Don't allow yourself to become discouraged.

▼

4. COOPERATION. Remember that your instructor can't teach you unless you resolve to learn. Your cheerful assistance and hearty cooperation are necessary.

▼

5. PLAY THE GAME. Every chapter teaches a certain phase of bookkeeping and accounting which you will study under the direction of your instructor. Learn the game by playing it! Conscientious work on your part is playing the game.

▼ ▼ ▼

Work thoughtfully, accurately, and enthusiastically.
Do your level best all the time.

Introduction

Chapter 1—Recording Purchases

1. A merchant must purchase goods before he can sell them. When goods are purchased on account, an invoice which gives the amount of the purchase is prepared by the seller and sent to the purchaser. That invoice shows the amount which the purchaser owes the seller.

Illustration 1 shows an invoice received by Mr. Harper for merchandise which he purchased from Mr. Thompson.

		WIlkins 7865		No. 2
		GEORGE C. THOMPSON		
		Athletic Supplies		
		416-420 WILKINS AVENUE, GREENSBURG, PA.		

Sold to John R. Harper
Munhall, Pa.

Date   March 1, 19—
Terms 30 days

8	Reach Baseballs No. OJ		.90	7.20
5	Catchers' Mitts No. 33		5.48	27.40
10	Basemen's Mitts No. 4AB		5.75	57.50
2	Catchers' Masks No. 40S		2.20	4.40
				96.50

Illustration 1

PURCHASE INVOICE

2. Notice that the invoice gives the date of the purchase (March 1, 19—), the name and address of the purchaser (John R. Harper, Munhall, Pa.), the terms of the purchase (30 days), the quantity of each item purchased, the cost of each item, and the total amount of the invoice ($96.50). The expression *Terms 30 days* means that this bill becomes due and payable thirty days from its date.

11

Invoices are prepared by the seller and are received by the purchaser. It is from the invoices received by the purchaser that a record of his purchases is made in the book which the purchaser keeps for that purpose. It is called the *purchases book*, and only this one class of transactions—purchases—is entered in it.

3. Illustration 2 shows Mr. Harper's purchases book containing the entries for five purchases which he made during March. Notice that the total purchases are entered, and that the book is ruled to show that all the entries of this class for the month have been made. The first entry is for the invoice shown in Illustration 1.

PURCHASES BOOK

March, 19-

DATE	PAGE	ACCOUNT CREDITED	ADDRESS	TERMS	AMOUNT
2		George C Thompson	Greensburg, Pa.	3/1, 30 days	96 50
6		Charles A Frank	Butler, Pa.	3/5, 10 days	101 20
11		George C Thompson		3/9, 15 days	221 80
19		Robert B Weller	Franklin, Pa.	3/18, 20 days	182 40
27		Charles A Frank		3/26, 30 days	149 70
		Total Purchases			751 60

Illustration 2

Purchases Book

Note: The purpose of the column headed "Page" will be explained later.

How To Interpret Purchases Book Entries

4. Refer to Illustration 1. Mr. Harper's bookkeeper would read this invoice as follows: "Mr. Harper has purchased from George C. Thompson, 416-420 Wilkins Avenue, Greensburg, Pa., an invoice of goods dated March 1, amounting to $96.50, to be paid for in thirty days." He would pay no attention to the fact that Mr. Thompson is a dealer in athletic supplies. Neither is the other information on the invoice necessary to the record of *the essential facts of the transaction with Mr. Thompson.* If the bookkeeper were asked to make a memorandum of the transaction, he would write it about as follows: "Purchased from George C. Thompson, 416-420 Wilkins Avenue, Greensburg, Pa., an invoice of merchandise dated March 1, terms 30 days, amounting to $96.50."

5. By referring to Illustration 2, you will see that *all the essential facts* in the foregoing memorandum are included in the entry for this invoice.

The entry is dated March 2, the date on which the invoice was received. The items that make up the invoice are omitted from the entry because such invoices are kept on file by the purchaser and can be referred to for the items at any time. If the bookkeeper were asked when this invoice would become due, he would say, "Thirty days after the date of the invoice, or March 31"; that is, the invoice should be paid on or before that date. An invoice begins to mature from its date and *not from the date of its entry* in the purchases book.

Analysis of Purchases Book Record

6. Analyze the transactions recorded in the purchases book shown in Illustration 2 by answering the following questions. Write the answers in the form shown at the bottom of this page. Mr. Harper is transacting the business, and the transactions are to be studied from his viewpoint. In other words, you are acting as Mr. Harper's bookkeeper.

1. What were Mr. Harper's total purchases for the month, and how is the amount found?
2. If at the end of the month he had paid none of these invoices, how much would he have owed?
3. According to its terms, the invoice for the first purchase from George C. Thompson was due and payable in 30 days. On what date was it due?
4. What were the due dates of the invoices entered on the 6th, 11th, 19th, and 27th, respectively?
5. Which one of the invoices owed to Mr. Thompson became due first?
6. If Mr. Harper had paid each invoice as it fell due, how much cash would have been required to pay the invoices that matured during March?
7. If all invoices maturing during the month were paid by March 31, how much did Mr. Harper owe at the end of the month, whom did he owe, and how much did he owe to each?

Answers to Analysis of Purchases Book Record

1. $751.60. The amount is found by taking the sum of the items entered.
2. $751.60.
3. March 31.
4. March 15; March 24; April 7; April 25.
5. The invoice of March 9, due March 24.
6. $ 96.50
   101.20
   221.80
   $419.50, Total cash required.
7. Robert B. Weller $182.40
   Charles A. Frank   149.70
                $332.10, Amount owed at the end of the month.

Exercise 1

W. H. Fulton conducts a produce business. He buys from farmers and sells to grocers and other retailers.   He received invoices during the month of August for the following purchases:

Aug. 1 John Holmes, Woodlawn, Md., July 30, 15 days, $175.
      5 W. J. Dixon, Catonsville, Md., Aug. 4, 20 days, $155.40.
     14 John Holmes, Aug. 11, 30 days, $211.50.
     17 L. N. Wilson & Sons, Catonsville, Md., Aug. 16, 10 days, $98.70.
     21 W. J. Dixon, Aug. 20, 15 days, $74.85.
     24 John Holmes, Aug. 24, 30 days, $122.80.
     27 Walter Crampton, Ellicott City, Md., Aug. 27, 10 days, $74.20.

With the purchases book shown in Illustration 2 as a guide, write the entries for the foregoing transactions on a sheet of journal paper.   If necessary, rule additional vertical lines so that your journal paper will have the same rulings as are shown in Illustration 2.   When the seven items have been entered, find the total purchases and enter the amount as shown in Illustration 2.

In recording these transactions, be careful to make the writing neat and uniform in size.   Write the figures plainly and distinctly.   Do not make the capital letters too high.   They must be written within the ruled lines on the paper.   When you have completed your work, present it to your teacher for examination and criticism.

Analysis

On the bottom of the page containing the purchases book, write the answers to the following questions:

1. What were Mr. Fulton's total purchases for the month?
2. If on August 31 he had paid none of the invoices for goods purchased during August, how much would he have owed?
3. Do the total amount of purchases and the amount he would have owed agree?
4. What invoices became due and payable during the month?
5. If Mr. Fulton paid these invoices as they became due, how much did he owe on unpaid invoices on August 31?
6. What was the total amount of his purchases from each person during the month?
7. If he had paid the invoices as they fell due during the month, whom did he owe on August 31, and how much to each?
8. How much cash was required to pay the invoices that matured during the month?

Chapter 2—Recording Sales

7. After goods have been purchased and placed in stock, they are ready for sale. As the goods are sold, they are billed by the seller to the buyer. Illustration 3 shows an invoice sent by Mr. Mason to Mr. Andrews for goods which were sold to Mr. Andrews.

No. 1

AUTO
EVERYTHING FOR THE AUTO

ACCESSORIES

HENRY R. MASON

191-195 Jackson Street · Canton, Ohio

MAin 2567   ·   ·   **ROAD SERVICE**

Sold to R. L. Andrews
145 Walnut Street
Canton, Ohio

Date August 1, 19—

Terms 30 days

10	Super-Lift Hydraulic Jacks	3.50	35.00

Illustration 3
SALES INVOICE

8. Notice that this invoice gives all the details of the sale, and is similar in general form to invoices for goods purchased. A record of each invoice of goods sold is made in a book kept for that purpose. That book is called the *sales book*. Sales entries are, therefore, another *class* of entries in keeping books.

9. Illustration 4 on page 16 shows Mr. Mason's sales book containing entries for seven sales which he made during August. The total sales have been entered, and the book has been ruled to show that all the entries for the month have been made. The first entry is for the invoice shown in Illustration 3.

The form of the sales book differs little from that of the purchases book. The entry consists of the date, the name of the customer, his address, the terms of the sale, the number of the sale, and the amount. It is not necessary to show the items which make up the invoices because the billing clerk makes carbon copies of all invoices. The originals are sent to the

SALES BOOK

August, 19–

DATE	PAGE	NAME OF CUSTOMER	ADDRESS	TERMS	SALE NO.	AMOUNT
1		R. L. Andrews	145 Walnut St.	30 days	1	35 —
3		Manning & Co.	456 Elm St.	10 days	2	30 —
7		R. L. Andrews		15 days	3	1 28 25
13		Service Garage	Center Square	30 days	4	1 65 10
17		Archer & Crane	215 Poplar St.	10 days	5	4 22 50
20		Manning & Co.		30 days	6	2 67 10
27		R. L. Andrews		30 days	7	61 65
		Total Sales				11 09 60

Illustration 4
SALES BOOK

customers, and the carbon copies are kept by the seller and may be referred to if it is necessary to know the individual items that make up any invoice. A sale is entered *under the date it is billed*. The due date is determined *from the date of the invoice*.

Analysis of Sales Book Record

10. Transactions are analyzed in order to develop a thorough understanding of the *relations established* between the parties to the transactions. If you understand those relations, your work later on in the course will be greatly simplified.

In each analysis the questions presented should be considered from the viewpoint of the person whose books are being kept and not from that of the other party to the transaction.

1. What were Mr. Mason's total sales for the month, and how is the amount found?
2. If none of these invoices had been paid, how much would his customers have owed him at the end of the month?
3. Who owes for these sales, Mr. Mason or the purchasers?
4. What were the due dates of the invoices for goods sold?
5. What was the total of the amounts due from Mr. Mason's customers for invoices maturing in August?
6. What is the total of the amounts not due until the following month?
7. If Mr. Andrews paid his invoices when they became due, how much cash did Mr. Mason receive from him during August?
8. If all invoices falling due in August were paid, which customers continued to owe Mr. Mason on August 31? How much did each owe? What was the total owed to Mr. Mason at the end of the month?

Exercise 2

J. R. Carter is a wholesale dealer in radio supplies. He purchases his merchandise from various manufacturers, and sells to radio repairmen and retail dealers. His sales for the month of April are given below.

April 3 J. C. Warren, 211 Second Street, 10 days, 9 All-Wave Antenna Sets at $5.

  5 Thompson & Co., Market Place, 15 days, 3 10-watt A. C. Amplifiers at $30; 20 Type 6J7 Metal Amplifier tubes at $1.05.

  9 John H. Horner Co., 472 High Street, 20 days, 3 Cleartone Mantel Model Radio sets at $21.50.

  14 J. C. Warren, 15 days, 5 19-Plate Super Storage Batteries at $14.25; 10 RCA Duo Diode Tubes at $1.10.

  17 John H. Horner Co., 30 days, 2 Aero Generators at $46.25.

  18 J. C. Warren, 30 days, 3 Worldwide 5-Tube Receivers at $22.50; 25 RCA Super Power Tubes at $1.15.

  23 Thompson & Co., 30 days, 12 "B" and "C" Battery Packs at $7; 5 Console Model Acme Radio Sets at $44.

  26 Walker & Sons, 126 Paca Street, 30 days, 2 All-Wave Radios, Console Model, at $65.25; 50 "B" and "C" Battery Testers at $1.10; 20 Complete Antenna Kits at $2.

  29 John H. Horner Co., 15 days, 50 83-V Rectifier Tubes at 95c.

Record the foregoing sales in a sales book, using a sheet of journal paper. Foot and rule the book as shown in Illustration 4, page 16.

Analysis

1. What were Mr. Carter's total sales for the month?
2. If on April 30 none of the invoices for goods sold had been paid, how much would Mr. Carter's customers have owed him on that date?
3. Do the total sales and the amount that would be owed to him agree?
4. What invoices became due during the month?
5. If each invoice had been paid when due, how much would Mr. Carter's customers have owed him on April 30?
6. What were his total sales to each customer during the month?
7. If we assume that all invoices maturing during the month were paid on their maturity dates, how much did each customer owe him on unpaid invoices on April 30?
8. If Mr. Warren paid his invoices as they became due, how much of his indebtedness to Mr. Carter did he cancel?
9. If all invoices falling due in April had been paid, how much cash did Mr. Carter receive from his customers?
10. If the John H. Horner Co. had made no payments during the month except $100 on account, how much of the company's indebtedness to Mr. Carter would have remained uncanceled on April 30?

Chapter 3—Cash Receipts and Payments

11. Cash is received and paid in making settlement for goods bought and sold. Recording receipts and payments of cash is therefore another important part of the bookkeeper's work. Cash receipts and payments are recorded in the cash book.

Recording Cash Receipts

12. Cash receipts are entered on the *left-hand side* of the cash book. Each entry includes the *amount* (which should be written first), the *date*, the *name* of the party from whom the cash is received, and a brief *explanation* of the entry. Illustration 5 shows the entries for the cash received by A. S. Parker during January.

CASH RECEIPTS

DATE		PAGE	ACCOUNT CREDITED	EXPLANATION	AMOUNT	TOTAL
Jan.	2		Walter Brown	Inv. Dec. 22	50 —	
	5		F. H. Dixon	Inv. Dec. 7	126 19	
	11		J. B. Herrick & Co.	Inv. Jan. 3	35 20	
	14		Martel & Sons	¾ inv. Jan. 3	150 —	
	19		Walter Brown	Inv. Jan. 6	17 28	
	21		J. B. Herrick & Co.	Inv. Dec. 23	255 40	
	27		F. H. Dixon	Inv. Jan. 3	272 16	
	30		Martel & Sons	Inv. Jan. 3	61 45	
	31		Total Receipts for the month			967 68

Illustration 5

CASH BOOK (RECEIPTS)

Analysis

1. What was the total amount of Mr. Parker's cash receipts for the month?
2. What was the total amount of cash received from Walter Brown and from Herrick & Co. during the month?
3. The last receipt of cash from Martel & Son was in full. What was the total amount of the invoice of January 3, sold to Martel & Son?
4. How much cash was received for invoices sold in December?
5. How much was received for invoices sold in January?
6. How much of Mr. Dixon's indebtedness was canceled during the month?
7. If Mr. Parker paid out $500 of the total amount of cash received, what was the balance of cash on hand on January 31?

Exercise 3

On a sheet of journal paper, enter the following items of cash received by R. F. Emerson during July. Rule additional vertical lines if needed, as shown in Illustration 5. Foot the column in pencil, and then prove the addition. Next, write the total in ink, and rule the book as shown in Illustration 5.

July 2 F. B. Nelson, invoice June 22, $95.40.
     6 R. A. Fisher & Co., invoice June 12, $125.12.
    10 T. E. Young, invoice June 12, $57.50.
    12 F. B. Nelson, invoice June 11, $176.19.
    17 Carter & Harris, on account invoice July 7, $100.
    20 R. A. Fisher & Co., invoice July 3, $117.20.
    25 T. E. Young, invoice July 9, $67.28.
    28 G. E. Emery, invoice June 28, $189.45.
    31 Carter & Harris, in full invoice July 7, $76.20.

Analysis

1. What were the total receipts of cash for the month?
2. What were the amounts of cash received from F. B. Nelson, Fisher & Co., T. E. Young, Carter & Harris, and G. E. Emery?
3. If F. B. Nelson owed R. F. Emerson $345.12 on July 1, how much did Mr. Nelson owe on July 31?
4. If T. E. Young owed $124.78 on July 1, how much did he owe on July 31?
5. How much of the cash received from Fisher & Co. canceled the company's indebtedness on June invoices? on July invoices?
6. If the cash received from G. E. Emery on July 28 came on the day the money was due, what were the terms of the invoice?
7. How much did Carter & Harris owe on the invoice of July 7 after the payment of July 17 was received?
8. How much of the cash received applied on June invoices? on July invoices?
9. What is the difference between the meaning of "on account" and "in full of account"?
10. If Mr. Emerson had paid out $425.50 of the cash received during the month, what was the balance left on hand on July 31?

Recording Cash Payments

13. Cash payments are entered on the *right-hand side* of the cash book. The entries include the *amount* (which should be written first), the *date*, the *name* of the party to whom the cash is paid, and a brief *explanation* of the entry. Illustration 6 shows the cash payments made by Brown & Co. for the month of February.

CASH PAYMENTS

DATE		PAGE	ACCOUNT DEBITED	EXPLANATION	AMOUNT		TOTAL	
Feb.	1		James S. Allen	Inv. Jan. 22	75	—		
	5		Hill & Myers	a/c inv. Jan. 26	50	—		
	12		H.B. Thompson	Inv. Jan. 14	126	83		
	15		Hill & Myers	a/c inv. Jan. 26	75	—		
	17		James S. Allen	Inv. Feb. 3	103	20		
	20		H.B. Thompson	Inv. Feb. 12	62	19		
	25		Hill & Myers	Inv. Jan. 26	48	75		
	28		A.J. Bates & Co.	Inv. Feb. 2	225	40		
	28		Total Payments for the month				766	37

Illustration 6

CASH BOOK (PAYMENTS)

Analysis

1. What was the total of Brown & Co.'s cash payments for the month?
2. What was the total amount paid to each party?
3. The last payment to Hill & Myers was in full of account. What was the amount of the invoice purchased from the firm?
4. How much cash was paid for invoices purchased in January?
5. How much was paid for invoices purchased in February?
6. How much of Brown & Co.'s indebtedness to Mr. Allen was canceled during the month?
7. If the cash receipts for the month were $1,892.75, what was the cash balance on February 28?

Exercise 4

The following are the cash payments of John C. Watson for the month of July. Enter them in a cash book in the manner shown in Illustration 6, ruling on a sheet of journal paper additional lines if required. Then foot and rule the book.

July 1 Henry Miller, invoice June 5, $27.80.
      3 A. M. Gordon, invoice June 16, $36.25.
      7 Barnes & Co., to apply on June invoices, $100.
     12 Henry Miller, invoice June 14, $52.28.
     16 G. W. Richards & Co., on account invoice July 1, $125.
     19 Barnes & Co., in full of account, $89.23.
     25 Blake Bros. Co., invoice July 7, $142.82.

27 A. M. Gordon, invoice June 22, $59.20.
28 G. W. Richards & Co., in full invoice July 1, $69.90.
29 Henry Miller, invoice July 12, $97.50.
30 L. O. Cummins, invoice June 30, $105.60.

Analysis

1. What were the total payments for the month?
2. What were the total payments to Henry Miller, A. M. Gordon, Barnes & Co., G. W. Richards & Co., Blake Bros. Co., and L. O. Cummins?
3. If Mr. Watson owed A. M. Gordon $95.45 on July 1, what did he owe on July 31?
4. If Mr. Watson owed Henry Miller $211.85 on July 1, how much of this indebtedness remained uncanceled on July 31?
5. How much did Mr. Watson owe Barnes & Co. on July 15?
6. If L. O. Cummins was paid on the day his invoice became due, what were the terms of the invoice?
7. On July 31 how much did Mr. Watson owe G. W. Richards & Co. on the invoice of July 1? How much did he owe on July 20?
8. How much of the cash paid canceled June invoices? July invoices?
9. If Mr. Watson's cash receipts during the month were $972.66, what was the balance on hand on July 31?

Review Questions

1. Who prepares invoices for goods purchased, and who receives them?
2. Who prepares invoices for goods sold, and who receives them?
3. What does the expression *Terms 30 days* mean?
4. What is the purpose of the purchases book? of the sales book?
5. Why are the items omitted in purchases and sales book entries?
6. From what date is the due date of an invoice of goods purchased determined?
7. From what date is the due date of an invoice of goods sold determined?
8. What is the purpose of the cash book?
9. Where are cash receipts entered? cash payments?
10. What information does a cash book entry include?
11. Explain the meaning of the expression, "He canceled his indebtedness to me."

Chapter 4—Classification of Transactions

14. The transactions presented up to this point have been grouped in four classes; namely, purchases, sales, cash receipts, and cash payments. These four classes include by far the larger number of transactions in businesses in which profits are derived from the *buying and selling* of merchandise.

15. Grouping or classifying transactions is a part of the work of the bookkeeper. The transactions which follow are listed in the order in which they occurred without regard to their classification. They are classified and recorded properly in the purchases, sales, and cash books in the Model Set on pages 24 and 25. The transactions are those of J. M. Fuller, wholesale dealer in sporting goods, for the month of January.

Transactions—Model Set

Jan. 2 Bought of Samuel Howe, Greenfield, Pa., his invoice of December 31, terms 30 days, $125.

3 Sold to W. C. Archer, 12 Penn St., terms 10 days, 10 Select Cowhide Golf Bags at $13.60; total, $136.

5 Bought of J. K. Todd, Columbia, Pa., his invoice of Jan. 4, terms 30 days, $100.

8 Sold to Harry Carter, 219 Central Ave., terms 10 days, 15 Super Driver Tennis Rackets at $3.45, $51.75; 10 sets 9-ounce Boxing Gloves at $5, $50; total, $101.75.

10 Received cash from W. C. Archer to cancel invoice of Jan. 3, $136.

11 Sold to W. C. Archer, terms 20 days, 10 Regulation Size Volley Balls at $3.50, $35; 5 36-ft. Tennis Nets at $6.25, $31.25; total, $66.25.

16 Bought of Samuel Howe, his invoice of Jan. 15, terms 20 days, $156.

17 Received cash from Harry Carter in full payment of invoices sold him on Jan. 8, $101.75.

21 Sold William Martin, 925 Elm Street, terms 15 days, 5 doz. Medal Play Golf Balls at $6, $30; 5 sets Golf Driving Clubs at $6.25, $31.25; total, $61.25.

22 Sold to Harry Carter, terms 20 days, 15 pairs Tennis Shoes at $1.30, $19.50; 10 sets 3-piece Baseball Uniforms at $10.50, $105; total, $124.50.

24 Paid J. K. Todd to cancel invoice of Jan. 4, $100.

27 Received cash from Wm. Martin in partial cancellation of his invoice of Jan. 21, $35.

28 Paid Samuel Howe in full to cancel invoice of Dec. 31, $125.

31 Sold to W. C. Archer, terms 30 days, 5 Cowhide Striking Bags at $3.40; total, $17.

Illustration 7
A MODERN ACCOUNTING DEPARTMENT

Footing and Ruling Books in Model Set

16. Notice that the purchases and sales books are footed and ruled in the same manner as formerly. In footing and ruling the cash book, however, the *cash balance*, which is found by taking the difference between the total receipts and the total payments, is entered on the payments side and added to the total payments, as illustrated in the model cash book. This is done in order to show that the sum of the payments and the balance is equal to the total receipts. This process is called "balancing" the cash book. The footings showing this equality should always be entered on the corresponding line on the two sides of the book, even if several lines on one side or the other must be left blank in order to do so. The balance is then brought down to the receipts side under the footing.

PURCHASES BOOK

January, 19–

DATE	PAGE	ACCOUNT CREDITED	ADDRESS	TERMS	AMOUNT
2	1	Samuel Howe	Greenfield	30 days	1 25 –
5	1	J. K. Todd	Columbia	30 days	1 00 –
16	1	Samuel Howe		20 days	1 56 –
31		Purchases Dr.	Total Purchases		3 81 –

Illustration 8
Purchases Book (Model Set)

Analysis of Model Set Entries

By following the analysis below, trace each transaction below and on page 25 to the corresponding entry in the books.

Jan. 2 In this transaction merchandise is purchased; therefore, the entry is made in the purchases book, where such transactions are recorded.

  3 In this transaction merchandise is sold; therefore, the entry is made in the sales book, where such transactions are recorded.

  5 Merchandise is purchased—purchases book.

  8 Merchandise is sold—sales book.

  10 In this transaction cash is received; therefore, the entry is made on the receipts side of the cash book, where such transactions are recorded.

  11 Merchandise is sold—sales book.

  16 Merchandise is purchased—purchases book.

  17 Cash is received—cash book, receipts side.

  21 Merchandise is sold—sales book.

  22 Merchandise is sold—sales book.

  24 In this transaction cash is paid; therefore, the entry is made on the payments side of the cash book, where such transactions are recorded.

CASH RECEIPTS

DATE	PAGE	ACCOUNT CREDITED	EXPLANATION	AMOUNT	TOTAL
Jan. 19– 10	1	W. C. Archer	Inv. Jan. 3	1 36 –	
17	1	Harry Carter	Inv. Jan. 8	1 01 75	
27	1	William Martin	Inv. Jan. 21	35 –	
31		Cash Dr	Total Receipts		2 72 75
					2 72 75
Feb. 19– 1	✓	Balance			47 75

Illustration 9
Cash Book—Receipts (Model Set)

SALES BOOK

January, 19–

DATE	PAGE	NAME OF CUSTOMER	ADDRESS	TERMS	SALE NO.	AMOUNT
3	1	W. C. Archer	12 Penn St.	10 days	1	1 36 —
8	1	Harry Carter	219 Central Ave.	10 days	2	1 01 75
11	1	W. C. Archer		20 days	3	66 25
21	1	William Martin	925 Elm St.	15 days	4	61 25
22	1	Harry Carter		20 days	5	1 24 50
31	1	W. C. Archer		30 days	6	17 —
31		Sales Cr.	Total Sales			5 06 75

Illustration 10

SALES BOOK (MODEL SET)

27 Cash is received—cash book, receipts side.
28 Cash is paid—cash book, payments side.
31 Merchandise is sold—sales book.

Analysis

1. What were Mr. Fuller's total purchases from Mr. Howe for the month? What were the total payments to him? How much did Mr. Fuller owe Mr. Howe on January 31?
2. What were Mr. Fuller's total sales to Mr. Archer? How much cash was received from Mr. Archer? How much did Mr. Archer owe Mr. Fuller on January 31?
3. Which invoice was canceled by the cash receipt entered on January 17?
4. Which invoice was canceled by the payment entered on January 24?
5. Who received the money for the cash payment entered on January 28? Who paid it?
6. Who received the money for the cash receipt entered on January 27? Who paid it?

CASH PAYMENTS

DATE	PAGE	ACCOUNT DEBITED	EXPLANATION	AMOUNT	TOTAL
Jan. 24	1	J. K. Todd	Inv. Jan. 4	1 00 —	
28	1	Samuel Howe	Inv. Dec. 31	1 25 —	
31		Cash Cr.	Total Payments		2 25 —
31	✓	Balance			47 75
					2 72 75

Illustration 11

CASH BOOK—PAYMENTS (MODEL SET)

Chapter 5—The Ledger

17. Grouping transactions with persons. When you made the analysis of the transactions for the Model Set, called for on pages 24 and 25, it was necessary for you to refer to the purchases, sales, and cash books for the items of merchandise bought and sold, and of cash received and paid. You also found it necessary to make separate calculations to determine the final result of the transactions with each party. This work would have been greatly simplified if a separate record, grouping all the transactions with each party, had been kept. Such a record is provided in bookkeeping by keeping an *account* with each party with whom business is transacted. That record is kept in a book called the *ledger*. Accounts show similar items arranged in the most convenient form for arithmetical solution and analysis. The ledger is the book of accounts.

18. Personal accounts are records kept in the ledger with parties with whom business is transacted. The *object* in keeping personal accounts is to ascertain the amounts *others owe to us* on account, and the amounts *we owe to others* on account at any given time. All accounts with *individuals*, *firms*, or *corporations* showing amounts owed to or by them are classed, for bookkeeping purposes, as personal accounts.

Personal accounts are divided into two classes: (1) those showing what others *owe to us*, known as *accounts receivable;* and (2) those showing what we *owe to others*, known as *accounts payable.*

Posting

19. Any book which receives the *first entry* of a transaction, such as the purchases book, sales book, and cash book, is a *book of original entry*. The entries in books of original entry are transferred to the accounts in the ledger by a process called *posting*. The ledger is the book of *final entry*.

20. Posting from the Purchases and Sales Books. Illustration 12, page 27, shows the postings to the personal accounts in the ledger of the entries contained in the purchases book (Illustration 8) and the sales book (Illustration 10) of the Model Set on pages 24 and 25. Notice that all the entries in the purchases book are posted to the *right-hand*, or *credit*, side of the ledger accounts of the persons from whom goods were purchased, and that all entries in the sales book are posted to the *left-hand*, or *debit*, side of the accounts of the persons to whom goods were sold.

Samuel Howe

Greenfield, Pa.

					Jan.	2	12/31, 30 ds.	P	1		1 25	–
						16	1/15, 20 ds.	P	1		1 56	–

J. K. Todd

Columbia, Pa.

					Jan.	5	1/4, 30 ds.	P	1		1 00	–

W. C. Archer

12 Penn St.

Jan.	3	10 days	S	4		1 36	–					
	11	20 days	S	4		66 25						
	31	30 days	S	4		1 7	–					

Harry Carter

219 Central Ave.

Jan.	8	10 days	S	4		1 01 75						
	22	20 days	S	4		1 24 50						

William Martin

923 Elm St.

Jan.	21	15 days	S	4		6 1 25						

Illustration 12
LEDGER (MODEL SET)

21. As each entry is posted, the initial and page number of the book of original entry are entered in the ledger account, as shown in Illustration 12. The page number of the ledger account to which the item is posted is entered in the page column of the book of original entry. See Illustrations 8 and 10.

Analysis of Postings from Purchases and Sales Books

1. From what book is the credit of $125 to Mr. Howe's account posted?
2. What book contains the original entry for the posting to Mr. Howe's account dated January 16?
3. Where is the purchase item of January 5 posted?
4. From what book are the debit items to Mr. Archer's account posted?
5. What book contains the original entries for the items posted to the debit side of Mr. Carter's account?

6. From what book is the posting to Mr. Martin's account dated January 21 made?

7. What is the meaning of the symbols "S 4" and "P 1" in the accounts in Illustration ·12?

Debiting and Crediting Personal Accounts From the Purchases and Sales Books

22. Parties from whom goods are purchased on account are *creditors* of the buyer because he owes those parties until the goods are paid for. The buyer therefore *credits* the parties from whom he buys on account. The entries for such transactions in the accounts which he keeps with his creditors are *credit entries*. These credits record the buyer's indebtedness to his creditors. It is the universal custom to record credits on the *right-hand side* of ledger accounts.

23. Parties to whom goods are sold on account are *debtors* of the seller because those parties owe him until the goods are paid for. The seller therefore *debits* the parties to whom he sells on account, and the entries for such transactions in the accounts which he keeps with his debtors are *debit entries*. These debits record the debtor's indebtedness to the seller. It is the universal custom to record debits on the *left-hand side* of ledger accounts.

24. Posting from the cash book. The model ledger on page 29 shows the postings of the entries from the cash book in the Model Set (Illustrations 9 and 11) in addition to the postings from the purchases and sales books shown in Illustration 12. Note that all entries on the *receipts* side of the cash book are posted to the *right-hand* side of the ledger accounts of the persons from whom the cash was received, and that all entries on the *payments* side are posted to the *left-hand* side of the accounts of the persons to whom payments were made.

Analysis of Postings from the Cash Book

1. Where is the original entry for the debit of $125 to Samuel Howe's account?

2. Where is the original entry for the credit of January 9 in Mr. Archer's account?

3. To what account and to which side is the cash payment of January 24 posted?

4. To what account and to which side is the cash receipt of January 17 posted?

5. Where is the original entry for the credit of $35 to William Martin's account?

Samuel Howe
Greenfield, Pa.

| Jan. 28 | | C 3 | 125 – | Jan. 2 | 12/31, 30 ds P 1 | 125 – |
| | | | | 16 | 1/15, 20 ds P 1 | 156 – |

J. K. Todd
Columbia, Pa.

| Jan. 24 | | C 3 | 100 – | Jan. 5 | 1/4, 30 ds P 1 | 100 – |

W. C. Archer
12 Penn St.

Jan. 3	10 days S 4	136 –	Jan. 9	C 2	136 –
11	20 days S 4	66 25			
31	30 days S 4	17 –			
	83.25				

Harry Carter
219 Central Ave.

| Jan. 8 | 10 days S 4 | 101 75 | Jan. 17 | C 2 | 101 75 |
| 22 | 20 days S 4 | 124 50 | | | |

William Martin
925 Elm St.

| Jan. 21 | 15 days S 4 | 61 25 | Jan. 27 | C 2 | 35 – |
| | 26.25 | | | | |

Illustration 13
LEDGER (MODEL SET)

Debiting and Crediting Personal Accounts From the Cash Book

25. When cash is received from a debtor in full for a sum owed by him, that payment *cancels* the indebtedness; the party who makes payment ceases to be a debtor; and the parties stand in the same financial relation to each other as they did before they transacted business. The amount of the payment is entered in the cash receipts book, and is posted to the debtor's ledger account on the side *opposite* the debit entry to show that the indebtedness has been canceled and that the item has been closed out of the account.

26. When cash is paid to a creditor in full for a sum owed to him, the payment *cancels* the indebtedness; the party who receives payment ceases to be a creditor; and both parties stand in the same financial relation to each other as they did before they transacted business. The amount of the payment is entered in the cash payments book, and is posted to the creditor's ledger account on the side *opposite* the credit entry to show that the indebtedness has been canceled and that the item has been closed out of the account.

27. If a partial payment of an amount previously debited or credited to a personal account is made, that payment *partially* cancels the orginal debt, and the difference between the two amounts shows the balance still due on the original debt. This situation is illustrated in the account of William Martin (Illustration 13).

Ruling Out Canceling Items in Personal Accounts

28. Notice how the canceling items in the accounts in Illustration 13 are ruled out. The method of entering canceling items on the opposite side of an account and ruling them out has, therefore, been adopted to provide a convenient and permanent record.

Balancing Personal Accounts

29. The balance of an account is found by taking the difference between the sum of the debits and the sum of the credits. When there are two or more unpaid items on either side of an account, as in Mr. Archer's account (Illustration 13), the items are added and the total is written in small pencil figures directly underneath the last item. The balance is entered in the explanation column of the larger side on the line on which the last entry is made. If the debit side is the larger, the party owes the proprietor the amount of the balance. If the credit side is the larger, the proprietor owes the party the amount of the balance.

Rule for Debiting and Crediting Persons

Debit persons when we give them something on account (merchandise or cash).	*Credit persons when we receive something from them on account (merchandise or cash).*

Note: According to this rule, therefore, we *debit* our customers when we sell them merchandise on account, and we *credit* them when they pay us in full or on account. We *credit our creditors* when we purchase merchandise from them, and we *debit* them when we pay them in full or on account.

Procedure in Posting

The following procedure should invariably be followed in posting:

1. Post the amount first.

2. Next post the date and the explanation, if any. Make it a rule, when opening an account, to write *first* the year date in the date columns.

3. Enter in the ledger account the initial and the page number of the book of original entry from which the item is posted.

4. Write in the page column of the book of original entry the ledger page number of the account to which the item is posted.

5. Rule out canceling items as they are posted.

Impersonal Accounts

30. So far, the only ledger accounts considered have been accounts with persons; that is, *personal accounts*. In modern bookkeeping, records of the cost of merchandise purchased, of the income from merchandise sold, of the receipts of cash, of the payments of cash, and of the expenses of doing business are also kept in the ledger. These records are kept in the Purchases, Sales, Cash, and Expense accounts. Such accounts are *impersonal accounts*. Taken together, they show on one side the costs and receipts, and on the other the incomes and payments resulting from conducting a business. It is from the results of purchases, sales, and expense accounts that the final profit or loss is determined. Illustration 14 shows, in addition to the personal accounts previously illustrated, the impersonal accounts required in the ledger for the Model Set, pages 24 and 25.

31. The item on the debit side of the Purchases account is the posting of the total purchases from the purchases book. The item on the credit side of the Sales account is the posting of the total sales from the sales book. The debit item in the Cash account is the posting of the total receipts from the cash book, and the credit item is the posting of the total payments. As no expenses are recorded in the Model Set, no Expense account is required in the ledger.

Debiting and Crediting Impersonal Accounts

32. Purchases are invariably debited to the Purchases account. Sales are always credited to the Sales account. The total receipts of cash are invariably debited to the Cash account, and the total payments are always credited to the Cash account.

Samuel Howe
Greenfield, Pa.

Jan '19	28		C	3		1 25	-	Jan '19	2	12/31, 30ds	P	1		1 25	-
									16	1/15, 20ds	P	1		1 56	-

J. K. Todd
Columbia, Pa.

Jan '19	24		C	3		1 00	-	Jan '19	5	1/4, 30ds	P	1		1 00	-

W. C. Archer
12 Penn St.

Jan '19	3	10 days	S	4		1 36	-	Jan '19	9		C	2		1 36	-
	11	20 days	S	4		6	25								
	31	30 days	S	4		17	-								
		83.25													

Harry Carter
219 Central Ave.

Jan '19	8	10 days	S	4		1 01	75	Jan '19	17		C	2		1 01	75
	22	20 days	S	4		1 24	50								

William Martin
975 Elm St.

Jan '19	21	15 days	S	4		6	25	Jan '19	27		C	2		35	-
		26 25													

Purchases

Jan '19	31	Pur Bk Tot	P	1		3 81	-								

Sales

								Jan '19	31	Sales Bk Tot.	S	4		5 06	75

Cash

Jan '19	31	Total Rec.	C	2		2 72	50	Jan '19	31	Total Pay	C	3		2 25	-
		47 75													

Illustration 14
LEDGER (MODEL SET)

Equality of Debits and Credits

33. Refer to the purchases book (Illustration 8) and the ledger (Illustration 14) of the Model Set, and notice that the sum of the three items posted to the credit of the personal accounts from the purchases book is equal to the debit to the Purchases account for the posting of the total purchases. The entries in the purchases book, as posted to the ledger, expressed in itemized ledger form are therefore equivalent to the items shown under (3) on the next page.

Note: In modern bookkeeping, the total debits must equal the total credits. For every credit there must be one or more debits of equal value; for every debit there must be one or more credits of equal value.

Illustration 15
AN ACCOUNTANT AT WORK

(1) Purchases Book		(2) Ledger as posted		(3) Which is equivalent to—	
Samuel Howe 125.00		*Samuel Howe*		*Samuel Howe*	
J. K. Todd 100.00			125.00		125.00
Samuel Howe 156.00			156.00		156.00
Total Purchases	381.00	*J. K. Todd*		*J. K. Todd*	
			100.00		100.00
		Purchases		*Purchases*	
		381.00		125.00	
				100.00	
				156.00	
		Total debits 381.00	Total credits 381.00	Total debits 381.00	Total credits 381.00

34. Posting the *total* of the purchases book to the Purchases account, instead of posting *each item separately*, saved two postings. If there had been one hundred purchases during the month instead of three, ninety-nine postings would have been saved.

35. In like manner, the sum of the six debits to persons posted from the sales book is equal to or balanced by the total sales posted to the Sales account, and five postings are saved by posting the *total* instead of posting each item. Thus:

(1) Sales Book		(2) Ledger as posted		(3) Which is equivalent to—	
W. C. Archer 136.00		*W. C. Archer*		*W. C. Archer*	
Harry Carter 101.75		136.00		136.00	
W. C. Archer 66.25		66.25		66.25	
William Martin 61.25		17.00		17.00	
Harry Carter 124.50		*Harry Carter*		*Harry Carter*	
W. C. Archer 17.00		101.75		101.75	
		124.50		124.50	
Total Sales	506.75	*William Martin*		*William Martin*	
		61.25		61.25	
		Sales		*Sales*	
			506.75		136.00
					101.75
					66.25
					61.25
					124.50
					17.00
		Total debits 506.75	Total credits 506.75	Total debits 506.75	Total credits 506.75

36. Similarly, the three credits to personal accounts posted from the cash receipts book are balanced by the total receipts posted to the debit of Cash account, and the two debits to personal accounts posted from the cash payments book are balanced by the total payments posted to the credit of that account. If each item of cash received and paid had been posted separately to the Cash account, five postings would have been required instead of two postings for the totals, or three additional postings as shown on page 32.

(1)		(2)		(3)	
Cash Receipts		Ledger as posted		Which is equivalent to—	
W. C. Archer	136.00	Samuel Howe		Samuel Howe	
Harry Carter	101.75	125.00		125.00	
William Martin	35.00				
		J. K. Todd		J. K. Todd	
Total Receipts	272.75	100.00		100.00	
Cash Payments		W. C. Archer		W. C. Archer	
J. K. Todd	100.00		136.00		136.00
Samuel Howe	125.00				
		Harry Carter		Harry Carter	
Total Payments	225.00		101.75		101.75
		William Martin		William Martin	
			35.00		35.00
		Cash		Cash	
		272.75	225.00	136.00	100.00
				101.75	125.00
				35.00	
		Total debits	Total credits	Total debits	Total credits
		497.75	497.75	497.75	497.75

37. One of the objects, therefore, in classifying and recording transactions in the purchases, sales, and cash books is to reduce posting to the minimum, because the totals instead of the individual items can be posted to the Purchases, Sales, and Cash accounts.

38. If all the debit and credit items included in the three illustrations on pages 34 and 35 are brought together in their respective accounts, the accounts will appear exactly as they are in the Model Ledger, page 32. The right-hand columns headed (3) show a detailed analysis of the postings in the Model Ledger.

39. It follows, therefore, that when all items and totals in the books of original entry have been correctly posted to the ledger accounts, the total debits will equal the total credits.   It is for this reason that this method of keeping books is called *double entry bookkeeping;* that is, for each debit entry there are one or more credit entries of equal amount, or *vice versa.*

40. After studying the posting of the Model Set, you should understand, and be able to explain, the *double entry* posting of (1) the purchases book, (2) the sales book, and (3) the cash receipts and cash payments book.

Chapter 6—Preparation of Statements

41. The trial balance. Since the debit and credit items posted from each book of original entry are equal, it follows that after all balancing items have been ruled out of the accounts, the sum of the debit balances must equal the sum of the credit balances, as shown by the following list of accounts, with their balances, taken from the model ledger (Illustration 14).

Samuel Howe		156.00
W. C. Archer	83.25	
Harry Carter	124.50	
William Martin	26.25	
Purchases	381.00	
Sales		506.75
Cash	47.75	
	662.75	662.75

42. A trial balance is a list of *open* accounts in the ledger, with the balance of each account set opposite its name. The trial balance shows that the sum of the debit balances is equal to the sum of the credit balances. The foregoing list of balances is in reality a trial balance. Accounts that are in balance are not included in the trial balance. Illustration 16 shows the balances of the accounts in the model ledger set up in the regular form of a trial balance. The figures in the page column are the ledger page numbers of the accounts.

	J. M. Fuller			
	Trial Balance, Jan. 31, 19—			
1	Samuel Howe			156 —
1	W. C. Archer	83 25		
1	Harry Carter	124 50		
1	William Martin	26 25		
1	Purchases	381 —		
1	Sales			506 75
1	Cash	47 75		
		662 75		662 75

Illustration 16

TRIAL BALANCE (MODEL SET)

The trial balance shows the following results:

1. J. M. Fuller, the proprietor, owes Samuel Howe $156.   (Amounts owed by us to others are *liabilities*.)
2. Mr. Archer owes Mr. Fuller $83.25.   (Amounts owed to us by others are *assets*.)
3. Mr. Carter owes Mr. Fuller $124.50, which is an asset.
4. Mr. Martin owes Mr. Fuller $26.25, which is an asset.
5. Mr. Fuller's purchases for the month cost him $381.
6. His sales for the month were $506.75.
7. His cash balance is $47.75, which is an asset.   Assets also include what a person owns or possesses.

43. Profit and Loss Statement.   Since all the merchandise that Mr. Fuller bought during the month was sold, the cost of purchases as shown by the balance of the Purchases account, $381, is therefore the cost of goods sold.   Since the income from goods sold, as shown by the balance of the Sales account, is $506.75, the gross trading profit is the difference between these two amounts, thus:

Income from Goods Sold	$506.75
Cost of Goods Sold	381.00
Gross Trading Profit	125.75

This statement would be set up in bookkeeping form as follows:

J. M. Fuller
Statement of Profit & Loss for month of January, 19—

Income		
Total sales for the month	506 75	
Costs		
Less cost of goods sold	381 —	
Gross Trading Profit		125 75

Illustration 17
STATEMENT OF INCOME (MODEL SET)

44.   This profit is designated as the *Gross Trading Profit* because it is the profit which results from the buying and selling of, or trading in, merchandise.   Gross trading profit is defined as the difference between the *Income from Sales* and the *Cost of Goods Sold*.   If the cost of goods sold exceeds the income from sales, the difference is the *Gross Trading Loss*.

45.   It will now be of interest to ascertain where this profit of $125.75 is.   As Mr. Fuller began business without capital and now has a cash

_chap 6

balance of $47.75, which is so much capital, that much of his profit is accounted for in his Cash account, leaving $78 still unaccounted for. The trial balance shows that three of his customers still owe him for goods sold, and that he owes one creditor for goods purchased, thus:

Amounts Owed to Mr. Fuller (Assets)

W. C. Archer	$83.25	
Harry Carter	124.50	
William Martin	26.25	
Total		$234.00

Amount Owed by Mr. Fuller (Liabilities)

Samuel Howe		156.00
Net Amount Owed to Mr. Fuller		78.00

46. You will see that the remainder of Mr. Fuller's profit is represented in the difference between what others owe him and what he owes others. This exact amount would have been realized in cash if all sums owed to him and all sums he owed to others had been paid on or before January 31.

47. Balance sheet. When profits are determined, it is also customary to ascertain one's financial standing by preparing a Balance Sheet (also sometimes called a *Statement of Assets and Liabilities*). This statement is prepared from the accounts in the trial balance which show assets and liabilities. If the cash balance were included, the foregoing tabulation of amounts owed to and by Mr. Fuller would be his Balance Sheet. A complete statement, arranged in proper bookkeeping form, appears below.

J. M. Fuller
Balance Sheet, Jan. 31, 19—

Assets		
Cash	47 75	
W C Archer	83 25	
Harry Carter	1 24 50	
William Martin	26 25	
Total Assets		2 81 75
Liabilities		
Samuel Howe		1 56 -
Net Assets, or J. M. Fuller's Net Capital		1 25 75

Illustration 18
BALANCE SHEET (MODEL SET)

48. The difference between the sum of the assets and the sum of the liabilities is the *Net Assets*. Capital consists of assets. The net assets constitute the proprietor's *capital investment*, or *net capital*. In this instance the net assets are represented by, and are equal to, the profit for the month. Capital is accumulated out of profits. Losses, on the other hand, decrease capital.

Gross Profits and Net Profits

49. If during the month Mr. Fuller had paid various expenses, such as rent, fuel, and supplies, amounting to $47.60, out of his personal funds for which he had turned in no report, what would have been his *net profit*, and how would it have been found? The answer would naturally be $78.15, which is found by taking the difference between the gross trading profit and the total expenses.

There is a distinct difference between *gross profits* and *net profits*. The gross profits are the difference between the total sales and the cost of goods sold; the net profits are gross profits *less expenses*. There can be no gross profit unless the goods are sold for more than they cost. There can be no net profit if the expenses are greater than the gross profit. In the latter case the difference would be a *net loss*.

Review Questions

1. What is the object of keeping personal accounts?
2. Define *debtor; creditor*.
3. What are books of original entry?   Name those which have been discussed.
4. How are debit and credit items in the books of original entry transferred to the ledger?
5. On which side of ledger accounts are debit items posted?   credit items?
6. To which side of the personal accounts are the individual entries in the purchases book always posted?   Are the personal accounts debited or credited from this book?
7. To what account is the total of the purchases book always posted?   Is this total a debit or a credit item?
8. To which side of the personal accounts are the individual entries in the sales book always posted?   Are these accounts debited or credited?
9. To what account is the total of the sales book always posted?   Is this total a debit or a credit item?
10. To which side of the personal accounts are the individual entries in the cash book always posted?   Are these accounts debited or credited?
11. To what account are the totals in the cash book posted?   Which total is a debit item and which is a credit item?
12. What result does the Purchases account show?   the Sales account?   the Cash account?

Chapter 7—Practice Sets

Set 1

R. L. Clark began business in Springfield, Mass., on January 1, as a dealer in fruits and vegetables. He entered into a contract with John Reed, a farmer of Fairview, Mass., to supply him with fruits and vegetables for which Mr. Clark is to pay as soon as he receives returns from sales of these goods. Although he has no ready money to invest in his business, he hopes soon to accumulate out of his profits a sufficient cash capital with which to finance his operations.

While Mr. Clark is beginning business without any *capital*, such as *money* or *property*, the *accumulated profits of previous industry*—he has the advantage of a good *credit*. Credit consists of a good name—*a reputation for honesty, ability, and trustworthiness.* A good credit is essential in the successful operation of business enterprises because a large part of the world's commerce is conducted on a credit basis. In this instance, Mr. Clark's good reputation enables him to start in business for himself. If he is successful in his venture and through his industry earns profits and saves them, he will thus accumulate capital, or wealth.

The following is a memorandum of the business Mr. Clark transacted in January. Record these transactions properly in a set of books. Using a double sheet of journal paper, open the purchases book on the front outside page (page 1), the cash book on the two inside pages (pages 2 and 3), and the sales book on the back outside page (page 4). Rule the additional perpendicular lines required, as instructed in previous exercises.

Transactions

Jan. 2 Bought first invoice of fruits and vegetables from John Reed, Fairview, Mass., dated Dec. 30, terms 30 days, $180.

3 Sold W. B. Morgan, 240 Second Ave., terms 10 days, 25 bbls. Baldwin Apples at $3.30.

5 Bought of John Reed, invoice of Jan. 4, terms 30 days, $95.

8 Sold Heald & Co., 9 Exchange Way, terms 10 days, 50 bu. Potatoes at $1.20; 30 bbls. Baldwin Apples at $3.50.

13 Received cash from W. B. Morgan to cancel invoice of Jan. 3, $82.50.

14 Sold W. B. Morgan, terms 20 days, 10 bbls. Baldwin Apples at $3.35; 20 bu. potatoes at 95¢.

17 Bought of John Reed, invoice of Jan. 16, terms 30 days, $167.50.

17 Received cash from Heald & Co. to cancel invoice of Jan. 8, $165.

20 Sold Walter Williams, 316 Washington St., terms 10 days, 45 bbls. Baldwin Apples at $3.30; 60 bu. Potatoes at 97¢.

23 Bought of J. H. Cooper, Merrick, Mass., invoice of Jan. 21, terms 10 days, $27.

25 Received cash from Walter Williams to cancel invoice of Jan. 20, $206.70.

26 Paid cash to J. H. Cooper to cancel invoice of Jan. 21, $27.

30 Paid John Reed cash to cancel invoice of Dec. 30, $180.

30 Sold remainder of goods on hand to Walter Williams, terms 30 days, 50 bu. Potatoes at 95¢; 15 bbls. Baldwin Apples at $2.42.

31 Paid cash to John Reed to cancel invoice of Jan. 4, $95.

Footing and Ruling Books

Foot and rule the purchases and sales books as instructed previously. In the cash book enter the total receipts and the total payments in the right-hand money columns as formerly. Subtract the payments from the receipts to find the balance of cash on hand, enter the amount on the payments side, write the footings, rule the book, and bring down the balance in the manner shown in the cash book of the model set.

Analysis of Set 1

1. What were the total purchases from John Reed during the month? What were the total payments to him? How much did Mr. Clark owe him on Jan. 31?

2. What were the total purchases from Mr. Cooper? What were the total payments to him? How much did Mr. Clark owe him on January 31?

3. What were the total sales to Mr. Morgan? What were the total receipts of cash from him? How much did he owe Mr. Clark on January 31?

4. What were the total sales to Heald & Co? What were the cash receipts from the company? How much did the company owe Mr. Clark on January 31?

5. What were the total sales to Walter Williams? What were the cash receipts from him? How much did he owe Mr. Clark on January 31?

6. What invoice was canceled by the cash payment entered on January 30?

7. What invoice was canceled by the cash receipt entered on January 25?

8. For what amount did Mr. Clark become indebted to Mr. Reed, and how much of this indebtedness did he cancel during the month?

Note: The teacher should retain all papers handed in by the students for this set and the succeeding sets, because they must be returned to the students later on when additional work on the sets is called for.

On a single sheet of ledger paper open the personal accounts required. Allow six lines for each account, and post the entries from the purchases, sales, and cash books in the order named. Follow the procedure in posting described on pages 26 and 28.

When the posting has been completed, present the books of original entry and the ledger to your teacher for approval. After the posting has been approved, take a trial balance, and prepare (1) an Income Statement and (2) a Balance Sheet. Use Illustrations 17 and 18, pages 38 and 39, as Models.

When your work has been completed, hand it to your teacher for approval, together with answers to the following questions.

1. What is a trial balance? When is a trial balance prepared?
2. What is an Income Statement? a Balance Sheet?
3. From what source did you secure the information contained in the statements you prepared?
4. To what is the net capital equivalent?

Set 2

Adam Richards, of Marshalltown, Iowa, has made an arrangement with his friends among the farmers in his community to cooperate with them in securing satisfactory prices for their crops. As he does not have any capital, they agreed to sell him their grain, fruits, and vegetables on open account at prices which would cover the cost of production and a fair profit. Mr. Richards on his part agreed to devote all his time to finding a market for the crops at prices which would enable him to make a profit over and above the cost to him and the value of his time and labor. He has further agreed to pay the farmers as soon as he receives returns from the products sold.

His transactions for October are given below. Record them in the proper books, using a double sheet of journal paper as in Set 1. After all the entries are made, total and rule the books of original entry. Then post the items from the books of original entry to the ledger in the following order: purchases book, sales book, and cash book. Use a single sheet of ledger paper, allowing six lines for each account. Rule out balancing items as they are posted; then enter the balances of the open accounts in pencil figures on the proper side. Take a trial balance, and prepare an Income Statement and a Balance Sheet as in Set 1. When completed, present the work to the teacher for approval.

Transactions

Oct. 1 Received shipment of wheat, corn, and oats from J. H. Burch, Albion, Iowa, his invoice of Sept. 28, on account, $232.50.

     2 Sold Frank J. Darling, 12 Main St., on account 10 days, 25 bu. wheat at $1.60; 50 bu. oats at 75¢.

     3 Sold Muscatine Flour Mills, Muscatine, Iowa, on account 15 days, 125 bu. wheat at $1.58; 20 bu. corn at $1.25.

     6 Received shipment from John Roberts, Marietta, Iowa, his invoice of Oct. 5, on account, $249.

    10 Sold Henry Miller, Melbourne, Iowa, on account 15 days, 5 tons baled hay at $21.50; 50 bu. rye at $1.85; 40 bu. corn at 1.27\frac{1}{2}$.

    11 Received from Frank J. Darling cash for invoice of Oct. 2, $77.50.

    17 Received cash from Muscatine Flour Mills in full of account, $222.50.

    18 Paid J. H. Burch on account, $100.

    20 Sold Frank J. Darling, on account 15 days, 50 bu. oats at 77$\frac{1}{2}$¢; 3 tons baled hay at $21.50.

    21 Bought from Evan Douglas, Three Hills, Iowa, his invoice of Oct. 19, on account, $47.50.

    22 Received cash from Henry Miller to apply on invoice of October 10, $200.

    23 Sold Henry Miller, terms 15 days, 30 bu. wheat at $1.61; 15 bu. corn at $1.25.

    25 Paid John Roberts on account, $150.

    26 Sold Muscatine Flour Mills, on account 30 days, 50 bu. corn at $1.20.

    27 Paid J. H. Burch on account, $75.

    28 Received cash from Henry Miller on account, $100.

    29 Paid Evan Douglas in full for invoice of October 19, $47.50.

    31 Paid John Roberts on account, $50.

Chapter 8—The Journal

50. Three books of original entry—the purchases, sales, and cash books—have been introduced up to this point. In these books purchases, sales, and cash transactions, respectively, are classified and recorded. Another book of original entry, called the *journal*, is required in which to make entries for transactions which cannot be classified in the above-named books.

51. The journal was formerly used as a chronological record of business transactions, as shown in Illustration 19, page 46. The transactions from which the items in this illustration are recorded follow.

Jan.   2   C. C. Downs invested $6,000 in the electrical supply business.

      3   Purchased merchandise on 30 days' time from the Columbus Mfg. Company, $240.

      4   Paid rent for store, $125.

      5   Sold Jas. T. Brown merchandise, $210.

      8   Purchased merchandise for cash, $225.

    10   Received from Jas. T. Brown, $150 to apply on account.

    11   Cash sales for the day, $300.

    12   Jas. T. Brown reported defective merchandise included in his purchase of January 5. Mr. Downs allowed him a credit of $16.80.

    12   Paid Columbus Mfg. Company, $140 on account.

You can see that the journal form of record-keeping adds to the time, labor, and space needed. In actual practice, therefore, the journal is used only for the following kinds of entries:

1. Entries for unusual transactions and transactions which do not occur with sufficient frequency to justify the keeping of a special book in which to classify them.

2. Entries for goods purchased or goods sold which are returned for credit.

3. Entries for rebates and allowances on purchases and sales resulting from errors in pricing, or from shortage and damage claims.

Note: The page of the ledger to which each transaction is posted is shown in the page column (the column at the left). These figures are entered as each transaction is posted.

Illustration 20 shows the entries for C. D. Clarkson's unclassified transactions for April, which require entries in the journal. Mr. Clarkson is a retail dealer in chinaware and glassware.

January 2, 19—

Cash	6000 —	
C. C. Downs, Capital		6000 —
Investment in electrical		
supply business		
3		
Purchases	240 —	
Columbus Mfg. Co		240 —
Mdse. on 30 days' time		
4		
Expense	125 —	
Cash		125 —
Paid rent for store		
5		
Jas. T. Brown	210 —	
Sales		210 —
Sold mdse. on account		
8		
Purchases	225 —	
Cash		225 —
Purchased mdse		
10		
Cash	150 —	
Jas. T. Brown		150 —
Received cash on account		
11		
Cash	300 —	
Sales		300 —
Cash sales		
12		
Sales	16 80	
Jas. T. Brown		16 80
Allowed credit		
12		
Columbus Mfg. Co.	140 —	
Cash		140 —
Paid on account		

Illustration 19

April 5, 19—.

Sales			32	50	
F. G. Allen					32 50
Allowed credit on damaged					
water goblets					
6					
Forbes & Co.			21	25	
Purchases					21 25
Allowed credit on 5 chipped					
dinner sets					
17					
Sales			1	50	
Arthur Walker					1 50
Allowed credit for shortage					
of plates					
21					
Harrison Glass Co.			11	60	
Purchases					11 60
Rebate on salt and pepper					
shakers					

Illustration 20

MODEL JOURNAL

The journal entries in this illustration record the following transactions:

April 5 F. G. Allen returned to Mr. Clarkson for credit 5 doz. water goblets which were billed to him at $6.50 a doz. The glassware had been damaged in transit and was unsalable. Credit, $32.50.

      6 Mr. Clarkson returned 5 dinner sets to Forbes & Co., for credit at the cost price, $4.25 a set, $21.25.

   17 Arthur Walker claimed a shortage of 5 salad plates sold him on April 14. As he was charged 30¢ for each plate, Mr. Clarkson allowed him credit for $1.50.

   21 For selling over 100 sets of salt and pepper shakers during a special sales campaign in April, Mr. Clarkson received a credit of $11.60 from the Harrison Glass Co.

Analysis of Model Journal Entries

April 5 By returning these goblets Mr. Allen has decreased, or partially canceled, his indebtedness to Mr. Clarkson incurred when the goblets were sold to him. As Mr. Allen's account was debited at the time the sale was made, his account must now be credited, at the selling price, for the goblets returned. As Mr. Clarkson credited his sales account for the amount of the original sale, he must now debit that account for the selling price of the goblets returned because his income from sales is decreased by that amount.

The original sale amounted to $100. After the required sales book entry and the foregoing journal entry were made and posted to Mr. Allen's account and to the Sales account, these accounts would show a debit and a credit balance, respectively, of $67.50, as far as these two transactions are concerned, thus:

F. G. Allen		Sales	
100.00	32.50	32.50	100.00

April 6 By returning these dinner sets to Forbes & Co. Mr. Clarkson has decreased, or partially canceled, his indebtedness incurred when he bought the china. As Mr. Clarkson credited Forbes & Co. at the time he made the purchase, he now debits Forbes & Co. for the dinner sets returned, at their cost price. As he debited his Purchases account when he bought the china, he now credits that account because his cost of purchases is decreased by that amount.

17 The shortage in the sale decreases or partially cancels Mr. Walker's indebtedness to Mr. Clarkson, and therefore his account is credited. Mr. Clarkson's income from sales is decreased, and therefore he debits his Sales account.

21 The rebate partially cancels Mr. Clarkson's indebtedness to the Harrison Glass Co., and therefore he debits that account. The rebate decreases the cost of his purchases, and therefore Purchases account is credited.

52. Each debit and credit item is posted *separately* from the journal to the proper account in the ledger. It is not possible to post totals in a two-column journal because the items entered in this book are miscellaneous items affecting various accounts; that is, they are not all of one class such as the transactions grouped in the purchases, sales, and cash books.

Exercise 5

Make journal entries for the following transactions of C. B. Aiken, a wholesale drug dealer.

Aug. 4 He allowed J. M. Rose credit for a shortage of 25 lbs. of Powdered Boric Acid at 30¢, included in a sale to him on July 29, $7.50.

11 Clarke & Co. overcharged him 15¢ a bottle on 25 bottles of Cod Liver Oil which he purchased on July 28. He called attention to the overcharge and received a credit of $3.75.

15 Melton & Dane returned for credit 10 doz. Rolls of Adhesive Tape at $1.65 a doz., ordered by mistake. Mr. Aiken has allowed a credit of $16.50.

18 H. A. Rollins reported an overcharge of $1 a doz. on 5 doz. bottles of Red Cross Mouth Wash sold him on August 15. Mr. Aiken allowed him a credit of $5.

27 H. B. Knight returned 10 doz. tooth brushes, which were unsalable. Mr. Aiken gave him credit at $1.85 a doz., $18.50.

28 Mr. Aiken returned the tooth brushes to Fitch & Sons, and received credit at the cost price, $1.35 a doz., $13.50.

Comparison of Classified Entries and Journal Entries

53. Journalizing is the process of determining the accounts to be debited and credited in any transaction. It is closely related to determining the particular classification to which a transaction belongs. For instance, when a purchase is made, it is classified as a purchase transaction and consequently is entered in the purchases book. This procedure is *classification*. As a result of this entry, the party from whom the purchase is made is *credited* in his ledger account from the purchases book for the amount, and Purchases account will be *debited* for the same amount when the footing of the purchases book is posted, because it is included in that footing. This procedure is *journalizing*.

54. It was originally the practice to enter all transactions in the journal. This method required a separate debit for every purchase, a separate credit for every sale, a separate debit for every cash receipt, and a separate credit for every cash payment. It also required separate postings to the ledger for all these entries. This practice is unnecessary when the purchases, sales, and cash books are used.

55. It has been shown that posting the totals of the purchases, sales, and cash books to the Purchases, Sales, and Cash accounts in the ledger is equivalent to posting each item separately. In other words, posting these totals results in an equality of debits and credits in the ledger. It follows that an entry in the purchases book, sales book, or cash book is equivalent to a journal entry, so far as the final result in the ledger is concerned. For this reason these books are frequently referred to as the purchases journal, sales journal, and cash journal. For instance, the

Purchases

| "19– Aug | 1 | Inventory | | | 4286 | 25 | | | | | | |

Sales

| | | | | | | | "19– Aug | 1 | | | 825 | – |

J. M. Rose

| July | 29 | | | | 67 | 50 | | | | | | |

Clarke & Co.

| | | | | | | | "19– July | 28 | | | 250 | – |

Melton & Dane

| "19– Aug | 2 | | | | 165 | – | | | | | | |

H. A. Rollins

| "19– Aug | 15 | | | | 150 | – | | | | | | |

H. B. Knight

| "19– Aug | 7 | | | | 148 | – | | | | | | |

Fitch & Sons

| | | | | | | | "19– Aug | 3 | | | 118 | – |

Illustration 21
MODEL LEDGER

entry in the purchases book for the first purchase in the Model Set (Illustration 8) is equivalent to the following journal entry.

Purchases	*125.00*	
Samuel Howe		*125.00*

The entry for the first sale is equivalent to this entry.

W. C. Archer	*136.00*	
Sales		*136.00*

The entry for the first cash receipt is equivalent to this entry.

Cash	*136.00*	
W. C. Archer		*136.00*

The entry for the first cash payment is equivalent to this entry.

J. K. Todd	*100.00*	
Cash		*100.00*

56. Thus you will see that in whatever book of original entry transactions may be recorded the sum of the debits will equal the sum of the credits if the items are correctly posted to the ledger; consequently, an equality of debits and credits will exist, and a trial balance can be taken from the ledger accounts.

Exercise 6

1. Copy on ledger paper the accounts in Illustration 21.
2. Post to these accounts the items from C. B. Aiken's journal, which you have prepared.
3. Discuss the effect that these adjusting items have on each account.

Chapter 9—Cash

57. Cash includes coins, bank notes, U. S. Treasury notes, money orders, bank drafts, checks, and whatever else is received or given as money. Cash is the most important of the *mediums of exchange*. The objects in keeping the Cash account are to record the *receipts* and *payments* of cash, and to ascertain the *amount of cash that should be on hand*.

58. Cash receipts are entered on the left-hand, or debit, side of the cash book. Entries for cash receipts result in *debits to Cash account*, and *credits to the accounts named*, when the items of cash received are posted. Cash payments are entered on the right-hand, or credit, side. Entries for cash payments result in *credits to Cash account*, and *debits to the accounts named*, when the items of cash paid are posted.

59. The cash receipts and payments heretofore considered have been confined to cash received or paid in settlement of personal accounts. In many businesses money is also frequently received for merchandise sold for cash. The receipts from cash sales are entered as one item in the cash book, Sales account being credited.

60. Merchandise is also frequently *bought* for cash. As in the case of cash sales, the personal accounts are eliminated by charging the Purchases account and crediting Cash directly through a cash book entry.

61. Expenses such as rent, heat, light, insurance, taxes, salaries, and wages of employees, office and store supplies and stationery, are always incurred in conducting a business. The bills for such expense items are usually not entered on the books until they are paid, at which time they

Cash Receipts

19–					
Nov.	1	Balance			572 80
	2	Howard Black	Invoice of Oct. 23	55 40	
	6	Sales	Cash sales to date	14 25	
	30	Sales	Cash sales to date	10 20	
	30	Total Receipts			876 24
					1449 04
19–					
Dec.	1	Balance			466 83

Illustration 22
Cash Book (Receipts)

are charged directly to the Expense account. Some business men pay such bills immediately on their receipt, but in most cases it is the practice to pay them between the first and tenth of each month. The parties from whom expense bills are received, although they are creditors until these bills are paid, should be distinguished from the parties from whom merchandise comprising the stock in trade is bought. Bills from such parties are for supplies and services necessary in the conduct of the business, and do not cover commodities purchased for resale to customers. Personal accounts are not opened to record the indebtedness arising out of expense transactions. The bills serve as records of such indebtedness until paid.

Exercise 7

F. J. Ralston & Co.'s cash receipts and payments for November are given on this page and on page 54. The correct entries for the first six transactions are shown at the top of Illustrations 22 and 23. Classify the transactions mentally under the following classes:

(a) Receipt or payment in settlement of a personal account.

(b) Receipt or payment for merchandise bought or sold.

(c) Payment for an expense item.

Next, make the proper entries for the transactions in a cash book. Use a sheet of journal paper.

Exercise 8

Nov. 1 Balance of cash on hand, $572.80.

1 Paid Miles & Co. in full for invoice of Oct. 2, $26.70.

1 Paid the Jones Realty Co. for rent for store for November, $72.50.

2 Received cash from Howard Black for invoice of October 23, $55.40.

Cash Payments

19–					
Nov.	1	Miles & Co.	Invoice Oct. 2	26 70	
	1	Expense	Rent for November	72 50	
	3	Purchases	Cash purchase	8 —	
	5	Expense	Gas and light bill	5 40	
	25	Expense	Oil bill	37 50	
	30	Expense	Salaries, office force	372 —	
	30	Expense	Manager's salary	130 —	
	30	Total Payments			982 21
	30	Balance			466 83
					1 449 04

Illustration 23

CASH BOOK (PAYMENTS)

3 Paid Samuel Boggs, a huckster, $8 for 3 bbls. of apples, which were placed in stock.

5 Paid City Gas & Electric Co. for gas and electric light bill for October, $5.40.

6 Cash sales to date, $14.25.

8 Paid Central Provision Co. on account, $100.

9 Paid Chesapeake & Potomac Telephone Co.'s bill for telephone service for October, $6.45.

9 Received cash from Allen & Boyce for invoice of Oct. 21, $226.36.

11 Cash sales to date, $9.42.

12 Paid Office Supply Co.'s bill for office stationery and supplies, $13.26.

12 Received cash from Morton & King in full of account to date, $311.78.

17 Paid O. H. Barnes & Co. for invoice of November 8, $175.60.

20 Cash sales to date, $27.40.

22 Received cash from Howard Black in full of account, $175.19.

23 Cash purchases to date, $34.80.

25 Paid Enterprise Fuel Co.'s bill for fuel oil, $37.50.

28 Received cash from E. Brown & Sons for invoice of October 30, $46.24.

30 Paid salaries of clerks and office force, $372.

30 Paid manager's salary, $130.

30 Cash sales to date, $10.20.

62. The lower part of Illustrations 22 and 23 shows the way in which the cash book should be balanced. The balance at the beginning of the month is added to the total receipts to get the total footing on the receipts side, just as the balance at the close of the month is added to the total payments to get the total footing on the payments side. After these footings are entered and the book is ruled, the balance at the close of the

Cash Receipts

19–						
Jan.	1	*	Balance			129 85
	1		W. B. Ward, Capital	Additional cash investment	1500 —	
	11		Walter Crane	Invoice Dec. 3	78 22	
	18		W. B. Ward, Personal	Received for debt due him	10 —	
	31		Cash Dr.	Total Receipts		1588 22
						1717 07
19–						
Feb.	1		Balance			863 41

Illustration 24
CASH BOOK (RECEIPTS)

* Page numbers would be inserted when the accounts are posted.

month should be brought down under the date of the first day of the
following month.   The balance on November 1 is entered in the right-
hand column so that the left-hand column will show the total receipts for
the month.   Compare Illustration 9, page 24.

The cash receipts and payments of W. B. Ward for the month of
January are listed below and are recorded in the cash book, Illustrations
24 and 25.

Jan. 1 Balance on hand, $129.85.
    1 Mr. Ward made an additional cash investment of $1,500, to be
       credited to his Capital account.
    2 Paid Jameson & Fox for invoice December 5, $218.78.
    3 Paid rent for store for January, $50.   This is an expense item to be
       debited to Expense account.
    8 Paid Bowen & Co. to apply on invoice December 27, $275.
   11 Received from Walter Crane for invoice December 3, $78.22.
   11 Paid a bill of $20 for Mr. Ward, to be charged to his Personal account.
   15 Paid traveling expenses of Mr. Ward for a business trip out of the
       city.   This amount is an expense item, $11.60.
   18 Mr. Ward collected a personal debt due him of $10, and turned the
       money over to the business.   It is to be credited to his Personal
       account.
   22 Paid Bowen & Co. in full for invoice December 27, $269.60.
   28 Paid gas and light bill, $8.68.   This amount is an expense item.

Analysis

1. What was the cash balance on January 1?
2. What were the total receipts for the month?
3. How much cash would have been on hand January 31 if none had been
    paid out?

Cash Payments

19— Jan.						
	2	*	Jameson & Fox	Invoice Dec. 5	218 78	
	3		Expense	Rent of store for Jan.	50 —	
	8		Bowen & Co.	account invoice Dec. 27	275 —	
	11		W. B. Ward, Personal	Personal doctor's bill	20 —	
	15		Expense	Traveling expenses	11 60	
	22		Bowen & Co.	In full invoice Dec. 27	269 60	
	28		Expense	Gas and light bill	8 68	
	31		Cash Cr.	Total payments		853 66
	31		Balance			863 41
						1717 07

Illustration 25

CASH BOOK (PAYMENTS)

* Page numbers would be inserted when the accounts are posted.

4. What were the total payments for the month?

5. What were the total debits and credits to cash for the month?

6. To which side of the ledger accounts named are cash receipts posted? To which side are cash payments posted?

The following account shows how the total receipts and total payments are posted from the cash book to the Cash account in the ledger:

Cash

19–					19–				
Jan.	1	Balance		129 85	Jan.	31	Total payments		853 66
	31	Total receipts		1588 22					

Rules for Debiting and Crediting Cash Account

Debit Cash account for receipts.	Credit Cash account for payments.

63. The balance of the Cash account should always be a *debit* balance, *and should equal the amount of cash on hand.* It is a *current asset* that should be included in the Balance Sheet. The credit side of the account can never properly be the larger because it is impossible to pay out more cash than is received. "Overchecking" on the bank may result in a larger amount on the credit side. Overchecking, however, is a violation of banking rules, and the cash book should never be closed showing an overdraft.

64. To close. Find the balance and enter it on the credit side. Then foot and rule the book, and bring down the balance on the *opposite* side under the date of the next business day.

Exercise 9

Record the following receipts and payments of J. H. Bond in a cash book. Then balance the cash book.

Jan. 2 Balance on hand, $211.36.

     2 Mr. Bond made an additional cash investment of $2000 to be credited to his Capital account.

     3 Paid R. J. Hunt & Co. for invoice December 28, $179.20.

     4 Paid H. B. Wilson & Co. for invoice December 29, $139.85.

     5 Paid personal bill for Mr. Bond, which is to be charged to his Personal account, $36.

Jan. 6 Paid rent for store for January, $47.50.

8 Received from Charles Clyde for invoice January 2, $78.52.

11 Paid Archer & Crane, on account invoice January 6, $150.

15 Received from J. C. Lane for invoice January 6, $22.13.

17 Paid bill for office supplies, $18.25.

18 Received from A. H. Morton for invoice January 4, $135.42.

20 Paid Mr. Bond $75 to apply on his January salary, which is to be charged to his Personal account.

20 Received from Allen & Blake, on account invoice January 4, $100.

22 Paid H. B. Wilson & Co., in full of invoice of December 29, $275.80.

24 Mr. Bond sold some second-hand furniture, belonging to him, for $20 and turned the money over to the business to be credited to his Personal account.

24 Paid Archer & Crane in full for invoice January 6, $95.60.

26 Paid R. F. Fulton, on account invoice January 4, $125.

27 Received from Cole & Co. for invoice January 3, $187.50.

30 Received from Allen & Blake in full for invoice January 4, $72.16.

31 Paid clerk's wages for the month, $60.

Chapter 10—Practice Sets and Statements

Set 3

The farmers and truckmen residing in the vicinity of Jamestown, New York, have established a community canning factory in that city under the name of the "Cooperative Canning Company."

H. C. Miller, of Jamestown, has contracted with the canning company to assist in the marketing of the output of the factory. He will establish a trade among the stores in Jamestown and nearby towns and among the summer resort hotels located about Lake Chautauqua. That part of the factory's product which Mr. Miller does not sell will be disposed of to other dealers in canned goods.

Certain stocks of goods will be set aside in the factory for Mr. Miller, for which he will be billed at the time. As he is beginning business without capital, he will be allowed a term of credit of 60 days on his first month's purchases, which will give him time to collect for his sales before his bills for purchases become due. He will deliver orders directly from the factory to his customers at his own expense. His profit will be the difference between the price to him at the factory and the price he secures from his customers, less his expense of doing business.

His transactions for the month of September follow. Record them in the proper books of original entry. Use a double sheet for the purchases, sales, and cash books and a single sheet, numbered page 5, for the journal.

Transactions

Sept. 1 Received invoice dated Sept. 1, terms 60 days, from Cooperative Canning Co. for the first allotment of 180 cases of canned peas, corn, beans, and tomatoes, $624.50.

2 Sold E. W. Spencer, Ashville, N. Y., terms 10 days, 10 cases peas, 30 doz., at $2; 5 cases corn, 15 doz., at $1.75.

Note: Canned goods are usually packed at the canning factories in cases containing two or three dozen cans, depending on the size of the cans. They are always bought and sold by the dozen and should be billed accordingly.

3 Sold for cash one case tomatoes, $3.30.

4 Paid cash for billheads and postage stamps, $1.15.

5 Sold Chautauqua Lake Hotel, Bay View, N. Y., terms 20 days, 15 cases beans, 45 doz., at $1.85; 20 cases tomatoes, 40 doz., at $1.55; 6 cases peas, 18 doz., at $2.05.

8 Received cash from E. W. Spencer in full for invoice of Sept. 2, $86.25.

9 As Mr. Miller secured an order for canned cherries and the canning company had none in stock, he bought 5 cases for cash, $18.

Sept. 11 Sold L. M. Duff, Bemus Point, N. Y., terms 20 days, 25 cases corn, 75 doz., at $1.75; 20 cases tomatoes, 40 doz., at $1.57½; 12 cases peaches, 24 doz., at $2.65; 5 cases cherries,10 doz., at $2.55.

12 Paid cash for warehouse tools, $13.60.

13 Received invoice dated Sept. 11, terms 60 days, from Cooperative Canning Co. for 50 cases of canned peaches and pears purchased on that date, $181.

16 Sold for cash 2 cases peas, $12, and one case pears, $4.90; total $16.90.

17 Sold Chautauqua Lake Hotel, terms 30 days, 8 cases peaches, 16 doz., at $2.62½; 8 cases pears, 16 doz., at $2.55; 10 cases corn, 30 doz., at $1.75.

18 L. M. Duff returned for credit 10 cases corn, 30 doz., sold to him on Sept. 11. Mr. Miller has given him credit for $52.50.

20 Sold E. W. Spencer, terms 30 days, 15 cases peas, 45 doz., at $2; 20 cases corn. 60 doz., at $1.72½; 10 cases beans, 30 doz., at $1.85.

22 Chautauqua Lake Hotel claims an overcharge of 22½¢ a dozen on the 8 cases of peaches sold on Sept. 17. As the price agreed upon was $2.40, Mr. Miller has allowed a rebate on 16 dozen, amounting to $3.60.

24 Received cash from Chautauqua Lake Hotel in full for invoice of Sept. 5, $182.15.

25 E. W. Spencer reported that 1 case of corn (3 doz. cans) sold him on Sept. 2 was spoiled. Mr. Spencer was allowed a rebate at the selling price, $5.25.

25 Mr. Miller reported the case of spoiled corn to the canning company and was allowed a rebate for the cost price, $4.20.

26 Mr. Miller has purchased a supply of tomatoes from the Dunkirk Cannery, Dunkirk, N. Y., and has received invoice dated Sept. 20, terms 30 days, for $38.

27 Sold for cash to John Ensor, Ross Mill, N. Y., 8 cases peas and 5 cases beans; total sale, $70.65.

29 Mr. Miller has returned 21 cases peas, 42 doz., to the Cooperative Canning Co., and has received credit for them at the cost price, $1.75; total, $73.50.

29 Sold Central Hotel, Harfield, N. Y., terms 30 days, 9 cases tomatoes, 18 doz., at $1.55; 10 cases peaches, 20 doz., at $2.65; 9 cases peas, 27 doz., at $1.95.

30 Mr. Miller paid the canning company the September rent for the space in the warehouse occupied by his stock, $12.50.

30 L. M. Duff paid $150 on account.

30 Paid Cooperative Canning Co., to apply on account, $250.

30 Paid bill of Jamestown Transfer Co., for delivering orders to customers during September, $35.80.

30 Mr. Miller took out as his salary for September, $100.

After entering the foregoing transactions, foot and rule the books with the exception of the journal. Balance the cash book in the manner shown in Illustration 24. The journal is not ruled and footed because totals are not posted from this book.

Then post from the purchases book, sales book, journal, and cash book in the order named. Use a single sheet for the ledger, number the pages 1 and 2, and allow 8 lines for each account. Post the individual items first and then the totals. In posting to the Purchases, Sales, and Expense accounts, write an appropriate explanation of each item, such as "Cash purchase," "Cash sale," "Return," "Rebate," "Office supplies," "Tools," "Pchs. Bk. total," or "Sales Bk. total," in the explanation column.

After posting, find the balance of each account as previously instructed. Then take a trial balance, and present all papers to your teacher for approval. Save them carefully for future reference, when they are returned.

Statement of Profits

65. Mr. Miller sold all the goods purchased during the month. The accounts in the trial balance showing the results from which his profits are to be ascertained are the Purchases, Sales, and Expense accounts. His profit is determined thus:

Income from Goods Sold	*$1099.10*
Cost of Goods Sold	*783.80*
Gross Trading Profit	*315.30*
Expenses	*163.05*
Net Profit	*152.25*

Formal Profit and Loss Statement

66. Such a statement, containing trial balance figures only does not provide all the essential details of results from operations. It is the custom, therefore, in preparing such statements, to include a detailed analysis of the accounts showing incomes, costs, and expenses so as to show all the units of information, facts, and figures relating to the business transacted. This *Profit and Loss Statement* plays a most important part in the decisions of the management with regard to future operations and business policies, because it demonstrates to what extent past policies and methods of operation have been successful or unsuccessful.

67. The statement on page 61, showing the same final result as the foregoing Income Statement, was prepared from the same trial balance and from the data shown by the Purchases, Sales, and Expense accounts in the ledger.   It supplies in approved form the information lacking in the first statement.

Analysis of Profit and Loss Statement

1. This statement is divided into three sections under the captions, "Income from Sales," "Cost of Goods Sold," and "General Expenses."
2. The Sales account is analyzed in the "Income from Sales" section.   The item *Total Sales* is the credit footing of the account.   The items under *Deductions from Sales* are the *returned sales* debited to the account on September 18, and the sum of the *rebates on sales* debited on September 22 and 25.   The difference between the *Total Sales* and the sum of the *Deductions* is the *Net Income from Sales*.
3. The Purchases account is analyzed in the "Cost of Goods Sold" section. The debit footing of the account shows the *Total Purchases*.   The items under *Deductions from Cost* are the *purchases returned*, credited to the account on September 29, and the *rebate on purchases*, credited on September 25.   Since all the goods purchased have been sold, the difference between the *Total Purchases* and the sum of the *Deductions* is the *Net Cost of Goods Sold*.
4. The difference between the Net Income from Sales and the Net Cost of Goods Sold is the Gross Profit resulting from the buying and selling, or trading, operations and is therefore designated as the *Gross Trading Profit*.

H. C. Miller

Statement of Profit and Loss for month of September, 19 .

Income from Sales:			
Total Sales		1160 45	
Deductions from Sales:			
Returns	52.50		
Rebates and allowances	8.85	61 35	
Net Income from Sales			1099 10
Cost of Goods Sold:			
Total Purchases		861 50	
Deductions from Cost			
Returns	4.20		
Rebates and allowances	73.50	77 70	
Net Cost of Goods Sold			783 80
Gross Trading Profit			315 30
General Expenses:			
Tools and Supplies		14 75	
Rent		12 50	
Drayage Charges		35 80	
Proprietor's Salary		100 —	
Total Expenses			163 05
Net Profit for the period			152 25

5. The Expense account is analyzed in the "General Expenses" section. General expenses are the expenditures for services, materials, and supplies required in conducting the business as a whole. Notice that the first two items in the Expense account are grouped in the statement as "Tools and Supplies."
6. The difference between the Gross Trading Profit and the General Expenses is the *Net Profit* for the month.
7. Observe that the Net Income from Sales and the Net Cost of Goods Sold are the same amounts, respectively, as the balances of the Sales and Purchases accounts in the trial balance.
8. If the General Expenses had exceeded the Gross Trading Profit, the difference would have been the *Net Loss*. If the Net Cost of Goods Sold had exceeded the Net Income from Sales, the difference would have been the Gross Trading Loss, in which case the General Expenses would have been *added* to the Gross Trading Loss to find the Net Loss.
9. Observe that the preparation of this statement depends on an orderly and proper arrangement of the items, as well as on correct addition and subtraction. The statement is really a systematically arranged solution of an arithmetical problem.

From the trial balance and the ledger for Set 3, prepare a Profit and Loss Statement and a Balance Sheet. Refer to Illustrations 17 and 18, if necessary, for the proper arrangement of the items. Then submit the statements to your teacher for approval. The preparation of these statements completes the work of Set 3.

Exercise 10

From the following trial balance and ledger accounts, prepare the proper statements and present them to the teacher for approval:

A. B. Mellon
TRIAL BALANCE, JUNE 30, 19 .

Browning & Co.		316 28
Frank Ward	176 85	
Lee C. Lang Co.	26 20	
Hudson Grocery Co.		119 76
R. C. Lake	122 17	
Marton & King		59 60
Samuel Blake	38 40	
Butler & Co.	116 22	
Purchases	876 90	
Sales		1182 45
Expense	168 44	
Cash	152 91	
	1678 09	1678 09

LEDGER ACCOUNTS

Purchases

Cash Purchase	20 —	Rebate		5 25
Cash Purchase	5 60	Return		41 80
Pchs. Bk. Total	927 51	Rebate		29 16

Sales

Rebate	9 25	Cash Sale		5 80
Return	1 60	Cash Sale		3 20
Rebate	2 35	Cash Sale		8 46
Rebate	5 21	Sales Bk. Total		1186 40
Return	3 —			

Expense

Gas and Light	7 84
Drayage Charges	24 75
Rent	30 —
Sundry Repairs	15 85
Prop. Salary	90 —

Exercise 11

Refer to the comparison of classified entries and journal entries on pages 49 and 51 of the text. From this comparison you will observe that the entry for any transaction can be set up in journal form. For practice in determining the debit and credit items arising out of transactions, make journal entries for all the transactions in Set 3. In other words, work the set again, using the journal as the only book of original entry. Omit all explanations. This is a journalizing drill.

After all the entries are made, post them to a new set of ledger accounts, just as the items from the journal in the classified or regular set were posted. Allow twelve lines for the Sales and Cash accounts, and eight lines for the other accounts. Then take a trial balance. It should agree with the trial balance of the classified set.

With both sets before you, prepare answers to the following questions:

Comparison of Classified and Journalized Sets

1. Count the individual debit and credit entries in the classified set. How many are there?
2. How many postings to the ledger were required in this set?
3. Count the individual debit and credit entries in the journalized set. How many are there?

4. How many postings to the ledger were required for this set?

5. If you consider each individual entry and its posting to the ledger as two operations, how many operations were required to record and post the transactions in the classified set and how many in the journalized set?

6. Do the accounts in the two ledgers show the same balances? Do they show the same items?

7. Are there any differences between the personal accounts in the two ledgers as to the number and amounts of the items?

8. How do you account for the differences, if any, between the Purchases, Sales, Cash, and Expense accounts in the two ledgers as to the number and amounts of the items?

68. From the foregoing comparison you will observe that while the processes of recording transactions differ, the same final results are shown by the classified set and the journalized set. You will also see that the classified set is the more efficient method because of the saving in time and effort in making entries and posting them.

Set 4

Record the business transactions of J. T. Johnson, retail coal dealer. Follow the procedure outlined for Set 3.

Jan. 2 Mr. Johnson invested $7,000 in business.
    3 Bought coal of Scott Coal Co., Pottsville, Pa., $380.
    4 Sold Jas. M. Bowen, 18 Monroe St., terms 10 days, $54.
    4 Bought coal and coke of Best Coal Co., Pittsburgh, Pa., $450.
    6 Paid $85 for rent, and $6.50 for telephone service.
    6 Bought coal of Keystone Coal Co., Shamokin, Pa., terms 30 days, $250.
    8 Paid Best Coal Co. $250 on account.
    8 Sold C. C. Canady, 10 Main St., 10 days, $136.
    8 Received $195 for cash sales.
    9 Received $215 for cash sales.
  10 Paid City Transfer Co., $78.60.
  10 The Best Coal Co. allowed us $16 overcharge on invoice of Jan. 4.
  12 Sold Melbourne Hotel, terms 10 days, $220.
  12 Paid Best Coal Co., $184.
  16 Paid bill for stationery, $6.80.
  17 Received for cash sales, $128.
  17 Received $50 from C. C. Canady on account.

Jan. 18 Allowed Jas. M. Bowen $9 credit. We should have billed him $45 instead of $54.

19 Paid the Scott Coal Co. $180 on account.

20 The Scott Coal Co. has allowed us $28 credit. We reported that the coal shipped us was of a lower grade than the coal ordered.

21 Received from Melbourne Hotel $65 on account.

21 Received $250 for cash sales.

23 Sold T. G. Harper on account, $87.50.

24 Allowed T. G. Harper $2.50, error in weight of coal.

25 Received $290 for cash sales.

Exercise 12

After entering the foregoing transactions, foot and rule the books, etc., as in Set 3. Post, take a trial balance, and make out a Profit and Loss Statement. Present all papers to your teacher for approval.

From the trial balance and the ledger for Set 4, prepare a Balance Sheet. Submit it to your teacher for approval.

Summary of Principles

1. Bookkeeping is the art of classifying and recording business transactions and facts systematically.

2. The function of books of original entry is to provide a convenient and efficient method of classifying and recording the transactions of a business as they occur from day to day. They also serve as posting mediums from which the debit and credit items resulting from transactions can be readily transferred to ledger accounts.

3. When books are kept by double entry, an equality of debits and credits in the ledger is maintained by posting all entries in the books of original entry to the ledger accounts in such a manner that debit items will always be offset by credit items, or *vice versa*.

4. Entries in books of original entry do not assume the status of debits and credits until they are posted to and appear in ledger accounts.

5. The purpose of recording the various classes of transactions in separate books of original entry is to reduce posting to the minimum, because the totals of such books can be posted as offsetting debits or credits to the individual items posted from them.

6. The journal is the book in which are recorded the transactions that cannot be classified in other books of original entry.

7. Any entry in a book in which transactions are classified is the equivalent of a journal entry so far as the final result in the ledger is concerned.

8. No item should appear in the ledger that is not posted from some book of original entry, except cross entries which balance accounts.

9. The purpose of ledger accounts is to group the financial records of all transactions under their proper classifications.

10. With respect to the manner in which the rules of debit and credit apply to them, accounts may be classified as personal and impersonal.

11. Personal accounts include all accounts receivable with individuals, firms, and corporations showing what they owe to us, and all accounts payable with individuals, firms, and corporations showing what we owe to them.

12. Impersonal accounts include all other asset, liability, capital, income, profit, and loss accounts.

13. Capital is treated as a credit for bookkeeping purposes for the purpose of maintaining an equality between the debits for assets and the credits for liabilities.

14. A trial balance merely shows that in the ledger the total debits are equal to the total credits, but it does not prove the correctness of the ledger accounts, or of the balances which compose it.

Part One
Elementary Accounting

Part One (pages 67 to 161) provides material which correlates with Practice Set One. As the student proceeds with the work of that Set, he is referred to explanations and exercises in this Part of the text.

The following schedule gives a list of the accounts treated in Elementary Accounting, and shows the classification of accounts required for Set One.

ASSET, LIABILITY, AND CAPITAL ACCOUNTS

Current Assets:

Cash*
Merchandise inventory
Notes receivable
Accounts receivable

Fixed Assets:

Real estate
Furniture and fixtures

Current Liabilities:

Notes payable
Accounts payable

Capital:

Proprietor's capital account
Proprietor's personal account

PROFIT AND LOSS ACCOUNTS

Cost of Goods Sold:

Purchases
Freight in
Warehouse expense

Operating Expenses:

General expense
Real estate expense

Deductions from Income:

Interest expense

Income from Sales:

Sales

Additions to Income:

Interest income
Real estate income

* See Chapter 9, page 52.

Chapter 11—Principles and Practice

69. A business transaction is a matter, affair, or item of business completed or in process of completion. A financial transaction is a business transaction which involves an amount to be recorded in the books of account.

70. Transactions result from an agreement, or contract, between two parties. Each party under the terms of an agreement obligates himself to do certain things. For instance, a seller obligates himself to sell certain goods at a certain price and to ship or deliver them to the purchaser. The buyer obligates himself to accept delivery of the goods he purchases and to pay the seller for them.

71. "The essential idea of contract is that two or more persons voluntarily enter upon some engagement as to one another, which gives each person some right as to the future conduct of the other party or parties. By the same token, each party assumes some duty or obligation toward the other or others—an obligation which the law recognizes and enforces."

—Business Law.

72. When both parties to a contract discharge their obligations at the same time, they usually fulfil the terms of their agreement in one transaction. Frequently, however, one party does not perform his part of the agreement until some time after the other party has done so. The first party thus becomes indebted to the other until he does perform his part and thereby discharges his obligation under the agreement. In such cases two or more transactions are required to carry out the terms of the agreement.

73. Obligations or debts are thus created and discharged by the parties to the transactions which result from agreements between them. Records of the creation and discharge of such obligations or debts are kept in *personal accounts*.

Personal Accounts

74. Personal Accounts are accounts kept with *debtors* and *creditors*. The object in keeping personal accounts is to ascertain what our debtors owe us on account, and what we owe creditors on account, at any given time. The book in which accounts are kept is called the *ledger*.

75. A debtor is one who owes or is in debt. The amounts he owes are known as *debit* items in the account kept with him by his creditor.

76. A creditor is one who is owed. The amounts that are owed to him are known as *credit* items in the account kept with him by his debtor.

77. Only persons can be debtors and creditors, and the terms *debit* and *credit* in the sense of owing or being owed can be used only in connection with personal accounts. All accounts with individuals, firms, or corporations showing amounts owed to or by them are treated, for bookkeeping purposes, as personal accounts.

Accounts with Debtors

78. Accounts with debtors are those kept with parties who owe us and who will later *cancel their indebtedness* by paying us the amounts they owe. They will then cease to be our debtors.

The following transactions with A. J. Cloud are correctly recorded in the account with him which appears below:

Oct. 12 Sold him merchandise, terms 10 days, $375.80.
     20 Sold him merchandise, terms 30 days, $162.75.
     23 Received cash from him for invoice of October 12, $375.80.
     31 Sold him merchandise, terms 30 days, $441.20.
Nov. 19 Received cash from him for invoice of October 20, $162.75.

			A. J. Cloud	796 Market St.						
				San Francisco Calif.						
Oct. '19	12	10 days	S		375	80	Oct. '19	23	Cancelled	C		375	80
	20	30 days	S		162	75	Nov.	19		C		162	75
	31	30 days	S		441	20							

Illustration 26
DEBTOR'S ACCOUNT

Analysis

1. Is this an account with a debtor or with a creditor?
2. For what amounts did Mr. Cloud become indebted to us?
3. How much of this indebtedness has been paid and canceled?
4. How much remains unpaid?
5. Is Mr. Cloud a debtor or a creditor for this amount?

79. It is therefore evident that in accounts with debtors there are two classes of items—*debit* items for the amounts for which they have become indebted to us, and *credit* items which wholly or partially cancel such indebtedness. As a matter of custom, debit items are always entered on the left-hand side and credit items on the right-hand side of ledger accounts. Canceling, or balancing, items are ruled out when they are entered, as shown in Illustration 26.

Rules for Debiting and Crediting Accounts with Debtors

Debit their accounts for all amounts they owe us.	*Credit their accounts for all items which wholly or partially cancel debit items in their accounts.*

Exercise 13

Prepare an account from the following transactions with Robert G. Burns, 120 N. Green St., your town or city. Rule out balancing items as they are entered.

Sept. 2 Sold him merchandise, $40.
    4 Sold him merchandise, $126.42.
    9 Received cash for invoice of Sept. 2, $40.
   10 He returned goods for credit on invoice of Sept. 4, $12.30.
   12 Sold him merchandise, $56.20.
   14 Received cash for balance due on invoice of Sept. 4, $114.12.
   15 Sold him merchandise, $125.90.
   16 Billed him for undercharge on invoice of Sept. 15, $3.68.
   23 Sold him merchandise, $176.80.
   27 Allowed him credit for defective goods on invoice of Sept. 12, $7.50.

Exercise 14

Transactions with Bell Bros., 19 Exchange Way, Columbus, Ohio.

Oct. 1 Sold them merchandise, $126.40.
    2 Billed them for freight prepaid on goods billed Oct. 1, $5.42.
    7 Sold them merchandise, $198.25.
    8 Allowed them credit for overcharge on invoice of Oct. 1, $9.36.
   12 Received cash for balance due on invoice of Oct. 1, including freight charged on the shipment, $122.46.
   15 Sold them merchandise, $272.80.
   17 They billed us for goods returned for credit on invoice of Oct. 7, $17.09.
   23 Sold them merchandise, $85.40.
   24 Billed them for express charges prepaid on invoice of Oct. 23, $4.75.
   27 Received cash for invoice of Oct. 15, $272.80.
   30 Received bill from them for shortage on invoice of Oct. 23 and allowed credit, $3.75.

Accounts with Creditors

80. Accounts with creditors are those kept with parties whom we owe and to whom we shall later *cancel our indebtedness* by paying them the amounts we owe. They will then cease to be our creditors.

The following transactions with the John S. Wilson Company are correctly recorded in the account shown below.

Aug. 12 Bought merchandise from the company, invoice of Aug. 6, terms 30 days, $74.20.

Sept. 3 Bought merchandise, invoice of Aug. 30, terms 30 days, $316.12.
5 Paid cash for invoice of August 6, $74.20.

John S. Wilson Co. Catonsville, Md.									
Sept. 5			C		74 20	Aug. 12	Aug. 6, 30 ds. P		74 20
						Sept. 3	Aug. 30, 30 ds. P		316 12

Illustration 27
CREDITOR'S ACCOUNT

Analysis

1. Is this an acount with a debtor or with a creditor?
2. For what amounts did we become indebted to the John S. Wilson Co.?
3. How much of this indebtedess has been paid and canceled?
4. How much remains unpaid?
5. Is the John S. Wilson Co. a debtor or a creditor for this amount?

81. It is evident that in accounts with creditors there are two classes of items—*credit* items for the amounts for which we have become indebted to them, and *debit* items which wholly or partially cancel such indebtedness.

Rules for Debiting and Crediting Accounts with Creditors

Debit their accounts for all items which wholly or partially cancel credit items in their accounts.	*Credit their accounts for all amounts owed to them.*

Exercise 15

Prepare an account from the following transactions with M. C. Morgan, 1242 Eighth Ave., your town or city. Rule out canceling items as they are entered.

Sept. 3 Bought merchandise from him, $342.50.
       7 Bought merchandise from him, $72.16.
      10 Paid cash for bill of Sept. 3, $342.50.
      12 Received credit for goods returned on invoice of Sept. 7, $12.40.
      15 Bought merchandise from him, $158.55.
      19 Paid cash for balance due him on invoice of Sept. 7, $59.76.
      21 Bought merchandise from him, $221.20.
      24 Billed him for overcharge on invoice of Sept. 15, $28.80.
      28 Bought merchandise from him, $36.25.
      30 Received credit for damaged goods on invoice of Sept. 21, $11.80.

Exercise 16

Transactions with Rodney, Gates & Co., 12 Pine St., Philadelphia, Pa.

Oct. 2 Bought merchandise from the company, $278.50.
      3 Received bill for freight prepaid on bill of Oct. 2, $21.46.
      7 Bought merchandise, $109.21.
      8 Billed the company for goods returned because they were not of the grade ordered, $35.27.
      8 Paid cash for balance due on invoice of Oct. 2, $264.69.
     10 Bought merchandise, $326.18.
     11 Billed for freight on invoice of Oct. 7 which the company was to prepay according to the terms of the purchase, $5.92.
     12 Bought merchandise, $158.20.
     20 Received credit for overcharge on invoice of Oct. 12, $28.80.
     22 Paid balance due on invoice of Oct. 7, $103.29.
     26 Bought merchandise, $37.50.
     30 Paid balance due on invoice of Oct. 12, $129.40.

82. The balance of an account is the difference between the sum of the debits and the sum of the credits. When the balance of a personal account is to be determined, canceled items may usually be eliminated from the calculation, in which case the difference between the sums of the uncanceled items on the two sides of the account is the balance of the account.

What the Balance of a Personal Account Shows

83. The balance of a personal account is the amount owed to us or by us. If the *debit* side is the larger, the balance is the amount owed to us, which, if it is not past due, is a *current asset*. Current assets are cash and other assets which can be quickly converted into cash. If the *credit* side is the larger, the balance is the amount owed by us, which is a *current liability*. Current liabilities are short-time debts. In either case the balance should appear as an item in the Balance Sheet. Accounts with debtors and accounts with creditors are often referred to as *accounts receivable* and *accounts payable*, respectively.

Ruling Personal Accounts

84. The proper ruling for a personal account depends on the method followed in the payment of invoices. Accounts are usually paid in one of four ways: (1) each item or invoice may be paid separately; (2) several items or invoices may be paid at one time; (3) one item or invoice may be paid in two or more payments; and (4) payments may be made "on account" but not in full settlement of any particular item or invoice. The latter is the method employed in "running accounts." Any one or more of these various methods of payment may be shown in a single account. The accounts shown in Illustrations 28, 29, and 30 illustrate the various methods of payment referred to and the proper rulings for each.

The Park Grocery Co. account illustrates the methods of payments described in (1) and (2). It shows that the item debited on March 6 was paid on March 16; that the item debited on March 12 was paid on March 23; and that the item debited on March 15 was paid on March 30. The items of March 25 and 29 were paid on April 7 in one amount. The lines were ruled underneath the balancing items as each credit entry was made. The items of April 5 and 24 are unpaid, and their sum, shown in pencil figures, is the balance of the account. This is an *account receivable*.

Park Grocery Co.

33 Elm St.

Mar. 19	6	Mdse.		34	40	Mar. 19	16	Cash	34	40
	12	"		109	48		23	"	109	48
	15	"		68	19		30	"	68	19
	25	"		16	45	Apr.	7	"	145	32
	29	"		128	87					
Apr.	5	"		83	37					
	24	"		12	21					

Illustration 28

Dodge Electrical Supply Co. 139 Water St.

19—						19					
Sept.	5	Cash		45	95	Aug.	12	Mdse.		12	98
							16	"		23	36
							25	"		9	61
						Sept	3	"		43	18
							30	"		11	90

Illustration 29

The items of August 12, 16, and 25 are for purchases which were paid in one amount on September 5, at which time the lines were ruled under the balancing items. The pencil footing on the credit side shows the balance of the account on September 30. This is an *account payable*. It illustrates the method of payment described in (2).

An examination of the entries in Gordon & Buchanan's account (Illustration 30) in the order of their dates will explain the rulings shown. It is an *account receivable*, and illustrates the practice of many bookkeepers. It will be noticed that when all items balance above a given point, they are ruled out, as shown by the items marked "*a*," "*b*," and "*c*," whether they are on the same line or not. The letters also show the method of indicating canceling items. The balance is found by taking the difference between the two sides of the account after the canceled items are excluded, as shown in the small pencil figures in the left-hand explanation column. This account illustrates the methods of payment described in (2), (3), and (4).

Gordon & Buchanan 371 Front St.

19							19					
Apr.	3	Mdse.		a	216	50	Apr.	14	Cash	a	150	—
	24	"		b	154	60		19	"	a	66	50
	27	"		b	31	77		26	"	b	100	—
	30	"		c	41	75		27	"	b	50	—
May	5	"		c	16	48		30	"	b	36	37
	12	"		c	141	41	May	15	"	c	150	—
	22	"		c	39	50		25	"			89	14
	26	"			106	20		29	"		100	—
	28	"	13.42		7	22						

Illustration 30

Note: The small cross mark (x) may be used instead of letters for indicating canceling items.

85. A debtor may overpay what he owes, in which case the amount overpaid becomes a credit balance in the debtor's account. He becomes a creditor until the overpayment is canceled. In like manner a creditor would become a debtor until the amount overpaid to him is returned or otherwise canceled.

86. Mixed personal accounts are accounts of persons who both buy from and sell to each other; consequently, they show both debtor and creditor items with the corresponding canceling items. It is not good accounting practice to keep mixed accounts. The best practice is to keep separate debtor and creditor accounts. The practice of indicating canceling items by letters, as explained on page 74, will be found exceedingly helpful in analyzing and adjusting such accounts. Illustration 31 shows a mixed personal account, with a proper segregation of the items in separate debtor and creditor accounts.

(Mixed Account) P. S. Spangler   Pittsburgh, Pa.

June 19	Mdse. 60ds.	S	Dr	346 45	July 1	Cash	C	Dr	100 —
30	" 20ds.	S	Dr	712 17	18	Mdse. 10ds.	P	Cr	185 40
July 20	Cash	C	Dr	185 40	24	Mdse. 30ds.	P	Dr	485 23
Aug. 16	Mdse. 30ds.	S	Dr	220 65	30	Cash on a/c	C	Dr	200 —
20	Cash	C	Cr	400 —	Aug. 3	"	C	Dr	200 —
					30	"	C	Dr	400 —

P. S. Spangler   (Debtor)

June 12	S	346 45	July 1	C	100 —
30	S	712 17	31	C	200 —
Aug. 16	S	220 65	Aug. 3	C	200 —
			Aug. 30	C	400 —

P. S. Spangler   (Creditor)

July 28	C	185 40	July 18	P	185 40
Aug. 20	C	400 —	24	P	485 23

Illustration 31

Chapter 12—Ownership Accounts

87. An investment of funds or property by the *owner* of a business is usually necessary to provide working capital to finance his operations, and to secure his creditors for the payment of debts which he may contract with them. Such investments of capital may be increased by additional investments; or they may be decreased by withdrawals of funds at any time the owner may so desire or circumstances permit.

88. Business is conducted *to earn profits.* If profits are allowed to remain in the business, they increase the proprietor's invested capital. Losses must be met out of the owner's capital, and hence decrease it. Profits which are withdrawn as they are earned and ascertained do not affect invested capital one way or the other.

89. Invested capital is the excess of assets over liabilities. It represents the owner's interest or equity in the assets of his business after all claims of creditors, which are represented by the liabilities, have been paid.

90. Usually the owner should have two accounts—a *Capital* account, showing his interest in the business, and a *Personal* account. In the Capital account only those items affecting the permanent investment of the owner should be recorded. His personal account should receive entries for only such items as withdrawals of money for salary, goods taken for private use, etc.

Owner's Capital Account

91. This account, while widely different in its purpose, is kept much like an ordinary personal account. It is, however, affected by the profits and losses resulting from the conduct of the business and therefore is not closed *until after the final profit or loss has been ascertained.* It should be kept in the general ledger or in a private ledger.

92. The object in keeping the Capital account is to show the owner's investment, interest, or equity in the business. The title of the account is usually the owner's name, followed by the word "Capital."

The following transactions affecting F. A. Raymond's Capital account are properly recorded in the account which appears below:

March   1 Mr. Raymond began business with a cash investment of $8,000.

March   1 At the time he began business he owed on personal accounts, $140.

May   1 He made an additional cash investment of $5,000.

Sept.   1 He withdrew in cash $1,500.

Nov. 1 He made an additional cash investment of $6,000.

Dec. 1 He paid a personal note amounting to $100 out of the cash invested, which he considered as a withdrawal of invested capital.

Dec. 31 His net loss for the first ten months he was in business was $453.

Jan. 12 He withdrew in cash $1,000.

Jan. 31 His Capital account was charged for the debit balance of his Personal account, representing charges for incidental personal expense bills paid out of the funds of the business, amounting to $200.

Jan. 31 His net profit for the month of January was $1,202.46.

F. A. Raymond, Capital Account

Date		Item		Amount	Date		Item		Amount
Mar.	1	Owed to others	J	140 —	Mar.	1	Investment	c	8000 —
Sept.	1	Withdrawn	c	1500 —	May	1	"	c	5000 —
Dec.	1	Personal note	c	100 —	Nov.	1	" (17260)		6000 —
	31	Net loss 10 mos.	J	453 —					19000
	31	Net Capital		16807 —					
				19000 —					19000 —
Jan.	12	Withdrawal	c	1000 —	Jan.	1	Net Capital 16807		16807 —
	31	Personal acct.	J	200 —		31	Net profit 1 mo.	J	1202 46
	31	Net Capital		16809 46					
				18009 46					18009 46
					Feb.	1	Net Capital		16809 46

Illustration 32
CAPITAL ACCOUNT

Note: Mr. Raymond ascertained his Net Capital as of January 31 because he entered into a partnership with another merchant on February 1.

Analysis

1. How much capital did Mr. Raymond invest during the first ten months he was in business?
2. How much did he withdraw from his invested capital during that time?
3. Did the loss on the business transacted during this period increase or decrease his capital?
4. What was his net capital at the beginning of the second year?
5. How much did he increase or decrease his capital during January?
6. What items entered into the final adjustment on January 31 when his net capital was again determined? Did these items increase or decrease his net capital?

Rules for Debiting and Crediting Proprietor's Capital Account

Debit the proprietor's Capital account for items which decrease his invested capital.	*Credit the proprietor's Capital account for his investments and for items which increase his invested capital.*

93. The balance of an owner's capital account, after the net profit or the net loss and any other amounts affecting it have been closed into it, shows the owner's net capital or net insolvency—*net capital* when the credit side is the larger, and *net insolvency* when the debit side is the larger. The capital account should be shown in the last section of the Balance Sheet.

Closing the Capital Account

94. The object in closing the proprietor's Capital account is to show in one amount the net capital or the net insolvency at the close of a fiscal period and at the beginning of the next period. After the Profit and Loss Statement has been prepared, the account is credited by a journal entry for the net profit, or debited for the net loss shown by that statement. After this entry has been posted, if the credit side is the larger, the balance of the account is the net capital. It is entered on the debit side to balance the account, which is then footed and ruled, and the net capital is brought down to the credit side under the date of the next business day, as shown in Illustration 32.

95. If the debit side is the larger after the net profit or the net loss has been posted to the account, the balance shows the net insolvency, which should be entered on the credit side to balance the account. The account is then footed and ruled, and the balance brought down under the date of the next business day.

Exercise 17

Jan.   1 Henry B. Walters invested $2000.

Feb. 15 He withdrew $500.

July   1 He invested $1000.

Oct. 22 He withdrew $200.

Dec. 10 He purchased for his business, out of his private funds, a store building and lot costing $6250.

Dec. 31 His profit for the year, which he left in the business, was $1346.12.

Exercise 18

Jan. 1 Charles E. Ford invested $3200 in cash; merchandise worth $900; notes made in his favor by his debtors $750; and accounts receivable from his debtors, $500.

Jan. 1 His liabilities to be paid on their maturity out of the cash capital of his business were accounts payable to his creditors, $375; and notes payable, $800.

April 1 He invested $1000.

May 15 He bought an automobile for his personal use, which was paid for with money he withdrew from the business, $750.

Nov. 20 He withdrew $500.

Dec. 31 His net loss for the year was $275.40.

Proprietor's Personal Account

96. The personal account of an owner is treated as any other personal account. It is kept under the name of the owner, followed by the word "Personal." It is opened for the purpose of keeping incidental items separate from the more permanent investment items entered in the owner's Capital account.

97. The personal account of an owner is *debited* for—

1. All sums withdrawn for private use which are not to be deducted from the investment;
2. Any personal debts paid from the funds of the business; and
3. All sums collected from customers and retained by the owner.

It is *credited* for—

1. Any sums paid in subject to immediate withdrawal;
2. Any debts of the business paid from private funds which are not to apply on the investment;
3. The owner's full monthly salary when it is paid to him in partial payments as needed and charged to his personal account as drawn; and
4. Such part of the net profit as the owner may direct.

The following bills for the personal expenses of F. A. Raymond were paid out of the funds of his business and charged to his Personal account, which is shown on page 80. The balance of this account was closed into the Capital account, as shown in Illustrations 32 and 33.

Jan. 5 Paid gas bill, $7.50.
10 Paid life insurance premiums, $47.52.
16 Paid grocery bill, $31.40.
21 He withdrew cash, $75.
25 Paid his house rent, $35.
31 Paid electric light bill, $3.58.

F. A. Raymond, Personal

'19						'19				
Jan.	5	Gas bill	c	7	50	Jan.	31	Capital Acct. J	200	—
	10	Life Ins. premium		47	52					
	16	Grocery bill	c	31	40					
	21	Cash	c	75	—					
	25	House rent	c	35	—					
	31	Elec. lgt. bill	c	3	58					
				200	—				200	—

Illustration 33
PROPRIETOR'S PERSONAL ACCOUNT

98. The balance shows the amount to be paid to or by the owner, or to be closed into his Capital account, as a final adjustment. When the Personal account is to be closed into the Capital account, a separate journal entry must be made.

99. The final disposition of the balance shown by the owner's Personal account *is determined entirely by the wishes of the owner.* If it shows a debit balance, he may pay into the business out of his personal funds the amount of the balance, which will close the Personal account. On the other hand, he might prefer to debit his Capital account and credit the Personal account for the balance of the latter, which likewise would close it. If his Personal account shows a credit balance, he can draw out the amount in cash, or close the account by debiting it for its balance and crediting his Capital account.

Exercise 19

Record the following items affecting the personal account of John A. Butler.

Dec.   1   Paid his house rent, $45.
      2   He withdrew $100 to apply on his salary.
      5   Paid provision bill, $35.20.
      8   Paid auto license, $12.50.
    10   He collected $22.50 from a customer and kept the money.
    15   He made a temporary loan to the business of $175 to pay a note maturing today.
    22   He withdrew $150 to apply on his salary.
    28   He paid an account of the business from his private funds, $32.75.
    31   His account is to be credited for his monthly salary, $250.
    31   His Personal account is to be credited for his net profit, $928.16.
    31   The balance of his Personal account is to be closed into his Capital account.

Chapter 13—Banking Procedure

100. Money is the standard medium of exchange. Dependence on actual money as the only medium of exchange, however, would be a disadvantage to the community. A large amount of cash would have to be kept on hand, and the possibility of loss and theft would be great. To meet payments, money of all denominations would need to be on hand at all times. Banks have been organized to do away with such a condition.

There are two kinds of banks: (1) the savings bank, which accepts money from depositors and pays a fixed rate of interest to the depositors; and (2) the commercial bank, which accepts and pays out money to an identified person on the written order of the depositor.

101. Opening a bank account. Suppose you wanted to open a bank account. After you have investigated the financial standing and responsibility of the bank, you will usually be "introduced" by someone who knows both you and the bank officers. You will be asked to fill out an application blank giving certain information about yourself; then you will write your signature on signature cards which are supplied by the bank. The form of signature you write on these cards should be followed on all written demands on the bank for payment.

A deposit slip containing a detailed description of your deposit will then be prepared by you. On this slip should be listed separately the total bills, total amount of coin, and the individual checks.

Most commercial banks require a deposit of at least $200 on opening an account. A monthly service charge is made by many banks on all accounts that carry an average daily balance of less than a stated amount.

Your deposit will then be entered in a book called the passbook, which you will keep as evidence from the bank that the deposit has been made.

The bank will give you a checkbook containing blank checks attached to stubs. A check is a written order on a bank by a depositor to pay some party on demand a fixed sum of money.

102. Checks. The parties to a check are called (1) the *drawer*, the person who signs the check or makes the order; (2) the *drawee*, the one on whom the order is made; and (3) the *payee*, the one who is to receive the money.

Extraordinary care should be exercised in preparing checks. Every precaution should be taken to prevent forgery. Forgery is the changing of a material fact on a legal instrument with intent to defraud, and is severely punished by law. The amount in dollars should be written close to the dollar sign. The amount is also written out in longhand, and any

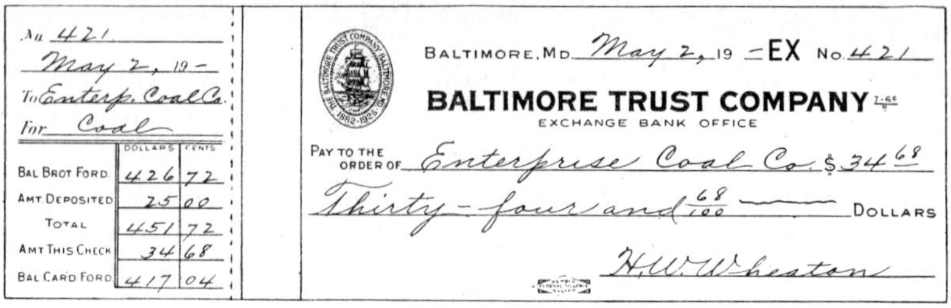

Illustration 34
Check with Stub

blank space remaining should be filled in by a wavy line. If possible, a check machine should be used to write out the amount. This machine cuts the desired amount into the paper.

103. Certified checks. Some state or Federal departments, as well as some individuals, will accept only certified checks in payment of obligations due them. When a bank certifies a check, it guarantees that there is money to the depositor's credit to pay for it. Before certifying a check, the bank will deduct the amount from the depositor's account and thus make sure that the money to pay it will be available when the check is presented.

Illustration 35
Certified Check

104. Cashier's checks. In meeting their own obligations, banks make payments by cashier's or treasurer's checks. These are orders drawn by the cashier or treasurer of the bank on his own bank to pay a third party. Instead of certifying a check, the bank will sometimes issue a cashier's check and retain the depositor's check.

Illustration 36
CASHIER'S CHECK

105. Federal Insurance of Bank Deposits.   By an Act of Congress approved July 16, 1933, a Corporation was created for the purpose of insuring bank deposits.   Insurance of bank deposits became effective January 1, 1934, under a temporary plan.   A permanent plan of insurance, as revised by the Banking Act of 1935, became effective on August 23, 1935.

In order to have your deposits insured, deposits must be made in banks which have become members of the *Federal Deposit Insurance Corporation*. Banks which are members of the Corporation are supplied with membership certificates and are required to display official metal signs at all windows where deposits are received.   Here is an illustration of this sign.

Illustration 37

At the right is an illustration of the emblem which many insured banks use in their advertising matter and on stationery, checks, etc., to announce their participation in deposit insurance.

This insurance covers deposits of money or its equivalent, received by a bank in the usual course of business, up to a maximum of $5,000 for each depositor. All types of deposits are protected, including Savings Deposits, Checking Deposits, Commercial Deposits, Certificates of Deposits, Time and Thrift Deposits, Christmas Savings Deposits, Certified Checks, Cashier's Checks, Drafts, etc. Travelers' Checks and Letters of Credit for which an insured bank is primarily liable, if issued in exchange for money or for a charge against the depositor's account, are also included.

Bank Reconciliation Statement

106. A comparison of the balance shown by the bank with your balance may often reveal differences. This situation is usually to be attributed to entries made by the bank which were not made in your book, or *vice versa*. If you issue a check on the last day of the month, your balance will be reduced by the amount of the check. The bank, however, has not as yet received your check, and the statement rendered will show a larger balance than the balance which your checkbook shows. To determine which checks have not been returned to the bank, it will be necessary to check each canceled voucher against the stub of the checkbook. The items which are unchecked may be considered outstanding.

A reconciliation statement should be prepared to verify the bank's balance with yours. Such a statement will be in the following form.

Bank Reconciliation Statement
First National Bank
June 1, 19—

Balance as shown by checkbook...$3452
Add outstanding checks

Date	Check Number	Amount	
June 6	367	$ 42	
June 10	392	165	
June 30	487	215	422

Balance as shown by bank statement..$3874

Exercise 20

On April 30, Mr. Anderson received from his bank a statement showing his balance to be $4540.18, together with his canceled checks. His checkbook shows a balance of $4287.30.

The checks outstanding are as follows:

April 9 No. 26....................$42.50
16 No. 54.................... 69.75
30 No. 92.................... 83.45
30 No. 93.................... 57.18

Prepare a reconciliation statement.

107. Indorsements. In depositing or cashing checks received from others, indorsements must be written on the back of the instrument. Checks made payable to bearer, cash, expense, etc., do not require an indorsement in order to be cashed and therefore are dangerous to issue. In case such a check is lost, the finder may cash it without the formality of an indorsement. The purpose of an indosement is to transfer the rights to the check to the endorsee.

Indorsements may be divided into four classes; (1) blank, (2) special or full, (3) restrictive, and (4) qualified.

A *blank indorsement* requires the name of the holder only and is payable to bearer. In case a check with a blank indorsement is lost, the finder may easily cash it.

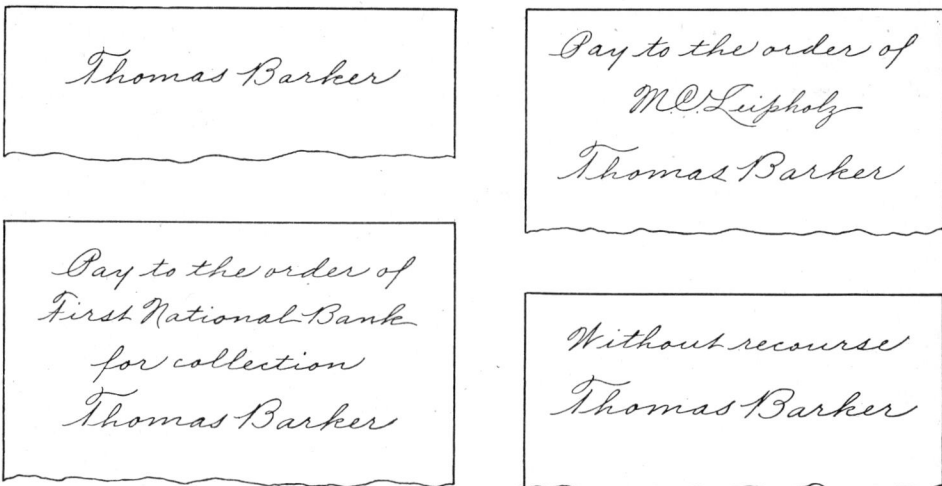

Illustration 38
KINDS OF INDORSEMENTS

A *special* or *full* indorsement names the person or company to whom the instrument is transferred.

A *restrictive* indorsement specifies what the transferrer desires to do with the instrument and is used principally when depositing checks.

A *qualified* indorsement limits the legal responsibility of the transferrer. The effect of this indorsement is to transfer the title to the instrument without assuming responsibility for payment.

108. A promissory note is an unconditional written promise to pay a specified sum of money at a definite future time. It is a *medium of exchange.* There are two principal original parties to a note—the *maker* and the *payee.* The maker is the party who signs the note—who makes the promise to pay. The payee is the party in whose favor the note is made—the one to whom the amount is to be paid.

In Illustration 39 John P. Stewart is the maker and Henry M. Prentiss is the payee. The maker of a note usually *owes* or is *in debt* to the payee of the note; that is, the maker is a *debtor* of the payee.

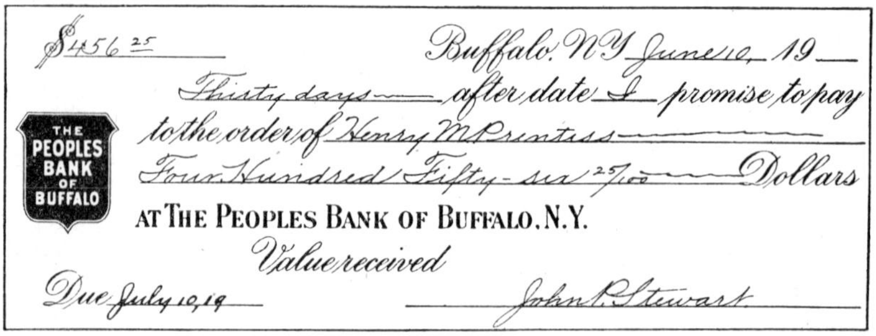

Illustration 39
Promissory Note

109. A draft is a written request to pay a specified sum of money on demand or at a certain future time. It is a *medium of exchange.* There are three parties to a draft—the *drawer*, the *drawee*, and the *payee.* The drawer is the party *who makes the request.* The drawee is the party *upon whom the request is made* and who, if he accepts the request, *becomes the payer or "acceptor" of the draft.* The payee is the party *in whose favor the draft is drawn;* that is, the one to whom the amount of the draft is to be paid when due.

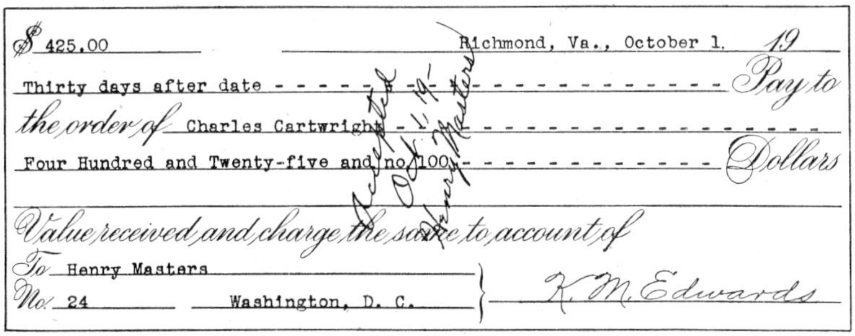
$ 425.00 Richmond, Va., October 1. 19

Thirty days after date Pay to

the order of Charles Cartwright

Four Hundred and Twenty-five and no/100 Dollars

Value received and charge the same to account of

To Henry Masters

No. 24 Washington, D. C. K. M. Edwards

Accepted Oct. 1, 19 Henry Masters

Illustration 40

DRAFT

110. In Illustration 40 K. M Edwards is the drawer, Henry Masters is the drawee and acceptor, and Charles Cartwright is the payee. The drawee of a draft usually *owes* or is *in debt* to the drawer; that is, the drawee is a *debtor* of the drawer. The payee is usually a creditor of the drawer.

111. When the drawer makes a draft payable to a third party, it is generally spoken of as a "three-party" draft. In such a case it may be assumed that the drawer *owes* the payee.

112. When the drawer and payee are the same person, the draft is usually drawn for the purpose of collecting a debt. If the draft is drawn in favor of the payee's bank, the same purpose is indicated.

113. Drafts are of two kinds as to time of payment. Those payable "at sight" are known as *sights drafts* and are usually payable on presentation. Those payable "after sight" or "after date" are known as *time drafts.* After a time draft has been accepted, it is known as *an acceptance.*

114. Accepting a draft is agreeing to pay it when it is due by writing the word "Accepted" across the face, followed by the date and the name of the drawee, who thus becomes the "acceptor," and the draft is known thereafter as an "acceptance," as stated in the preceding paragraph. (See Illustration 40).

115. The date of maturity is the date on which the note or draft falls due. When the time is indicated in days, the *exact number* of days is meant, not counting the date of making or of acceptance, but counting the date of maturity. When the time is indicated in months, the *same day of the maturing month* is the date of maturity. Drafts and notes are called *negotiable instruments.*

116. A draft drawn "after sight" begins to mature *from the date of the acceptance*. When drawn "after date", it begins to mature from the date the draft was drawn without regard to the date of acceptance. A note begins to mature from the date it is made.

117. Paper due on Sunday or on a legal holiday. The law in nearly all states is that when the due date falls on Sunday or a legal holiday, the paper falls due on the *next following business day*.

118. Negotiable checks, notes, and drafts can be *transferred* by one party to another. To be negotiable, a commercial paper must contain the words "or order" or "or bearer." When the paper does not contain these words, it is said to be non-negotiable, which means that it cannot be transferred by simple indorsement and delivery.

Questions

1. What is a check? a note? a draft?
   Why are they called "mediums of exchange"?
   How are they transferred?
2. Discuss the following forms of indorsement:
   (a) blank, (b) special, (c) restrictive, (d) qualified.
3. What words indicate negotiability?
4. Why should checks never be indorsed until they are deposited or transferred to others?

Chapter 14—Notes Receivable and Notes Payable

119. Notes receivable are the written promises of others to pay, which are *received* by us. They consist of notes and accepted drafts the value of which we are to receive when they become due.

120. Notes payable are our own written promises to pay, *given* (issued) to others. They consist of notes and accepted drafts the value of which we are to pay when they become due.

121. Both show a condition of indebtedness, notes receivable corresponding to accounts receivable and notes payable corresponding to accounts payable. The principal difference between a note receivable or a note payable and an account receivable or an account payable is that the note is a *written* promise to pay, and the account indicates an *oral* or *implied* promise to pay.

122. Notes and acceptances are generally received and issued in settlement of personal accounts, thus changing oral promises into written promises, which are in fact written contracts.

> *Note:* If A owes B on account and afterwards A gives B his note or acceptance in settlement, while the record of A's indebtedness in B's books is transferred from A's personal account to the Notes Receivable account, A's indebtedness to B remains just the same. Under some circumstances the written promise (note or acceptance) may be more binding on A.

123. The principal advantage of notes and acceptances is that they are *negotiable;* that is, they are transferable from one person to another a fact which lends to them the characteristics of *mediums of exchange* and greatly increases their usefulness in the transaction of business.

124. Because of their negotiability, notes and acceptances are frequently bought and sold, are discounted at bank to raise funds, are transferred "on account," and are sometimes given as security for loans or debts.

Notes Receivable Account

125. Notes Receivable account is one of the accounts in which items relating to *mediums of exchange* are recorded. The object in keeping the account is to show—

(1) The face value of notes and acceptances *received* from debtors;

(2) The face value of such notes and acceptances which have been paid by their makers, or transferred by us before maturity to others to apply on debts owed to them; and

(3) The face value of notes and acceptances receivable *on hand* at any date, which amount is a *current asset.*

89

126. Notes and acceptances receivable are considered to be "on hand" until actual payment of them has been received, even though some of them may have been sent to banks or placed in attorneys' hands for collection.

127. All items must first appear on the debit side of this account before they can appear on the credit side. *As notes and acceptances of others are received*, they are entered on the debit side of the Notes Receivable account *at their face value. As they are paid and returned to those who issued them*, or *are transferred to others*, they are entered as *canceling items* on the credit side *at their face value.*

128. When a debtor issues to his creditor a note or acceptance covering a debt already recorded in their respective personal accounts, the creditor debits Notes Receivable account and credits his debtor's Personal account for the face value of the paper. The debtor's record of the transaction is a debit to his creditor's Personal account and a credit to Notes Payable account. Regardless of these bookkeeping entries, however, the debtor still continues to owe his debt until the note or acceptance is paid. He has simply changed an implied or oral promise to pay into a written promise to pay. Accordingly, the bookkeeping entries referred to merely transfer the record of the indebtedness from the debtor's Personal account to the Notes Receivable account on the books of the creditor, and from the creditor's Personal account to the Notes Payable account on the books of the debtor.

129. The act of giving a written promise to pay, whether in the form of a note or acceptance, therefore, *does not pay the debt*. In case a note or draft is not paid at maturity (when it ceases to be negotiable), it is the best accounting practice to charge it back to the debtor's personal account. In such case, the note or acceptance becomes merely a written evidence of indebtedness over the signature of the debtor. The debtor continues to be responsible for his debt until the note is redeemed or the personal account is paid. The debit items in the personal accounts of the debtors are not canceled until the notes or acceptances are paid. Notes and acceptances issued, however, should invariably be credited to the Notes Payable account, and charged to the personal accounts of the parties to whom they were issued.

The following transactions are correctly recorded in the Notes Receivable account shown below:

Jan. 1 Received note for $500.
     4 Received note for $450.
     6 Received accepted draft for $375.

Jan. 15 Received cash for note entered on January 1.

15 Received note for $220.10.

17 Received acceptance for $360.75.

19 Received accepted draft for $900.

21 Received cash for draft entered on January 6.

23 Received note for $102.14.

24 Received cash for draft entered on January 4.

25 Transferred note entered on January 17 to a creditor in part payment of his account.

26 Received check for draft entered on January 19.

31 Received $200 in part payment of note entered on January 15.

Notes Receivable

19 Jan.	1		500	–	19 Jan.	15			500	–
	4		450	–		21			375	–
	6		375	–		24			450	–
	15		220	10		25			360	75
	17		360	75		26			900	–
	19		900	–		31			200	–
	23		102	14					2460	75
	30		377	76						
	31		400	–						
			3960	75						

Illustration 41
NOTES RECEIVABLE ACCOUNT

Analysis

1. On which side of this account are entered the amounts of the notes and accepted drafts received?
2. What do the amounts on the other side of the account show?
3. On what dates was it possible to rule out balancing items?
4. What do the footings on the debit and credit sides show?
5. What is the balance of the account, and what does it show?
6. Which are the balancing items below the rulings?
7. How may the balance of the account be proved?

Rules for Debiting and Crediting Notes Receivable Account

Debit for the face value of others' notes and acceptances received.	Credit for the face value of such notes and acceptances when paid or transferred.

130. The balance of the Notes Receivable account (if any) shows the amount of notes and acceptances receivable on hand, which amount is a *current asset* that should be included in the Balance Sheet. The sum of the unpaid notes and acceptances on hand must agree with the balance of the account.

131. When all items balance above a given point, they may be ruled out, as shown in Illustration 41, but the Notes Receivable account should never be closed except when it is necessary to forward the account to another page. In that case the balance is entered on the credit side, the account is footed and ruled, and the balance is forwarded to a new account on another page.

Exercise 21

George Warren's notes receivable transactions follow. Enter them in a Notes Receivable account.

Feb.   2 Received 30-day note for $250.
         5 Received 60-day note for $112.50.
     25 Received 10-day acceptance from customer for $96.50.
March   3 Received cash in payment of note entered on Feb. 2.
         4 Received two months' note for $165.70.
         7 Received cash in payment of acceptance entered on Feb. 25.
     10 Received 30-day note for $282.19.
     12 Received three months' note for $742.56.
April   4 Received cash for note entered on Feb. 5.
         9 Transferred note entered on March 10 to a creditor in part payment of his account.

Exercise 22

Enter the following notes receivable transactions of Blake & Ray in a Notes Receivable account.

May   2 Received 15-day accepted draft from customer for $92.68.
         4 Received 90-day note for $322.18.
     11 Received 60-day accepted draft from customer for $216.22.
     15 Had note entered on May 4 discounted at bank.
     16 Received one month's note for $112.70.
     17 Received cash for acceptance entered on May 2.
June   12 Received 30-day note for $175.90.
     15 Had acceptance entered on May 11 discounted at bank.
     16 Received cash for note entered on May 16.
July   2 Received 60-day note for $300.
     12 Transferred note entered on June 12 to a creditor to apply on account.
     28 Received accepted draft drawn at 10 days' sight for $211.18.

Notes Payable Account

132. Notes Payable account is one of the class in which items relating to *mediums of exchange* are recorded.   The object in keeping this account is to show—

(1) The face value of our notes and acceptances issued to creditors;
(2) The face value of these notes and acceptances which have been redeemed by and returned to us; and
(3) The face value we still owe on unpaid notes and acceptances at any date, which amount is a *current liability*.

133. All items must first appear on the credit side of this account before they can appear on the debit side, because our obligations to pay must be issued before they can be paid and redeemed. *As we pay these items and as they are returned* to us by those to whom they were issued or transferred, they are entered as *canceling items* on the debit side of the account.

The following transactions are correctly recorded in the Notes Payable account shown below:

Jan.   1 Gave note for $200.
     4 Gave note for $633.45.
     9 Accepted draft for $89.73.
   16 Gave note for $1,137.68.
   19 Paid draft entered on January 9.
   21 Accepted draft for $113.39.
   24 Paid note entered on January 4.
   24 Issued note for $150.
   26 Paid note issued January 1.
   30 Accepted draft for $212.32.
   31 Paid draft entered on January 21.

Notes Payable

Jan. '19					Jan. '19				
19		c	89	73	1		J	200	—
24		c	633	45	4		J	633	45
26		c	200	—	9		J	89	73
31		c	113	39	16		J	1137	68
					21		J	113	39
					24		J	150	—
					30	1500.	J	212	32
								1,613	39

Illustration 42
NOTES PAYABLE ACCOUNT

Analysis

1. On which side of this account are entered the amounts of notes and accepted drafts issued?
2. What do the amounts on the other side of the account show?
3. On what date was the account in balance?
4. What do the footings of the account show?
5. What is the balance of the account, and what does it show?
6. Which are the balancing items below the rulings?
7. How may the balance of the account be proved?
8. At what value are Notes Receivable and Notes Payable accounts always debited and credited?

Rules for Debiting and Crediting Notes Payable Account

Debit for the face value of our notes and acceptances when paid.	Credit for the face value of our notes and acceptances issued to others.

134. The balance of the Notes Payable account (if any) shows the amount of our notes and acceptances unpaid, which amount is a *current liability* that should be included in the Balance Sheet. The sum of the unpaid notes and acceptances must equal the balance of the account.

135. When all items balance above a given point, they may be ruled out, as shown in Illustration 42, but the Notes Payable account should never be closed except when it is necessary to forward the account to another page. In that case the balance is entered on the debit side, the account is footed and ruled, and the balance is forwarded to the credit side of a new account on another page.

Exercise 23

J. C. Bond's notes payable transactions are as follows. Enter them in a Notes Payable account.

Feb.   3 Gave 30-day note for $100.
      5 Gave 60-day note for $242.50.
    24 Accepted 10-day draft drawn on him by creditor for $52.60.
March   1 Paid cash in settlement of note entered on Feb. 3.
     3 Gave 30-day note for $133.90.
     6 Paid cash in settlement of draft entered on Feb. 24.
   13 Gave two months' note for $211.40.
   22 Gave 30-day note for $175.
April   2 Paid cash in settlement of note entered on March 3.
     6 Paid cash in settlement of note entered on Feb. 5.

Chapter 15—Merchandise Accounts

136. Merchandise is the general name given to commodities that are bought for the purpose of selling them at a profit.

137. As the principal profit of a mercantile or trading business is derived from the buying and selling of merchandise, those accounts in which are recorded the various items entering into the *cost of the goods purchased*, the *cost of goods sold*, and the *income from sales* are of first importance, because they provide the information from which the *gross trading profit* is determined.

138. The three principal operations in a trading business are *purchasing* merchandise, *selling* merchandise, which are more or less continuous operations, and taking the *inventory* at the time of closing the books, which operation occurs at the close of each fiscal period.

> *Note:* A fiscal period is any business period for which profits or losses are to be determined. That period is usually a year—either the calendar year or any other twelve months. Some businesses use six months as the fiscal period. For purposes of instruction in this text, a month is used.

139. Three principal trading accounts are kept to record the results of the three trading operations referred to in the preceding paragraph; namely, the *Purchases, Sales,* and *Inventory* accounts. Current purchases and sales are recorded in the first two accounts, and they are therefore referred to as *running* or *continuing* accounts. The Inventory account receives entries only when the books are closed at the end of a fiscal period and when they are opened at the beginning of the next period. The items included in these accounts relate only to the commodities bought and sold in trading operations.

Purchases Account

140. The object in keeping the purchases account is twofold:
(1) To ascertain the *invoice cost of merchandise* for a fiscal period; and
(2) To ascertain the *invoice cost of goods sold* for a fiscal period.

141. The invoice cost of goods purchased is debited to the Purchases account. *Invoice cost* is the price at which goods are *billed* when purchased. All items which *decrease* or *reduce* the invoice cost of purchases are credited to the Purchases account. Such items are designated as "deductions from cost," and consist of purchases returned for credit, rebates and allowances on purchases for defective or damaged goods, overcharges, and similar items.

95

142. In order to have the Purchases account show the *invoice cost of goods sold* for a fiscal period, it must include the *inventory at the beginning* and the *inventory at the close* of the current period. The inventory at the beginning of the period consists of goods which *were purchased but not sold* in the *preceding* fiscal period or periods. As these goods are on hand and available for sale at the beginning of the current period, their invoice cost is *debited* at that time to the Purchases account. The inventory at the *close* of the current period consists of the *unsold goods on hand*. Their invoice cost is therefore *credited* to the Purchases account at the close of the period, because *it is not a part of the cost of the goods sold or disposed of during the current period.*

143. When the Purchases account is debited for the beginning inventory and for the goods purchased during the period, the debit footing is the *total invoice cost of merchandise* for the period. The total invoice cost minus the sum of the deductions from invoice cost credited to the account is the *net invoice cost of merchandise*. When the account is credited for both deductions from invoice cost and the closing inventory, the balance is the *net invoice cost of goods sold* for the period.

The following transactions are properly recorded in the Purchases account which appears below:

Nov. 1 Inventory at beginning of period, $6842.19.
    10 Returned for credit goods which were ordered by mistake, $33.66.
    12 Bought merchandise for cash, $22.95.
    14 Received a rebate on goods purchased which were damaged because of defective packing, $9.45.
    17 Received rebate for overcharge on goods purchased, $13.72.
    26 Purchased goods for cash, $15.
    27 Returned defective goods for credit, $11.16.
    30 Total purchases on account, as shown by the purchases book total, $7002.91.
    30 Inventory of unsold goods on hand, $8716.42.

Purchases

19—						19—				
Nov.	1	Inventory		6842	19	Nov.	10	Goods ret'd	33	66
	12	Cash pur.		22	95		14	Rebate	9	45
	26	Cash pur.		15	—		17	Rebate	13	72
	30	Pur. book tot.		7002	91		27	Goods ret'd	11	16
		5098.64		13883	05		30	Inventory	8716	42
								8784 41		
							30	To close	5098	64
									13883	05

Illustration 43
Purchases Account

Analysis

1. If no merchandise had been purchased during the month, what would have been the invoice cost of the goods available for sale beginning with November 1?
2. What was the invoice cost of the goods purchased during November?
3. What was the total invoice cost of merchandise for the period?
4. What was the invoice cost of the goods returned? What was the amount of the rebates and allowances? What were the total deductions from cost for the period?
5. What was the net invoice cost of merchandise for the period?
6. What was the invoice cost of the goods remaining unsold on November 30?
7. What was the net invoice cost of the goods sold during the period?
8. What is the balance of the account, and what does it represent?

Rules for Debiting and Crediting Purchases Account

Debit for the invoice cost of merchandise on hand at the beginning of and purchased during a fiscal period.	Credit for deductions from invoice cost, and for the invoice cost of goods unsold at the close of the period.

To Close Purchases Account

144. After the Profit and Loss Statement has been prepared, the Purchases account is closed by a journal entry crediting it for the amount of its balance shown in the trial balance. When this entry is posted, the account will be in balance and can be footed and ruled as shown in Illustration 43.

Exercise 24

C. H. Miller's transactions for January affecting the Purchases account were as follows. Record them in an account.

Jan. 1 Inventory of merchandise on hand at beginning of business, $1892.73
7 Bought merchandise for cash, $175.
11 Received credit memorandum for purchases returned, $13.45.
18 Bought merchandise for cash, $112.42.
22 Received credit memorandum for defective goods purchased, $42.80.
25 Mr. Miller took, for his private use, merchandise which cost $11.85.
31 Total purchases of merchandise during month per total of purchases book, $3695.48.
31 Inventory of merchandise unsold at end of month, $1522.76.

Exercise 25

Walter E. Lee's transactions affecting the Purchases account for January, February, and March, in monthly totals, are as follows:

Jan.
- 1 Inventory at the beginning of the period, $12,472.16.
- 31 Total of purchases returned during January, $117.28.
- 31 Total of purchases book for January, $3,278.46.

Feb.
- 28 Total of rebates and allowances received during February, $96.19.
- 28 Total cash purchases during February, $276.80.
- 28 Total of purchases returned during February, $161.20.
- 28 Total of purchases book for February, $7,248.22.

March
- 31 Total of rebates and allowances received during March, $39.25.
- 31 Total of purchases returned during March, $185.40.
- 31 Mr. Lee donated to charity goods amounting at cost to $75.40.
- 31 Total purchases for March, as shown by the purchases book, $5,986.21.
- 31 Inventory of merchandise unsold at end of period, $13,786.28.

Additions to Invoice Cost of Goods Sold

145. The balance of the Purchases account shows the net invoice cost of goods sold, as explained in Section 143 and illustrated in the foregoing exercises. There are a number of other costs and expenses incurred in purchasing and handling merchandise which *increase* its cost; consequently, they must be *added* to the net invoice cost of goods sold in finding the *total cost of goods sold*. These additional costs and expenses include incoming freight, express, and drayage charges incurred in buying goods, etc. Such items are designated as "additions to cost." Warehouse wages, supplies, and expenses, if incurred in the purchase of goods, should also be considered as "additions to cost." In this text, these expenses are all to be considered as incurred in the buying operations. The best practice is to keep separate accounts for them. As this practice is observed in this text, such accounts will be introduced later as required.

Sales Account

146. The object in keeping the Sales account is to ascertain the net income from sales for a fiscal period. The account is credited for the selling price of all goods sold, which amount is the *income from sales*. It is debited for all items which *decrease* or *reduce* the income from sales. Such items are designated as "deductions from sales," and consist of goods returned for credit, rebates and allowances on sales for defective or damaged goods and overcharges, and similar items.

147. The credit footing of the Sales account is the *total sales*, or *gross sales*. The debit footing is the *total deductions from sales*. The amount of the total sales minus the total deductions is the *net income from sales*, which is the balance shown by the account.

The following transactions are correctly recorded in the Sales account which appears below.

Jan. 19 Allowed a customer a rebate of $7.56 for an overcharge on goods previously sold to him.

21 Allowed a customer a credit of $12.40 for damaged goods.

25 A customer reported a shortage in a shipment and was allowed a credit for $15.18.

31 A customer returned goods for credit amounting to $64.13.

31 The total sales for the month as shown by the total of the sales book were $7,124.38.

Sales

'19					'19					
Jan.	19	Overcharge	7	56	Jan.	31	Sales	7025.11	7124	38
	21	Damaged goods	12	40						
	25	Shortage	15	18						
	31	Goods rtd	64	13						
			99	27						
	31	To close	7025	11						
			7124	38					7124	38

Illustration 44
SALES ACCOUNT

Analysis

1. What were the total sales for the period?
2. What was the amount of the goods returned for credit? What was the total of the rebates and allowances on sales?
3. What were the total deductions from sales?
4. What were the net sales for the period?
5. What is the balance of the account, and what does it represent?

Rules for Debiting and Crediting Sales Account

Debit for all deductions from the selling price of goods sold.	*Credit for the selling price of all goods sold.*

To Close Sales Account

148. After the Profit and Loss Statement has been prepared, the Sales account is closed by a journal entry debiting it for the amount of its balance as shown in the trial balance. When this entry is posted, the account will be in balance and can be footed and ruled as shown in Illustration 44.

Exercise 26

C. G. Kirwan's transactions affecting the Sales account for January were as follows. Record them in an account.

Jan.   3 Sold merchandise for cash, $27.60.

       10 Allowed a customer credit for goods returned, $13.72.

       14 Sold merchandise for cash, $115.

       17 Allowed a customer credit for overcharge on goods sold him, $3.76.

       22 Allowed a customer credit for damaged goods, $21.75.

       25 Sold merchandise for cash, $12.70.

       31 Total sales for month, as shown by the sales book total, $4,278.89.

Exercise 27

Hynson & Westcott's transactions affecting the Sales account for the months of January, February, and March, in monthly totals, are as follows:

Jan.   31 Total cash sales during January, $211.83.

       31 Total sales, as shown by the sales book for January, $7,898.85.

       31 Total rebates and allowances on sales during January, $368.40.

Feb.   28 Total sales returned during February, $122.19.

       28 Total cash sales during February, $326.72.

       28 Total rebates and allowances on sales during February, $37.22.

       28 Total sales, as shown by the sales book for February, $8,688.78.

March 31 Total sales returned during March, $422.16.

       31 Total cash sales for March, $521.73.

       31 Total rebates and allowances on sales during March, $78.21.

       31 Total sales, as shown by the sales book for March, $9,972.43.

Other Deductions from Sales

149. There are other items in addition to those named which reduce the income from sales, but such items are not entered in the Sales account. The best practice is to keep separate accounts for them, and such accounts will be introduced later as they are required.

Cash Sales

150. Cash sales are those sales in which cash is received immediately for the goods sold. They are "spot cash" sales over the counter. When goods are paid for immediately, there is no reason for opening an account with the customer. When cash registers or cash drawers are used, the amount received for the cash sales during the day is entered as one item in the cash receipts book and credited to the Sales account. Disposition of cash sales in most lines of business is made in this manner. When goods are not paid for immediately, an account is opened with the customer.

```
MARKET
BASKET
GROCERY

DEC 10      2 3 7


$ 0 00.32 —
$ 0 00.10 —
$ 0 00.10 —

*$ 0 00.52 —


Total
Shown Above
```

CASH REGISTER IN OPERATION AND CASH REGISTER SLIP

Chapter 16—Inventory Account

151. A merchandise inventory is a list of merchandise or stock in trade on hand at any time. It is necessary to take an inventory of the merchandise on hand at the end of each fiscal period in order to ascertain the correct profit or loss on the goods sold, because the inventory of unsold goods must be deducted from the total invoice cost of merchandise to ascertain the net invoice cost of goods sold for the period.

152. The object in keeping the Inventory account is to record in the ledger the value of the merchandise on hand at the end of any fiscal period. The inventory is a *current asset* which should be included in the Balance Sheet. The account on page 103 shows the proper entries for inventories taken on October 31, November 30, and December 31.

When the books were closed on October 31, the Inventory account was debited and the Purchases account was credited in the following adjusting journal entry:

October 31

Inventory	To transfer invoice cost of unsold goods from	$6,842.19
Purchases	Purchases account to inventory account	$6,842.19

Reference to Illustrations 43 and 45 will show that when the books were opened again for the next period on November 1, this inventory was debited to the Purchases account and credited to the Inventory account by reversing the foregoing entry, thus:

November 1

Purchases	To charge Purchases account with inventory of	$6,842.19
Inventory	unsold goods on hand on this date	$6,842.19

As this entry balances the Inventory account, the balancing items were ruled out. On November 30, when the books were closed again, and on December 1, when they were opened again, similar adjustment entries were made for the inventory of $8,716.42. Illustration 43 does not show the debit to Purchases account for the inventory entry of December 1 because it includes November items only.

Inventory

Oct. 19 31			6842	19	Nov. 19 1					6842	19
Nov. 30			8716	42	Dec. 1					8716	42
Dec. 31			7516	45							

Illustration 45
INVENTORY ACCOUNT

Analysis

1. What account was credited when the Inventory account was debited on December 31 for $7516.45?
2. When the books are opened again on January 1, what account will be debited and what account will be credited for this amount?
3. Why is the Inventory account debited and the Purchases account credited for the inventory on hand at the close of a fiscal period?
4. Why is the Purchases account debited and the Inventory account credited for the inventory on hand at the beginning of a period?

Rules for Debiting and Crediting Inventory Accounts

Debit for the inventory on hand at the end of any fiscal period.	Credit for the same inventory at the beginning of the next fiscal period.

Exercise 28

Jan. 1, 19—(B). R. L. Johnson's inventory of merchandise debited to the Inventory account on his books at the beginning of the year was $3,278.42.
Dec. 31, 19—(B). His inventory at the end of the year was $4,391.12.
1. Open the Inventory Account, debiting it with the inventory of Jan. 1, 19—(B) under date of Dec. 31, 19—(A), when it was taken. Credit Purchases for it.
2. What entries are required to transfer this inventory from the Inventory account to the Purchases account at the beginning of business on Jan. 1? Make the entries in the two accounts and rule out any balancing items.
3. Make the entries required to transfer the inventory of Dec. 31, 19—(B), from the Purchases to the Inventory account.
4. Make the entries to adjust the account on Jan. 1, 19—(C).

Note: For (A) use the year date of last year; for (B) use this year; for (C) use next year.

Chapter 17—Freight, Express, and Drayage Charges

153. Freight and express charges are the amounts paid for the transportation of goods by public carriers. Drayage and cartage charges represent the cost of hauling goods from freight stations to the warehouse or to other freight stations, and from the warehouse to freight stations or other points of delivery. As understood by accountants, the term "freight" includes all freight, express, cartage, postage, and other costs paid for the transportation of goods.

154. The terms on which goods are bought and sold generally indicate which of the parties is to pay the transportation charges. When goods are shipped "f. o. b." (free on board) shipping point, the seller delivers the goods on board the cars, boat, or ship, after which they are transported at the expense of the buyer. The term "Charges prepaid" means that the seller of goods shipped f. o. b. pays the freight or express charges at the point of shipment for the buyer, and that the buyer becomes indebted to the seller for the amount. When goods are shipped "f. o. b. delivery point," the seller is to pay the carrying charges; if they are paid by the buyer, the seller becomes indebted to him for the amount. It is a matter of *agreement between the parties when the sale is made as to who is to bear the expense of the transportation charges.*

155. There are two kinds of freight from an accounting standpoint. *Incoming* freight (or "freight in") consists of all transportation charges on goods purchased. *Outgoing* freight (or "freight out") consists of all such charges on goods sold.

Freight In Account

156. Freight In account is one of the accounts included in the group designated as "additions to cost." The account is debited for the cost of the freight, express, and drayage charges paid on goods purchased. It is

Freight In

19—					19—				
Jan.	4	Freight	12	16	Jan.	17	Rebate on dra. 1/15	1	50
	7	Express	9	28		28	Rebate on frt. 1/9	6	12
	9	Freight	21	74		31	To close	82	96
	15	Drayage bill	22	50					
	27	Express	5	40					
	31	Drayage bill	19	50					
			90	58				90	58

Illustration 46
Freight In Account

credited for the amount of any of these charges rebated and returned because of overcharges resulting from mistakes in rating, etc. The balance of the account shows the *net increase in cost* for incoming freight to be added to the net invoice cost of goods sold, in finding the total cost of goods sold for a fiscal period. Inward freight is a *trading expense.*

Analysis

1. What should have been the charges for the freight entered on January 9?
2. What should have been the amount of the drayage bill entered on January 15?
3. What were the total freight, express, and drayage charges for the month?
4. What were the total rebates on these charges?
5. What is the balance of the account, and what does it show?

Rules for Debiting and Crediting Freight In Account

Debit for incoming freight, express, drayage, and postage charges.	Credit for rebates or allowances on such charges.

157. To close. After the Profit and Loss Statement has been prepared, this account is closed by a journal entry, crediting it for the amount of its balance shown in the trial balance. The account is then footed and ruled as shown in Illustration 46.

Exercise 29

H. A. Hamilton's transactions affecting the Freight In account are the following. Record them in an account.

June   2   Paid freight bill on goods purchased, $42.65.
        8   Paid express charges on incoming goods, $7.63.
      15   Paid freight on goods purchased, $35.72.
      21   Received rebate for overcharge on freight paid on June 2, $11.22.
      28   Paid express on incoming goods, $3.16.
      30   Paid bill of City Transfer Co. for hauling incoming goods from freight station to store, $8.50.

Warehouse Expense Account

158. Warehouse expenses consist of the expenditures for labor employed and supplies used in handling merchandise in the warehouse or store. They thus consist of the expenses of receiving, unpacking, and placing stock. This account is sometimes classified as a selling expense. This treatment would be correct only if the expenses consisted primarily of the cost of the labor in boxing, packing, and shipping materials and supplies.

159. The Warehouse Expense account is one of the accounts in the group designated as "additions to cost." It is debited for the cost of warehouse expenses. It is credited for rebates resulting from overcharges and any other items that reduce the cost of such expenses. The balance of the account shows the net increase in cost for warehouse expenses, which is to be added to the net invoice cost of goods sold, in finding the total cost of goods sold for a fiscal period. Warehouse expenses are *trading expenses.*

Warehouse Expense

19–					19–				
Jan.	1	Rent 1 month	50	—	Jan.	14	Sale of scrap	7	—
	5	Supplies	18	25		31	To close	261	55
	15	Wages	80	—					
	18	Materials	24	50					
	31	Light	15	80					
	31	Wages	80	—					

Illustration 47
WAREHOUSE EXPENSE ACCOUNT

Analysis

1. What was the expense for materials and supplies for the month?
2. What was the expense for warehouse labor for the month?
3. What were the total charges to warehouse expense?
4. By what amount were these charges reduced by the credits?
5. What is the balance of the account, and what does it show?

Rules for Debiting and Crediting Warehouse Expense Account

Debit for the cost of warehouse labor and supplies.	Credit for deductions from the cost of items charged to the account.

160. To close. After the Income and Profit and Loss Statement has been prepared, this account is closed by a journal entry crediting it for the amount of its balance shown in the trial balance. The account is then footed and ruled as shown in Illustration 47.

Exercise 30

Record the following transactions affecting R. L. Strong's Warehouse Expense account:

Aug. 3 Paid bill for supplies, $17.65.
   8 Paid bill for storage boxes, $79.60.
   11 Paid bill for repairs, $15.70.
   15 Paid wages of warehousemen, $110.
   27 Sold scrap (crates), $8.70.
   31 Paid wages due today, $110.

Gross Trading Profit

161. In a mercantile or trading business, the *gross trading profit* is the excess of *net income from sales* over the *total cost of goods sold*. It represents the profit resulting from the buying and selling operations. It is ascertained by deducting from the net income from sales the total cost of goods sold. If the total cost of goods sold should exceed the net income from sales, the difference is the *gross trading loss*.

The following tabulation, prepared for illustrative purposes from the accounts shown in Illustrations 43, 44, 45, 46, and 47, gives the gross trading profit resulting from the buying and selling operations recorded in those accounts:

Net Income from Sales		7025.11
Net Invoice Cost of Goods Sold	5098.64	
Additions to Cost:		
Freight In	82.96	
Warehouse Expense	261.55	
Total Cost of Goods Sold		5443.15
Gross Trading Profit		1581.96

Analysis

1. The net income from sales is the debit footing, credit footing, or balance of what account?
2. The net invoice cost of goods sold is the debit footing, credit footing, or balance of what account?
3. By what amount was the net invoice cost of goods sold increased by additions to cost?
4. If there had been no deductions from sales, what would have been the net income from sales?

5. If there had been no deductions from the invoice cost of merchandise, what would have been the net invoice cost of goods sold and the total cost of goods sold?
6. If the inventory of November 30 had been $7716.42, what would have been the gross trading profit?

Exercise 31

Prepare tabulations showing the gross trading profit or gross trading loss from the following groups of accounts:

(1)		(2)	
Sales	9728.60	Sales	15893.21
Purchases	7263.22	Purchases	14938.20
Freight In	236.78	Freight In	573.98
Warehouse Expense	498.16	Warehouse Expense	1216.93

Chapter 18—Expenses

162. In general, expenses are the expenditures for services and supplies required in conducting the activities and operations of a business, but for which no permanent value is secured. They consist of the expenditures of funds which necessarily must be made in carrying on the operations from which the profits of a business are derived. These expenditures do not represent permanent investments of funds, but, on the contrary, they represent the cost of services and of materials and supplies that are used or consumed. Expenses include the cost of such items as rent, fuel, light, taxes, insurance, postage, office supplies and stationery, telephone and telegraph charges, freight, express, and drayage charges, warehouse expenses, interest on borrowed money, salaries of the proprietor or manager, office help, etc.

163. When it is possible to determine accurately the expenses of any particular department or operation of a business, those expenses are classified or segregated in separate accounts so they can be charged against the department or operation in connection with which they were incurred. For instance, the Freight In and Warehouse Expense accounts include the cost of two classes of expense items incurred directly in connection with the merchandising operations, and hence are included in the cost of such operations.

164. Expenses which cannot properly be charged *entirely* to any particular department or operation, but which are applicable to and incurred by the business *as a whole*, are referred to, in small businesses, as general or operating expenses, and are recorded in one account under the title of "Expense" or "General Expense." These expenses include such items as rent, fuel, light, taxes, insurance, etc. If desired, the Expense account may be analyzed at any time to determine the cost of each separate item of expense.

Expense Account

165. The Expense account is debited for the cost of all general expenses. It is credited for any deductions in the cost of items charged to it. The balance of the account shows the net cost of the general expenses, which must be deducted from the gross trading profit in finding the net profit for a fiscal period. In case there is a gross trading loss, the expenses must be added in determining the net loss.

109

Expense

Jan.	10	Fuel Oil	11	50	Jan.	31	Rent			25	—
	14	Truck license	3	75		31	To close			85	56
	18	Telegram	1	50							
	31	Elec. bill	3	81							
	31	Rent	90	—							
			110	56						110	56

Illustration 48
EXPENSE ACCOUNT

Analysis

1. What were the total general expenses for January?
2. If the $25 credited to the account on January 31 was received for the space rented to another merchant, what was the net expense for rent for the month?
3. What is the balance of the account, and what does it represent?

Rules for Debiting and Crediting Expense Account

Debit for the cost of all general expenses.	Credit for deductions from the cost of items charged to the account.

166. To close. After the Income and Profit and Loss Statement has been prepared, this account is closed by a journal entry crediting it for the amount of its balance shown in the trial balance. The account is then footed and ruled as shown in Illustration 48.

Exercise 32

H. A. Bacon's expenses for October were as follows. Prepare an account for them.

Oct. 1 Paid rent of store for the month, $65.
    10 Bought 500 gallons fuel oil for heating, $37.50.
    13 Bought postage stamps, $5.
    18 Paid electric light bill, $2.48.
    24 Bought letterheads, envelopes, and office supplies, $22.40.
    28 Paid telephone bill, $5.30.
    31 Paid clerk's salary, $60.

Exercise 33

The Central Drug Company's expenses for February were as follows:

Feb. 1 Paid rent for store and warehouse, $135.
2 Paid gas and electric light bill, $11.86.
10 Paid bill for building new shelves and making sundry repairs, $45.
12 Paid printing bill for advertising matter, $75.60.
15 Paid clerks' salaries and wages, $265.
18 Paid bill for automobile oils and gasoline, $26.52.
20 Paid telephone bill, $7.85.
22 Received cash for overpayment on bill paid on Feb. 18, $2.
27 Paid traveling expenses of salesman, $35.80.
28 Paid clerks' salaries and wages, $265.

Interest and Discount

167. Interest and discount are charges paid for the use of money. When the charge is paid *after* the money has been used, it is called *interest;* when the charge is paid *before* the money is received, it is called *discount.* Discount is interest *paid in advance.* This is the only real difference in the terms; consequently, for bookkeeping purposes, the term "interest" applies to both interest and discount.

Example: If A borrows $100 from B for one year at 6% interest, at the expiration of that time (*after* he has had the use of the money) he will return to B $100 plus $6, or $106. The $100 is in payment of the loan. The $6 is in payment for the use of $100 for one year. If the $6 is deducted from the $100 when the loan is made, the interest is then called *discount*, because it is paid in advance, or *before* the borrower has had the use of the money.

168. Interest is received and paid in connection with many kinds of business transactions, the more common of which are—
(1) Interest paid by banks to depositors for funds on deposit with them;
(2) Interest paid by their customers to banks for funds borrowed;
(3) Interest received and paid on notes receivable and notes payable, representing debts arising out of current routine transactions between business concerns;
(4) Interest received and paid on past-due open book accounts;
(5) Interest received and paid on mortgages, bonded indebtedness, and other long-time obligations, which are *fixed liabilities.*

169. Most debts on which interest is to be received or paid are evidenced by notes receivable or notes payable, which stipulate the rate at which the interest is to be calculated. Such notes are called interest-bearing notes. In most states the legal rate of interest is 6%, but in some states the legal rate is higher.   The practice of charging interest in excess of the legal state rate is unlawful.

170. Interest is calculated on an interest-bearing note from the date of the note to the date on which it is paid.   Discount is calculated for the exact number of days from the date of discount to the due date.   An interest-bearing note is discounted for the *amount* of the note, which is the *face* of the note *plus* the *interest*.   The amount of the note less the discount equals the *proceeds*, which is the value of the note on the date it is discounted.   Interest on an open book account is calculated from the date on which the account is due to the date on which it is paid.

Let us assume that you are engaged in business and that on April 5, 19—, you sell merchandise for $350 to Martin Van Blarcom on terms of 2/10 n/30.   On May 5 Martin Van Blarcom gives you his 30-day note in payment of his account for $350.   On May 10 you decide to discount the note at 6%.   As the bank's charges are based on the number of days that it will have to wait for its money, the time is an important element.

171. Arithmetical steps in discounting a non-interest-bearing note.

1. Find the date of maturity by adding the number of days which the note has to run to the date on which the note was issued.

Date of Note, May 5	Balance in May, 26 days
Add 30 days	June, 4 days
	30 days

Date of maturity is June 4.

2. Find the term of discount by taking the exact number of days from the day of discount to the day of maturity.

Date of Discount is May 10	Balance in May, 21 days
Date of Maturity is June 4	June, 4 days
	25 days

Term of discount is 25 days.

3. Calculate the interest on the face of the note for the term of discount at the specified rate.

$3.50	equals the interest at 6% for 60 days
1.166	equals the interest at 6% for 20 days
.29	equals the interest at 6% for 5 days
$1.456	equals the interest at 6% for 25 days

The interest is $1.46.

4. Find the net proceeds by deducting the interest from the face of the note.

$$\begin{array}{ll} \text{Face of note} \ldots\ldots\ldots\ldots\ldots\ldots\ldots & \$350.00 \\ \text{Interest} \ldots\ldots\ldots\ldots\ldots\ldots\ldots\ldots & \underline{1.46} \\ & \$348.54 \\ \text{Net proceeds} \ldots\ldots\ldots\ldots\$348.54 & \end{array}$$

Exercise 34

(1) Find the bank discount and the proceeds of the following notes. the discount rate is 6%.

	Face	Date	Time	Interest	Discounted
(a)	$600	May 3	60 days	None	May 15
(b)	850	April 16	2 months	None	April 30
(c)	900	June 21	90 days	6%	July 2
(d)	165	March 12	3 months	5%	April 9
(e)	3000	Nov. 15	30 days	6%	Nov. 21

(2) Find the bank discount and the proceeds of the note in Illustration 39, page 86, if the note was discounted on June 25.

(3) If the note in Problem 2 was a 6% interest-bearing note, what would be the bank discount and the proceeds?

(4) Find the bank discount and the proceeds of the following drafts. The discount rate is 6%.

	Face	When payable	Date	Accepted	Discounted
(a)	$4,000	30 days after date	Jan. 1	Jan. 3	Jan. 11
(b)	600	60 days after date	March 20	March 22	April 1
(c)	480	90 days after date	Sept. 10	Sept. 12	Oct. 10
(d)	3,000	30 days after sight	July 6	July 8	July 17
(e)	880	2 months after sight	April 18	April 20	May 2

Interest Income Account

172. Interest received is income earned for the use of money which has been lent. From the standpoint of the business man who extends credit to his customers, it represents an earning of capital, because the capital he has invested in his business is sufficient to enable him to continue to carry the accounts of debtors when they fail to pay their debts within the usual term of credit. Under these circumstances a creditor indirectly lends money to his debtors by giving them the use of a part of his capital. Interest received is therefore frequently referred to as a *capital income*, to distinguish it from operating income.

173. Interest received is recorded in the Interest Income account, which is credited for all such interest and debited for any rebates to others resulting from overpayment of interest charges. The balance of the account is the net income from interest received. The account is included in the group designated as "additions to income," and its balance is added to the gross trading profit in finding the gross income for a fiscal period.

Interest Expense Account

174. Interest paid is an expense incurred for the use of money which it is necessary to borrow because the capital invested is not sufficient to meet all debts and obligations when they mature. It represents an expense which would not be incurred if the capital invested were sufficient to finance promptly all the operations of a business. Interest paid is therefore frequently referred to as a *capital expense*, to distinguish it from operating expenses.

175. Interest paid is recorded in the Interest Expense account, which is debited for such interest and credited for any rebates received from others resulting from overpayment of interest charges. The balance of the account is the net expense for interest paid. The account is included in the group designated as "deductions from income," and its balance is deducted from the gross income in finding the net profit for a fiscal period.

The following transactions are correctly classified and recorded in the Interest Expense and Interest Income accounts shown in Illustrations 49 and 50.

March 2 Paid interest on note due today at bank, $9.17.

        5 Received interest from a customer on note due today but renewed at his request, $4.48.

        7 The bank discounted a note for $300, deducting discount amounting to $3.

     12 Paid an interest-bearing note due today, the interest amounting to $5.72.

     17 Received interest on a past-due account amounting to $6.60.

     17 Allowed customer credit on the above interest for error in calculating, $3.30.

     25 Paid interest on a note due today, $7.80.

     31 Received credit from bank for interest accrued on daily bank balance for quarter ending March 31, $17.16.

Interest Income

19–					19–				
March	17			3	30	March	5		4	48
	31	To close		24	94		17		6	60
						31		17	16
				28	24				28	24

Illustration 49
INTEREST INCOME ACCOUNT

Interest Expense

19–					19–				
March	2			9	17	March	31	To close	25	69
	7			3	—				
	12,			5	72				
	25			7	80				
				25	69				25	69

Illustration 50
INTEREST EXPENSE ACCOUNT

Analysis

1. What was the total income from interest received for the month?
2. Were there any deductions from this income, and if so, what was the net income from interest received?
3. What is the balance of the Interest Income account, and what does it show?
4. What was the expense for interest paid during the month?
5. Were there any deductions from Interest Expense?
6. What is the balance of the Interest Expense account, and what does it show?

Rules for Debiting and Crediting Interest Income Account

Debit for items which reduce the income from interest received.	Credit for all income from interest received.

Rules for Debiting and Crediting Interest Expense Account

Debit for the expense incurred for interest paid.	Credit for any items which reduce the expense incurred for interest paid.

176. To close. After the Profit and Loss Statement has been prepared, the Interest Income account is closed by a journal entry debiting it for the amount of its balance shown in the trial balance. The Interest Expense account is closed by a journal entry crediting it for the amount of its balance. The accounts may then be footed and ruled as shown in Illustrations 49 and 50.

Exercise 35

C. J. Boone's transactions for July affecting the Interest Expense and Interest Income accounts are as follows. Record them in the proper accounts.

July 2 Paid interest on note due at bank, $7.45.

     5 Received interest on note due today, $5.20.

     8 The bank discounted a note, deducting discount amounting to $3.68.

   11 Received interest from a customer on a note due today but renewed at his request, $8.38.

   12 Paid interest-bearing note due today, the interest amounting to $9.22.

   15 Paid interest on an overdue account amounting to $7.48.

   15 Received interest from customer on overdue account, $9.62.

   15 Allowed customer credit on above interest for error in calculating it, $1.68.

   17 The bank discounted a note, deducting discount amounting to $6.42.

   18 Received rebate on interest paid on July 12, the interest being due for 30 days instead of 60 days, $4.61.

   21 Received interest on note due today, $7.43.

   31 Received credit from bank for interest accrued on bank balance, $16.21.

Selling Expense Account

176A. Selling expense is an expense incurred in selling merchandise. These expenses may be kept in one account, or a separate account may be maintained for each expense item. If such expenses are kept in one account, it will include the salaries of the sales manager and his assistants, sales clerks, and traveling salesmen; advertising cost, insurance on merchandise and store fixtures, etc.

The balance of this account shows the net cost of selling merchandise; it is usually shown on the Statement of Profit and Loss as one of the operating costs of the business. It is closed as all other expense accounts are closed.

Summary of Principles

1. Accountancy is the science which treats of the methods of classifying business transactions and accounts so that the facts they exhibit will be shown in their proper relations and expressed in terms that will most fully provide the information necessary to successful business and financial administration.

2. The two principal objects of accounting are (a) to determine at stated intervals the financial condition of an enterprise, and (b) to determine at stated intervals the net profit or loss resulting from conducting the enterprise.

3. Accounts are grouped into two principal classes: (a) asset, liability, and capital accounts, and (b) income and profit and loss accounts.

4. It is the function of the Balance Sheet to exhibit in complete detail the financial condition of an enterprise, as reflected by the relative condition and amounts of its various assets and liabilities, and invested capital.

5. The function of the Income and Profit and Loss Statement is to exhibit in their proper relations and in complete detail the sources and amounts of all costs, returns, expenses, incomes, losses, and profits which enter into the determination of the net profit or net loss for a fiscal period.

6. In an accounting sense, assets include all real and tangible personal property, the rights to such property, and claims against debtors.

7. In an accounting sense, liabilities include all claims of creditors and debts and obligations owed to others.

8. A trading account is one in which are recorded items that increase or decrease the cost of goods sold, or that increase or decrease the income from sales.

9. An income account is one in which are recorded the receipts, returns, proceeds, or income from a particular operation, activity, or transaction.

10. An expense account is one in which is recorded a certain class of expenditures for the services and supplies required in conducting the operations of a business that are necessarily incurred in order to earn incomes and profits, but from which no definite permanent value is derived.

11. A profit account is one in which is recorded an unusual, incidental, non-operating, or miscellaneous increase in income which does not result from the regular income-producing operations of a business.

12. A loss account is one in which is recorded an unusual, incidental, or miscellaneous decrease in income arising out of a non-operating source and which results in a pure waste, destruction, or forfeiture of capital and wealth.

13. Trading accounts are divided into two groups—those affecting the income from sales, and those affecting the cost of goods sold.

14. Accounts must be classified so that the balance of each account will show one definite financial result and unit of accounting information.

15. The only way to secure a subtraction in the ledger is to record the item to be subtracted on the opposite side of either the same or another account.

Chapter 19—Capital Investment Accounts

177. In almost every business some part of the invested capital is reinvested in the property and equipment of various kinds required in conducting it, such as real estate, furniture and fixtures, machinery and tools, delivery equipment, etc. Property of this kind is to be distinguished from the merchandise purchased and from the materials and supplies consumed in operating the business. The property required in conducting a business is used continuously over a period of years; consequently, the sums required to purchase it are more or less permanent investments of capital. Such investments constitute that part of the invested capital which is not immediately available for the payment of current debts and expenses. For these reasons such investments are referred to as *capital investments*, and the accounts in which they are recorded are called *capital investment accounts*. The properties themselves are referred to as *fixed assets*.

178. Capital Investment account should be debited for the *cost* of the capital asset acquired. It is credited only for the cost of the whole or any part of the asset that is *sold or otherwise disposed of*. The purpose is to have the balance of the account represent at all times the *cost of the property on hand*. Any profit or loss resulting from the sale of a fixed asset is recorded in a separate account opened for that purpose.

Expense and Income Accounts Relating to Capital Assets

179. Expenses are incurred and incomes are sometimes earned in connection with the ownership and use of capital assets. The various expenses incurred in their maintenance may be recorded in separate expense accounts, instead of being charged to the General Expense account, when it is desired to know the cost of maintaining each particular property. Likewise, some properties classed as capital assets produce incidental incomes which are not a part of the principal income resulting from the regular operations of the business, and hence are recorded in separate accounts. Such incomes are secured by renting vacant space in buildings, leasing idle machinery, hiring the use of equipment to others, etc.

180. The question arises frequently as to whether expenditures made in connection with capital assets should be charged to the Investment account or to the Expense account. The following rules are usually observed by accountants:

(1) All expenditures on a capital asset, whether for first cost or for improvements, *up to the time the property is ready for use or becomes productive* should be charged to the *Investment* account.

(2) All sums expended on a capital asset which *increases its efficiency as an income-producing factor or its market value as an investment* should be charged to the *Investment* account.

(3) All sums expended to *maintain* a capital asset at its *normal efficiency as an income-producing factor or at its original cost or investment value* should be charged to the *Expense* account.

Real Estate Account

181. Real estate is a general name that is applied to real property which consists of land and the houses, buildings, and permanent improvements that are erected on the land. An Investment account with all the real property owned may be kept under the title of "Real Estate," or "Real Estate Investment"; but it is the better practice, when more than one property is owned, to open an account with each piece of property under an appropriate heading, such as "House and Lot, 96 North Street," or "Elm Township Farm."

182. The Real Estate account is a typical capital investment account representing a permanent investment in a capital asset. The object in keeping it is to show the original cost of an investment in real property, which includes—

(1) The first cost of the property purchased, including the land, buildings, and other improvements, and the cost of surveying, examination of title, recording fees, etc.

(2) The cost of all permanent improvements which result in increasing the earning or rental value of the property, such as repairs and alterations, grading, sidewalks, etc.

(3) The cost of taxes, interest on mortgages, or other similar items incurred prior to the time the property becomes productive or is ready for use.

183. The cost of these items constitutes the *investment* in the property. The account is credited for the original cost of the whole or any part of the property sold or otherwise disposed of. The balance of the account at all times is the original cost of the property on hand, which is a fixed capital asset that should appear in the Balance Sheet.

The following transactions are recorded in the account shown in Illustration 51.

Jan. 1 Purchased an 80-ft. lot improved by a 40 x 60 ft. building known as 9 West Main Street for a purchase price of $11,500, the cost of the lot being $6,000 and of the building $5,500.

      5 Paid contractor's bill of $450 for permanent improvements and alterations on the store building.

      6 Paid for examining the title and recording the deed for the property, $63.75.

    12 Paid for repairing the sidewalk and putting in new front steps, $86.25. The property was ready for use on January 15.

    25 Sold the vacant half of the lot for cash, $3,000.

Real Estate, 9 W. Main St.

19—					19—				
Jan.	1		11500 —		Jan.	25		3000 —	
	5		450 —			31	Balance	9100 —	
	6		63 75						
	12	9100	86 25						
			12100						
			12100 —					12100 —	
Feb.	1	Balance	9100 —						

Illustration 51
Real Estate Account

Analysis

1. What was the purchase price of the property when it was taken over?
2. How much was spent for improvements and other outlays until the time the property was ready for use?
3. What was the original cost price of the entire investment?
4. Why was the account credited for $3,000?
5. What is the balance of the account, and what does it represent?

Furniture and Fixtures Account

184. Furniture and fixtures is a general name applied to the furniture, fixtures, machines, and appliances required to equip business offices and stores for the efficient transaction of business. The cost of such furniture and equipment is recorded in the Furniture and Fixtures account, which is another typical capital investment account. It is debited for the cost of all furniture and equipment. It is credited for the cost price of anything sold which has previously been charged to the account.

The balance of the account is at all times the cost of the furniture and equipment on hand, which is a fixed capital asset that should appear in the Balance Sheet.

Furniture and Fixtures

19—						19—					
Jan.	1	Mahog. desk		82	50	Jan.	31	Paper stapler		5	—
	1	Single desk		45	—		31	Balance		392	50
	1	3 chairs		17	50						
	1	Typewriter		75	—						
	1	Filing case		12	50						
	1	Paper stapler		5	—						
	1	Typewriter table		7	50						
	1	Rug for office		20	—						
	1	Telephone booth		7	50						
	15	Safe	392.50	125	—						
				397	50						
				397	50					397	50
Feb.	1	Balance		392	50						

Illustration 52
FURNITURE AND FIXTURES ACCOUNT

Analysis

1. What was the total cost of the furniture and fixtures charged to the foregoing account?
2. What reasons can be suggested for the credit to the account dated January 31 for $5?
3. At what price was the paper stapler credited to the account?
4. What is the balance of the account, and what does it represent?

Rules for Debiting and Crediting Capital Investment Accounts

Debit for the cost of capital assets, including all expenditures (if any) until the time they become productive or ready for use.	Credit for the cost price of the whole or any part of a capital asset sold or otherwise disposed of.

Closing Capital Investment Accounts

185. A capital investment account is never closed except—
(1) When the capital asset is sold or otherwise disposed of; and
(2) When the account contains so many items that is is desirable to restate them in one total amount, which is done by entering the balance of the account on the lesser side, footing and ruling it, and bringing the balance down on the opposite side as shown in Illustrations 51 and 52.

Exercise 36

J. K. Marston began business as a retail grocer on May 1. His transactions involving the purchase of capital assets are given below. Record them in the proper accounts.

May 1 Purchased a store and lot at 122 Pine Street. The cost of the store building was $4,250; of the lot, $2,500.

　　1 Paid for examining the title, recording the deed, and real estate agent's commission for negotiating the purchase, $172.50.

　　3 Purchased furniture and equipment required to equip the office and store. The bill amounted to $478.60. Mr. Marston desires to have but one account kept for both the office and store furniture and fixtures.

　　9 Paid carpenter's bill for building shelves and counters, $100. These shelves and counters are not permanent improvements to the building.

　　11 Paid plumber's bill for repairs and replacements required to put the plumbing in first-class condition, $16.20.

　　15 Mr. Marston opened his store for business on this date, all alterations and repairs having been completed.

　　18 He returned for credit a single typewriter desk included with the other furniture and fixtures purchased on May 3, the cost of which was $21.50, and purchased in place of it a combination typewriter and flat-top desk for $37.50, and paid the difference.

　　22 Paid for an electric coffee grinding machine, $75.

　　29 Sold a slightly used slicing machine for $15, the cost of which was $20.

Real Estate Expense

186. The Real Estate Expense account is kept to show the expenses incurred in maintaining real property. It is an expense account typical of the kind kept in connection with the investment account for a capital asset. The expenses of maintaining capital assets may properly be recorded in the General Expense account, but when it is desired to separate the expenses incurred in maintaining a particular property from other expenses, they should be recorded in a special expense account.

187. The Real Estate Expense account is debited for all expenses incurred in maintaining the real estate owned. It is credited for any rebates or deductions resulting from overcharges on the items debited to the account. The balance of the account is the net expense for a fiscal period of maintaining the real property owned. The expenses on real estate used in a business are part of its general or operating expenses. The expenses on real estate owned by but not used in a business are included in the group of accounts designated as "deductions from income," because in that case they are not operating expenses of the business.

The following transactions are properly recorded in the account shown in Illustration 53.

Jan. 15 Paid tinner's bill for repairing roof and rain spouts, $6.50.
     25 Paid plumber's bill for repairing frozen pipe, $2.56.
     31 Paid city tax bill for installing extra water hydrant, $3.50.
     31 Paid annual premium on fire insurance policy covering the store building, $8.50.

Real Estate Expense

19—						19—					
Jan.	15	Repairs		6	50	Jan.	31	To close		31	06
	25	"		2	56						
	31	Taxes		3	50						
	31	Insurance		8	50						
				31	06						
				31	06					31	06

Illustration 53
REAL ESTATE EXPENSE ACCOUNT

Analysis

1. What were the total real estate expenses paid during the month?
2. What is the balance of the account, and what does it represent?

188. To close. After the Income and Profit and Loss Statement has been prepared, the Real Estate Expense account is closed by a journal entry crediting it for the amount shown of its balance in the trial balance. The account may then be footed and ruled as shown in Illustration 53.

Real Estate Income Account

189. The Real Estate Income account is kept to show the income received from real property. It is an income account typical of the kind kept in connection with the investment and expense accounts for a capital asset. As the income from real property is not a part of the principal income derived from the regular income-producing operations of a business, it is recorded in a special account.

190. The Real Estate Income account is credited for all incomes received from real property, owned or rented. It is debited for any reductions from such income. The balance of the account is the net income from real estate for a fiscal period, which is included in the group of accounts designated as "additions to income."

124   Rowe Bookkeeping and Accounting Practice

The following transactions are properly recorded in the account which appears below:

Jan. 2 Received cash for rent of second floor of the store building, $22.50.
     20 Received cash for storing temporarily the surplus stock of another merchant, $10.
     25 Refunded $2.50 to the tenant on the second floor in consideration of his signing a year's lease for the space at a monthly rental of $20.

Real Estate Income

19—					19—				
Jan.	25		2	50	Jan.	2		22	50
	31	To close	30	—		20		10	—
			32	50				32	50

Illustration 54
REAL ESTATE INCOME ACCOUNT

Analysis

1. What was the total income received from real estate during the month?
2. What was the net income?
3. What is the balance of the account, and what does it represent?

191. To close. After the Profit and Loss Statement has been prepared, the Real Estate Income account is closed by a journal entry debiting it for the amount of its balance shown in the trial balance. The account may then be footed and ruled as shown in Illustration 54.

Exercise 37

Classify and record the following transactions in the General Expense, Real Estate Expense, and Real Estate Income accounts:

May 2 Paid bill for office supplies and stationery, $8.65.
     3 Received rent for offices on the second floor of the store building, $20.
     8 Paid city and state taxes on the assessed value of the building and lot for the current year, $211.83.
   10 Paid gas and electric light bill, $9.43.
   12 Paid carpenter's bill for repairs on floors, steps, weather stripping, etc., $18.
   15 Rented a vacant office on the second floor and received rent for one-half month, $6.25.
   15 Paid salaries and wages of office help and clerks, $170.
   21 Paid the premium on a fire insurance policy covering the building, $12.40.
   24 Paid advertising bill for the announcement of a special sale, $36.
   28 Paid bill for painting the front of the building, $20.
   31 Paid salaries and wages of office help and clerks, $170.
   31 Paid proprietor's salary, $175.

Chapter 20—Preparing Statements

Trial Balance

192. After all entries are posted to the ledger, the next step in book-keeping procedure is to take a trial balance. A trial balance is a list of open accounts in the ledger, with the balance of each account set opposite its name, showing that the sum of the debit balances is equal to the sum of the credit balances. Trial balances are usually taken on the last day of each month, and must always be taken before the statements which show the results of the business transacted for a fiscal period are prepared.

The following trial balance was prepared as of December 31, 19—, before the entry for merchandise inventory was made. It will serve as a basis for instruction in the preparation of statements.

John Spangler
Trial Balance, December 31, 19—

Cash	1187 52	
Notes Receivable	578 60	
Accounts Receivable	2975 43	
Real Estate Investment	7250 —	
Furniture and Fixtures Investment	428 75	
Notes Payable		3006 86
Accounts Payable		1635 80
John Spangler, Capital		10000 —
John Spangler, Personal	122 50	
Purchases	9015 21	
Freight In	91 72	
Warehouse Expense	275 84	
Sales		7719 16
General Expense	388 70	
Real Estate Expense	75 16	
Real Estate Income		35 —
Interest Expense	21 72	
Interest Income		14 33
	22411 15	22411 15

Illustration 55

The Accounts Receivable item in the trial balance includes the balances of all personal accounts showing debit balances. The Accounts Payable item includes the balances of all personal accounts showing credit balances. Accounts Receivable and Accounts Payable are grouped in this way to

125

shorten the trial balance. A detailed exhibit that includes the items which make up the balance of an account in a trial balance or statement is called a *supporting schedule*. The following schedules support the Accounts Receivable and Accounts Payable items referred to:

Schedule A—Accounts Receivable		Schedule B—Accounts Payable	
M. J. Forgan	782.91	Platt & Co.	313.18
Bronson Bros	598.26	James L. Vernon	209.76
R. C. Nelson & Co.	322.50	Matthews & Kling	778.96
Dodd Mercantile Co.	978.20	Bell & Bell	333.90
Wilson & Marcott	293 56		
Total Accounts Receivable	2975.43	Total Accounts Payable	1635.80

193. A trial balance does not necessarily prove that the accounts in the ledger are correct—it demonstrates merely that the sum of the debits is equal to the sum of the credits. Any one or more of the following errors might exist in a ledger and a trial balance could still be taken from it:

(1) A debit or a credit item posted to the wrong account; as for example, the posting of a debit of $10 to General Expense instead of to Real Estate Expense.

(2) The posting of a debit item to the credit side of the ledger and the posting of the corresponding credit item to the debit side; as, for example, debiting a debtor's Personal account and crediting Notes Receivable for a note received from him.

(3) An error in addition or subtraction in footing accounts and finding their balances, which is equalized by a similar error for the same amount on the opposite side of the ledger.

Therefore, if the trial balance totals do not balance, check for the following possible errors: (a) posting to the wrong side of the account; (b) posting to a wrong account; (c) posting the same item twice; (d) transposition of figures; (e) failure to post an item.

194. Such errors are detected by a process called "checking," which consists of comparing all postings with the entries in the books of original entry to determine whether each entry has been correctly posted. All figures should be checked as the footings and balance of each account are calculated.

The Working Sheet

195. Purpose of the Working Sheet. The Working Sheet, or Work Sheet, is a preliminary solution of the Profit and Loss Statement and of the Balance Sheet. Its purpose is to spread out on an analysis paper the Trial Balance and additional facts used in preparing the financial statements.

It is used by accountants when the work of preparing the financial statements must take into account so many items that the task becomes considerably involved. Although the use of the Working Sheet is not essential in elementary bookkeeping, it is introduced here in a simple form so that its purpose and use may be understood early in our study of financial statements.

Steps in Preparing the Working Sheet. The following steps are indicated in connection with the Working Sheet shown in Illustration 56, page 128.

(1) List the Trial Balance.

(2) Make "adjusting" journal entries on separate journal paper.

(3) Post the adjusting entries to the adjustment columns, adding new accounts if necessary.

(4) Make all extensions to the Profit and Loss and the Balance Sheet columns.

(5) Find the net profit or loss by adding the cost and income columns and ascertaining the difference between the totals of these two columns.

(6) Enter the net profit in the cost column and extend it to the liability column.

(7) Foot and prove the columns.

Adjusting Entries. The following adjusting journal entries are to be made. These entries support the Working Sheet.

December 31, 19—

Merchandise Inventory	2,736.84	
Purchases		2,736.84
To set up merchandise inventory and credit purchases.		

31

John Spangler, Capital	122.50	
John Spangler, Personal		122.50
To transfer the balance of his Personal account to his Capital account.		

John Spangler
Work Sheet, December 31, 19—

	Trial Balance		Adjustments		Profit & Loss		Balance Sheet	
Cash	1187 52						1187 52	
Merchandise Inventory			2736 84				2736 84	
Notes Receivable	578 60						578 60	
Accounts Receivable	2975 43						2975 43	
Real Estate Investment	7250 —						7250 —	
Furniture and Fixture Investment	428 75						428 75	
Notes Payable		3000 86						3000 86
Accounts Payable		1635 80						1635 80
John Spangler, Capital		10000 —	122 50					9877 50
John Spangler, Personal	122 50			122 50				
Purchases	9015 21			2736 84	6278 37			
Freight In	91 72				91 72			
Warehouse Expense	275 84				275 84			
Sales		7719 16				7719 16		
General Expense	388 70				388 70			
Real Estate Expense	75 16				75 16			
Real Estate Income		35 —				35 —		
Interest Expense	21 72				21 72			
Interest Income		14 33				14 33		
Net Profit					636 98			636 98
	22411 15	22411 15	2859 34	2859 34	7768 49	7768 49	15157 14	15157 14

Illustration 56

Executives Use Carefully Prepared Statements to Review Past
Business Operations and to Chart Future Policies.

196. Accounts may be grouped into two principal classes: (a) asset, liability, and capital accounts, and (b) income, cost, and expense accounts. The Balance Sheet is prepared from the asset, liability, and capital accounts. The Profit and Loss Statement is prepared from the income, cost, and expense accounts. Accounts showing assets, costs, expenses, and losses have debit balances. Accounts showing liabilities, invested capital, incomes, and profits have credit balances. Classify mentally the accounts in the trial balance shown in Illustration 55 under the two principal groups named above. Then reclassify them according to whether they represent assets, liabilities, capital, costs, expenses, losses, incomes, or profits.

Profit and Loss Statement

197. The Profit and Loss Statement is prepared at the close of each fiscal period to exhibit in detail the results of the income-producing operations of a business, which are expressed finally in terms of net profit or net loss. The net profit may be quickly found by adding the balances of the profit and loss accounts showing credit balances, and deducting from the total the sum of the balances of such accounts showing debit balances, as shown by the following tabulation prepared from the Working Sheet on page 128.

Sales	7719.16	
Real Estate Income	35.00	
Interest Income	14.33	
Total Credit Balances		7768.49
Purchases	6278.37	
Freight In	91.72	
Warehouse Expense	275.84	
General Expense	388.70	
Real Estate Expense	75.16	
Interest Expense	21.72	
Total Debit Balances		7131.51
Net Profit		636.98

198. A Profit and Loss Statement, however, should be arranged to exhibit *in their proper relations* all the *essential facts and figures* shown by the accounts, so as to provide the detailed and properly classified information that is necessary in managing a business intelligently. The statement on page 131, showing the same final result as the foregoing tabulation, was prepared from the same accounts in the Working Sheet, but includes an analysis of the Purchases and Sales accounts, which appear in the ledger as follows:

Purchases

19–					19–				
Dec.	1	Inventory	2276	80	Dec.	5	Rebate	12	16
	14	Cash Purchase	92	50		18	Return	32	20
	31	Pch. Bk. total	6724	11		27	Rebate	33	84
		6278.37	9093	41		31	Inventory	2736	84
								2815	04

Sales

19–					19–				
Dec.	3	Return	23	60	Dec.	9	Cash Sale	28	62
	17	Rebate	42	30		20	Cash Sale	21	80
	23	Return	45	12		31	Sales Bk. total	7779	76

The preparation of statements is facilitated when explanations such as the foregoing are included in posting to accounts which must be analyzed in a statement.

Construction and Interpretation of Profit and Loss Statement

199. This statement is arranged in "report" form. It is divided into five sections under the captions, "Income from Sales," "Cost of Goods Sold," "Operating Expenses," "Additions to Income," and "Deductions from Income."

1. *The Sales account* is analyzed in the "Income from Sales" section for the purpose of exhibiting certain units of information that are not shown in a statement prepared from trial balance figures only, such as the tabulation on page 107 and the statement on page 129. The *Gross Sales* is the credit footing of the account. This item is frequently designated as *Total Sales*. The items under *Deductions from Sales* are the *returned sales* and *rebates and allowances on sales* debited to the account. The difference between the total sales and the sum of the deductions is the *Net Income from Sales*, or the balance of the Sales account.

2. *The Purchases account* is analyzed in the "Cost of Goods Sold" section. *The Inventory of December 1* is the invoice cost of the goods which were on hand at the *beginning* of the fiscal period and which was consequently debited to the account at that time. To this inventory is added the invoice cost of goods purchased during the period to find the *Total Invoice Cost of Merchandise* for the period. From this amount is

deducted the invoice cost of the goods on hand at the *close* of the period, as shown in the adjusting journal entry represented by the credit to the Purchases account for the *Inventory of December 31*, to find the *Total Invoice Cost of Goods Sold* for the period. It is evident that the invoice cost of goods sold must be the inventory at the beginning of a period, plus the purchases during the period, minus the inventory at the close of the period.

John Spangler
Profit and Loss Statement for month of December, 19—

Income from Sales:			
Gross Sales		7830 18	
Deductions from Sales:			
Returns	68.72		
Rebates and Allowances	42.30	111 02	
Net Income from Sales			7719 16
Cost of Goods Sold:			
Inventory Dec. 1, 19 .		2276 80	
Purchases during month		6816 61	
Total Invoice Cost of Merchandise		9093 41	
Inventory Dec. 31, 19 .		2736 84	
Total Invoice Cost of Goods Sold		6356 57	
Deductions from Cost:			
Returns	32.20		
Rebates and Allowances	46.00	78 20	
Net Invoice Cost of Goods Sold		6278 37	
Additions to Cost:			
Freight In		91 72	
Warehouse Expense		275 84	
Total Cost of Goods Sold			6645 93
Gross Trading Income			1073 23
Operating Expenses:			
General Expense		388 70	
Real Estate Expense		75 16	463 86
Net Income from Operations			609 37
Additions to Income:			
Real Estate Income		35 —	
Interest Income		14 33	49 33
Total Income from Operations and all other sources			658 70
Deductions from Income:			
Interest Expense			21 72
Net Profit for the month			636 98

Illustration 57

After the Invoice Cost of Goods Sold has been determined, any deductions from such cost for *returned purchases* and *rebates and allowances on purchases* must be subtracted to find the *Net Invoice Cost of Goods Sold*, which is the balance of the Purchases account. To this amount must be added any additions to cost for *trading expenses*, such as *Freight In* and *Warehouse Expense*, to find the *Total Cost of Goods Sold*. Such expenses are called trading expenses; they *decrease* the Gross Trading Profit, because they must be included in the cost of goods sold.

The difference between the Net Income from Sales and the Total Cost of Goods Sold is the *Gross Trading Profit*. This profit is frequently referred to as the *Gross Trading Income*, and is so designated in this statement. It is the income derived directly from the buying and selling operations before any other incomes have been added or before any non-trading expenses have been deducted.

3. "Operating expenses" are the general expenses applicable to and incurred by a business as a whole and which therefore cannot properly be charged against any particular department or operation. They may be designated as *non-trading* expenses to distinguish them from *trading* expenses, which are included in the Cost of Goods Sold in finding the Gross Trading Income.

In other words, trading expenses must be included in the cost of goods sold, but operating expenses must be excluded from such cost and must be set up, in calculating the net profit, as one of the deductions from Gross Trading Income after it has been ascertained. Operating expenses must necessarily be incurred in order to earn income and profits. Some of them, such as rent, insurance, and taxes, are *fixed charges;* that is, they are incurred and must be paid regardless of whether a concern is earning profits or not. If earnings are not sufficient to meet such expenses, they must be paid out of capital. Other operating expenses, such as light, fuel, salaries and wages, public service charges, materials and supplies, etc., can be reduced or eliminated in case of low earnings, lack of business, or temporary suspension of operations.

The operating expenses included in this statement are the expenses recorded in the *General Expense* and *Real Estate Expense* accounts. The real estate expenses are included in operating expenses because the real estate is owned by and used in the business. If this real estate, while owned by the business as an investment, were not used in conducting it, the real estate expenses would not be considered as operating expenses, but would be included in "Deductions from Income" as a non-operating expense. The difference between the Gross Trading Income and Total Operating Expenses is the *Net Income from Operations*.

4. "Additions to Income" include the *incidental and miscellaneous incomes* which are not earned by the regular income-producing operations of a business. They are therefore *non-operating incomes*. The income from real estate is an incidental earning resulting from renting a portion of the space in the building in which the business is conducted. As the investment in the building is a capital asset, the income received from the investment in the form of rentals is a *capital income*. The income from interest is likewise an incidental income which results from having sufficient capital invested to lend money directly or indirectly to debtors temporarily. The sum of the net income from operations and the additions to income is the *Total Income from Operations and all other sources*.

5. "Deductions from Income" include *incidental expenses* which cannot properly be charged against the regular income-producing operations of a business as operating expenses in finding the net income from operations. They are therefore *non-operating expenses*. The Interest Expense included under this heading represents an expense that would not have been incurred had sufficient capital been invested to pay all debts and obligations when they matured. It represents the cost of borrowing money directly or indirectly with which to finance the business. For these reasons it is classified as a *capital expense*. The difference between the Total Income from operations and all other sources and the sum of the Deductions from Income is the *Net Income* for the fiscal period. The Net Income is generally referred to as the *Net Profit*, and is so designated in this statement.

Balance Sheet

200. The assets and liabilities of a business and its financial condition on a given date are set forth in the Balance Sheet. The difference between the Total Assets and the Total Liabilities is the *Net Assets* when the assets are the larger; *Net Liabilities* when the liabilities are the larger.

Cash	1187.52	
Merchandise Inventory	2736.84	
Notes Receivable	578.60	
Accounts Receivable	2975.43	
Real Estate Investment	7250.00	
Furniture and Fixtures Investment	428.75	
Total Assets		15157.14
Notes Payable	3006.86	
Accounts Payable	1635.80	
Total Liabilities		4642.66
Net Assets		10514.48

The Net Assets represent the proprietor's interest or equity in his business, and constitute his *Net Capital*. The Net Liabilities are the excess of creditors' claims over the assets available to meet them, and constitute the proprietor's *net insolvency*.

201. The Net Assets may be quickly ascertained by adding the balances of the asset accounts, and deducting from the total the sum of the balances of the liability accounts, as shown by the tabulation on page 129, which was prepared from the Working Sheet on page 128.

202. In a properly prepared Balance Sheet, however, the assets and liabilities are exhibited in classified order in their proper relations so as to provide all the units of information required to interpret the statement correctly. The following statement, showing the same final result as the tabulation referred to, was prepared from the same accounts:

John Spangler
Balance Sheet, December 31, 19—

Assets				
Current Assets:				
Cash	1187.52			
Merchandise Inventory	2736.84			
Notes Receivable	578.60			
Accounts Receivable	2975.43			
Total Current Assets		7478 39		
Fixed Assets:				
Real Estate Investment	7250.00			
Furniture and Fixtures Investment	428.75			
Total Fixed Capital Assets		7678 75		
Total Assets			15157 14	
Liabilities				
Current Liabilities:				
Notes Payable		3006 86		
Accounts Payable		1635 80		
Total Liabilities			4642 66	
Net Assets			10514 48	
Capital				
John Spangler, Capital	10000.00			
Add Net Profit for December per I. & P. & L. Statement	636.98	10636 98		
Deduct John Spangler, Personal		122 50		
John Spangler's Net Capital December 31, 19—			10514 48	

Illustration 58

Construction and Interpretation of
The Balance Sheet

203. The Balance Sheet is divided into three sections under the captions, "Assets," "Liabilities," and "Capital." It is arranged in "report" form, which requires that the assets, liabilities, and capital be listed in the order named. In setting up this statement, the assets are usually classified or grouped as *current assets* and *fixed assets*. Liabilities should be arranged in the same relative groups; namely, *current liabilities* and *fixed liabilities*. There are, however, no fixed liabilities to be considered in this instance.

1. *Current assets* consist of cash and such other assets as can be quickly converted into cash or its equivalent, if necessary, to meet maturing debts. They are frequently referred to as *quick*, *liquid*, or *floating* assets, because they are quickly convertible into cash or its equivalent and because they fluctuate continually in amount as a result of the daily transactions of a business.

Current assets should be listed in the order of their *availability* to meet maturing obligations or *convertibility* in securing working cash capital. As the cash on hand is always immediately available to pay debts, it is given first place in the statement. The Merchandise Inventory is given second place because the stock in trade is continually being converted into cash as goods are sold, and for the further reason that loans for a considerable part of the present market value of the goods on hand can usually be negotiated at bank when the stock in trade is offered as security.

Notes Receivable are listed next because they are short-time *contracts* to pay at a *specified date*, and because they can usually be readily discounted at bank if the notes are made and indorsed by responsible parties. Debtors' Accounts Receivable are listed next because they are usually short-time debts based on *implied promises* to pay at the expiration of the term of credit, and can ordinarily be collected sooner if a sufficient inducement in the way of a cash discount is offered for prepayment. They can also be offered to banks as security for loans for a part of their book value if they are "good" accounts. They may also be sold at a discount to concerns which make a business of buying accounts receivable from business men who are in need of funds. These concerns collect the accounts they buy at their *book value* at maturity, and their profit is the difference between the book value and the *discounted value* at which they were purchased. These concerns, however, charge back to the party from whom it was purchased, any part of an account which cannot be collected.

Accounts receivable that are past due and which therefore may not be collected should not be listed as current assets with such other accounts receivable as are not yet due, but should be included in the statement as "Doubtful Accounts Receivable" under the caption "Other Assets."

Fixed assets are the *permanent investments* in the various kinds of property and equipment required in conducting a business. They are to be distinguished from investments in stock in trade and such other assets that are purchased to be sold at a profit. As a rule, they are the kind of assets in which some part of the capital of a concern must first be invested before the income-producing operations can be started or maintained. They *do not fluctuate* in amount as a result of daily routine transactions and *cannot be so readily converted* into cash as current assets. However, because of their status as permanent investments in tangible real or personal property, most of them can be pledged as security for long-time loans when funds are borrowed to finance current obligations, new operations, or permanent improvements and betterments. Fixed capital assets are usually listed in the order of their importance and permanence as investments, the largest being listed first.

2. *Liabilities* should be grouped in the same relative order as assets. When current assets are stated first among the assets, current liabilities should be listed first among the liabilities. Current liabilities are the obligations and debts which will mature and be payable *in the near future*, and thus as a rule represent the first claims on assets. Careful management requires that care be taken at all times to have sufficient current assets available to pay current liabilities as they mature, in order to keep the credit of a concern unimpaired.

Current liabilities should be listed in the order in which they will have to be liquidated. Notes payable are listed first because they are usually short-time *written promises* or *contracts* to pay on *definitely specified dates*. Accounts payable are listed next because they are usually short-time debts based on *implied promises* to pay at the expiration of the term of credit. As previously stated, there are no fixed liabilities in this statement. The long-time loans referred to in connection with fixed assets, such as mortgages on real estate and bonded indebtedness, are examples of fixed liabilities.

3. *The capital* of a business at a given date is its owner's *net assets* invested in the business. The net assets are the *total assets* minus the *total liabilities*. The net assets are equal to the proprietor's Capital investment at the beginning of a given period plus the profit or minus the loss for the period, and plus or minus the balance (if any) of the proprietor's Personal account, which is usually closed into the Capital account at the close of the period.

Mr. Spangler's Income and Profit and Loss Statement shows that he has made a profit of $636.98. His *wealth* has been increased by the amount of this profit. Any part of the net profit may be *withdrawn*, or it may be allowed to *remain in the business* as an addition to invested capital. If Mr. Spangler had allowed his entire profit to remain in his business, his invested capital would have been increased by the amount of the profit. If he had withdrawn all the profit, his invested capital would have remained unchanged, because in that case the profit would no longer have been included in the assets of his business.

Mr. Spangler's books show that during the month there were paid out in settlement of his personal debts sums amounting to $122.50, which were charged to his personal account. Such items are to be regarded as withdrawals of profit made prior to the date on which the net profit is ascertained. The difference between $636.98 and $122.50, or $514.48, is the amount of the profit yet to be disposed of in the final adjustment of his accounts for this period. Mr. Spangler desires to have the amount credited to his Capital account as an addition to invested capital. This disposition and adjustment of his profit are provided for in the capital section of the Balance Sheet.

The proprietorship interest in a business, as set forth in the Balance Sheet, may therefore be stated in the form of an equation as follows:

$$\text{Assets} - \text{Liabilities} = \text{Capital}$$

In the ledger, however, assets are debits and liabilities are credits, because the only way to distinguish between them, in keeping books by double entry, is to record them on *opposite* sides of their respective ledger accounts. No provision is made in double-entry bookkeeping for the usual method of subtracting one item from another, as required in the foregoing equation. The only way to secure a subtraction in the ledger is to record the item to be subtracted on the opposite side of either the same or another account. For example, the credit items in debtors' accounts are subtractions from debit items. Likewise, the debit items in creditors' accounts are subtractions from credit items. Hence, transposing the negative quantity in the above equation results in a new equation which states the proprietorship interest in ledger form, thus:

$$\text{Capital} + \text{Liabilities} = \text{Assets}$$

Substituting the total assets, total liabilities, and net capital, as shown in the Balance Sheet, for the members of the foregoing equation, we have the following:

Total Assets	15157.14	Total Liabilities	4642.66
		Capital	10514.48
	15157.14		15157.14

As, in double-entry bookkeeping, an equality of debits and credits is to be maintained, and as assets are debits and liabilities are credits, it follows that capital must be treated as a credit for bookkeeping purposes. It is erroneous, however, to reason that because capital is a credit it is in any sense a liability of its owner or of the business in which he invested it, or that the business owes the proprietor the amount of the capital invested. An owner owns his business; hence, he cannot be owed for something which already belongs to him. The credit balance of his Capital account merely shows the *excess* of his assets over his liabilities, and represents *his interest* or *equity* in *his assets*. His liabilities represent the claims held by *his creditors* against his assets. If he has no liabilities, he is the *sole* owner of his assets, and the balance of his Capital account will be equal to the sum of his assets. That balance stands as a credit in the ledger as an off-setting or balancing item against the assets appearing on the debit side.

The accounting practice of treating assets as debits, and liabilities and capital as credits, is the equivalent of crediting a proprietor in his Capital account for his assets and debiting him for his liabilities, thus:

Assets

Total Assets	15157.14		

Liabilities

		Total Liabilities	4642.66

John Spangler, Capital

Total Liabilities	4642.66	Total Assets	15157.14

The Capital account as now set up above shows the same balance as it would show if the proprietor were credited with his net assets, or the difference between his total assets and total liabilities, thus:

John Spangler, Capital

		Net Assets	10514.48

A trial balance of the foregoing ledger accounts therefore shows:

Assets		15157 14	
Liabilities			4642 66
John Spangler, Capital			10514 48
		15157 14	15157 14

Reconciliation of Profit and Loss Statement with the Balance Sheet

204. The net profit or net loss for a fiscal period can be determined by taking the difference between the net capital at the beginning and the net capital at the close of the period. If the net capital at the close of the period is the larger, the difference is the net profit. If it is less than the net capital at the beginning of the period, the difference is the net loss. Stated in another way, as the net capital of a business is its net assets, the amount of the increase in net assets during the period is the net profit; or the amount of the decrease is the net loss. The following tabulation shows how the final results in the Profit and Loss Statement and the Balance Sheet are reconciled in proving the correctness of the net profit:

Net Capital at close of period	10514.48
Net Capital at beginning of period	10000.00
Profit credited to Capital account of proprietor	514.48
Profit withdrawn during period and charged to proprietor's Personal account	122.50
Net Profit shown by the Balance Sheet	636.98

Closing the Books

205. It is the best practice to post daily all current entries in the books of original entry and to post the totals of the books at the end of the month, after which they may be ruled and closed for the month. In order to make a periodical test of the equality of debits and credits in the ledger, it is customary to take a trial balance at the end of each month. By doing so, errors in original entries or in posting may be detected and corrected promptly.

206. As a rule, it is customary to prepare statements and ascertain the net profit or loss and the financial condition of a business annually at the end of each fiscal period, although in some instances such statements are prepared semi-annually, quarterly, or even monthly. The ledger should be closed at the end of each fiscal period, after the annual statements have been prepared, for the following purposes:

(1) To indicate the end of an accounting or fiscal period;

(2) To close the current income and profit and loss accounts and thus eliminate them as open accounts in the ledger so as to prepare them to receive entries for the next fiscal period;

(3) To record the final distribution of the net profit or net loss in the proper ledger accounts in accordance with the directions of the proprietor; and

(4) To close the proprietor's Capital account for the current period and to reopen it for the amount of the capital invested at the beginning of the next fiscal period.

207. It is the function of the income and profit and loss accounts to supply the classified data from which to ascertain the net profit or the net loss for each fiscal period. The various elements of cost, expense, loss, income, and profit shown by these accounts are summarized in the Profit and Loss Statement and are reduced, in that statement, to the single result of net profit or net loss. The profit and loss accounts should therefore be closed, or "written off the books," after the Profit and Loss Statement has been prepared. These accounts are frequently referred to as *fiscal* accounts because they are opened at the begining and closed at the end of each fiscal period.

208. On the other hand, asset and liability accounts are not closed because their function is to show at all times, regardless of fiscal periods, the amounts of the various assets and liabilities. They are *continuing* accounts and show the assets and liabilities not only at the close of one accounting period, but also at the beginning of the next period and during that period and succeeding periods, until the assets are finally disposed of or the liabilities are paid.

Chapter 21—Adjusting and
Closing Entries

209. The closing of the ledger is accomplished by means of certain closing and adjusting entries made in the journal, which, when posted, will *balance* and thus close out all accounts in the ledger except the asset, liability, and capital accounts. These entries summarize in one account all the profit and loss accounts in substantially the same manner in which they are summarized in the Profit and Loss Statement. This account is called the Profit and Loss Summary. It is set up by transfer entries which close the balances of the various profit and loss accounts into it, with the result that its balance is the net profit or the net loss shown on the statement. The balance of the profit and loss summary is closed into the proprietor's Capital account. The balance of his Personal account is then closed into his Capital account in most instances. The closing and adjusting entries referred to are prepared from the Adjustment and Profit and Loss columns in the Work Sheet.

210. The debits and credits in an account must be equal before the account can be closed. If an account shows a debit balance, it must be credited for the amount of its balance to close it; likewise, if it shows a credit balance, it must be debited for the amount of its balance. The profit and loss accounts can thus be closed by journal entries which transfer their balances to the Profit and Loss Summary account. The entries in the journal on page 142 set up the Profit and Loss Summary account in Mr. Spangler's ledger, and close the profit and loss accounts included in his trial balance on page 125.

211. Illustration 60 shows the income, cost, and expense accounts and the Profit and Loss Summary account in Mr. Spangler's ledger after the transfer and closing entries referred to have been posted. Notice that all the income, cost, and expense accounts are footed and ruled to show that they are closed, and that the Profit and Loss Summary has a credit balance equal to the amount of the net profit shown by the Profit and Loss Statement. These entries have therefore resulted finally in recording the net profit on the books as a credit to the Profit and Loss Summary.

Journal, December 31, 19—

Sales	7719 16	
Profit and Loss Summary		7719 16
To close Sales account and transfer income from Sales to P. & L. Summary		
31		
Real Estate Income	35 —	
Profit and Loss Summary		35 —
To close Real Estate Income account and transfer its balance to P. & L. Summary		
31		
Interest Income	14 33	
Profit and Loss Summary		14 33
To close Interest Income account and transfer its balance to P. & L. Summary		
31		
Profit and Loss Summary	6278 37	
Purchases		6278 37
To close Purchases account and transfer Cost of Goods Sold to P. & L. Summary		
31		
Profit and Loss Summary	91 72	
Freight In		91 72
To close Freight In account and transfer its balance to P. & L. Summary		
31		
Profit and Loss Summary	275 84	
Warehouse Expense		275 84
To close Warehouse Expense account and transfer its balance to P. & L. Summary		
31		
Profit and Loss Summary	388 70	
General Expense		388 70
To close General Expense account and close its balance into P. & L. Summary		
31		
Profit and Loss Summary	75 16	
Real Estate Expense		75 16
To close Real Estate Expense account and close its balance into P. & L. Summary		
31		
Profit and Loss Summary	21 72	
Interest Expense		21 72
To close Interest Expense account and transfer its balance to P. & L. Summary		

Illustration 59

212. The Profit and Loss Summary contains exactly the same data as the tabulation showing the net profit which appears on page 129. In the tabulation, the sum of the costs, expenses, and losses is deducted from the sum of the incomes and profits, while in the Summary account the costs, expenses, and losses are debits, and the incomes and profits are credits. In other words, the Profit and Loss Summary is an abbreviated or condensed Profit and Loss Statement in ledger form.

Purchases

19—					19—				
Dec.	1	Inventory	2276	80	Dec.	5	Rebate	12	16
	14	Cash Purchase	92	50		18	Return	32	20
	31	Pch. Bk. total	6724	11		27	Rebate	33	84
						31	Inventory	2736	84
						31	To close	6278	37
			9093	41				9093	41

Freight In

19—					19—				
Dec.	10	Freight	22	16	Dec.	21	Frt. rebate	3	46
	14	Express	9	37		31	To close	91	72
	22	Freight	39	15					
	31	Drayage	24	50					
			95	18				95	18

Warehouse Expense

19—					19—				
Dec.	12	Supplies	95	84	Dec.	31	To close	275	84
	31	Wages	180	—					
			275	84				275	84

Sales

19—					19—				
Dec.	3	Return	23	60	Dec.	9	Cash sale	28	62
	17	Rebate	42	30		20	Cash sale	21	80
	23	Return	45	12		31	Sales Bk. total	7779	76
	31	To close	7719	16					
			7830	18				7830	18

Illustration 60

General Expense

19–						19–				
Dec.	4	Coal	66	25		Dec.	31	To close	388	70
	15	Office Supplies	42	45						
	31	Salaries	280	—						
			388	70					388	70

Real Estate Expense

19–						19–				
Dec.	12	Taxes	52	42		Dec.	31	To close	75	16
	20	Repairs	22	74						
			75	16					75	16

Real Estate Income

19–						19–				
Dec.	31	To close	35	—		Dec.	10	Rent	10	—
							31	Rent	25	—
			35	—					35	—

Interest Expense

19–						19–				
Dec.	12	Interest	13	12		Dec.	31	To close	21	72
	24	Discount	8	60						
			21	72					21	72

Interest Income

19–						19–				
Dec.	31	To close	14	33		Dec.	19	Interest	3	21
							29	Interest	11	12
			14	33					14	33

Profit and Loss Summary

19–						19–				
Dec.	31	Purchases	6278	37		Dec.	31	Sales	7719	16
	31	Freight In	91	72			31	R. E. Income	35	—
	31	Ware. Expense	275	84			31	Int. Income	14	33
	31	Gen. Expense	388	70				636.98	7768	49
	31	R. E. Expense	75	16						
	31	Int. Expense	21	72						
			7131	51						

Illustration 6o (Continued)

213. The Profit and Loss Summary now stands open in the ledger with a credit balance equal to the amount of the net profit. The next step in the process of closing the ledger is to transfer this balance, which is the net profit, to the Capital account of the proprietor. The following journal entry will therefore close the Profit and Loss Summary into Mr. Spangler's Capital account:

31

Profit and Loss Summary		636 98	
John Spangler, Capital			636 98
To close P. & L. Summary and credit proprietor's Capital account			
for net profit shown on I. & P. & L. Statement, Dec. 31, 19—			

Illustration 61

When the foregoing entry is posted, the Summary account, after being footed and ruled, and the Capital account will appear as follows:

Profit and Loss Summary

19–					19–				
Dec.	31	Purchases	6278 37		Dec.	31	Sales	7719 16	
	31	Freight In	91 72			31	R. E. Income	35 —	
	31	Ware. Expense	275 84			31	Int. Income	14 33	
	31	Gen. Expense	388 70						
	31	R. E. Expense	75 16						
	31	Int. Expense	21 72						
	31	J. Spangler, Cap.	636 98						
			7768 49					7768 49	

John Spangler, Capital

					19–				
					Dec.	1	Investment	10000 —	
						31	Net Profit	636 98	

Illustration 62

214. After the net profit is carried to the credit of the Capital account, the next step in the closing process is to make such final adjustment of the owner's Personal account as he may direct. The Personal account may be closed into the Capital account; it may be allowed to stand as an open account for future adjustment; or it may be credited with such part of the net profit as is required to close it, or with such part of the net profit as the proprietor may elect to withdraw. In any case, that part of the net profit not withdrawn or applied against the debit balance of the owner's Personal account remains as a credit in his Capital account as an addition to invested capital. In case the owner has a credit balance in his Personal account, it may be closed by transferring the balance to his Capital account as an additional investment, by withdrawing the amount of the balance in cash or some other asset, or by charging it, in the case of a net loss, with that part of the loss required to close it.

215. Mr. Spangler has decided to credit his Personal account with such part of the net profit as is required to close it, and to allow the remainder of the net profit to remain in his business as an addition to invested capital. This adjustment is made by the following journal entry:

	31		
John Spangler, Capital		122 50	
John Spangler, Personal			122 50
To close balance of Personal account and credit Capital account			
with that part of net profit invested.			

Illustration 63

After the foregoing entry is posted, the Personal account, after being footed and ruled, and the Capital account will appear as follows:

John Spangler, Personal

19–					19–				
Dec.	1	House rent		75 —	Dec.	31	Capital account		122 50
	4	Coal		47 50					
				122 50					122 50

John Spangler, Capital

19–					19–				
Dec.	31	Personal		122 50	Dec.	1	Investment		10000 —
						31	Net profit		636 98

Illustration 64

216. The process of closing the ledger is completed when the final distribution of the net profit or net loss is recorded in the ledger and the accounts are footed and ruled. It is customary, however, to "balance" the proprietor's Capital account in order to restate his present invested capital, or net capital, in one amount. This object is accomplished by entering the credit balance on the debit side, footing and ruling the account, and bringing the balance down on the credit side under date of the next business day, as shown in Illustration 65.

John Spangler, Capital

19–					19–				
Dec.	31	Personal		122 50	Dec.	1	Investment		10000 —
	31	Net Capital		10514 48		31	Net Profit		636 98
				10636 98					10636 98
					19–				
					Jan.	1	Net Capital		10514 48

Illustration 65

217. Observe that a journal entry is not required in balancing an account in the manner described in ¶216. An account is balanced by a *cross entry* within the account itself—a credit above the ruling and a debit below, or *vice versa*. It is stated in ¶208 that asset and liability accounts are not *closed*. They may be *balanced*, however, at the close of each fiscal period, in the manner just described, if it is preferred to do so. As a rule, it is customary not to balance them until it is necessary to forward them to new pages in the ledger. Illustrations 51 and 52 on pages 120 and 121 show how such accounts may be balanced.

Compound Journal Entry to Close

218. The process of closing the ledger may be considerably simplified and shortened if the Profit and Loss Summary account is not opened. If the debits and credits to the Profit and Loss Summary included in Illustrations 60 and 62 are omitted and the remaining debits and credits in these entries are combined in one entry, a compound journal entry will result, which will include—

(1) All the debits and credits required to close the income and profit and loss accounts; and

(2) A credit to the proprietor's Capital account for the amount of the net profit, thus:

Journal, December 31, 19—

Sales	To close		7719 16	
Real Estate Income	" "		35 —	
Interest Income	" "		14 33	
Purchases	" "			6278 37
Freight In	" "			91 72
Warehouse Expense	" "			275 84
General Expense	" "			388 70
Real Estate Expense	" "			75 16
Interest Expense	" "			21 72
John Spangler, Capital	Net Profit for December			636 98

Illustration 66

219. In order to complete the closing of the ledger, a second entry adjusting the proprietor's Personal account is required. This entry is shown in Illustration 63. The method to be followed in closing the ledger is largely a matter of individual preference. Those who close by the first method illustrated prefer it because they wish to group all the elements of profit and loss in one account in the ledger. This method is to be preferred principally because it supplies a record in the ledger of all the amounts entering into the annual net profits or losses from year to year. That record can easily be checked when books are audited for income tax purposes. Those who use the compound journal entry believe that the Profit and Loss Summary account in the ledger is useless because the Profit and Loss Statement contains the same information in greater detail, and consequently the compound entry is to be preferred because of its brevity.

Chapter 22—Exercises

Exercise 38

From the following trial balance and other data, prepare a Profit and Loss Statement, a Balance Sheet, and the closing and adjusting entries required to close the ledger. Set up the Profit and Loss Summary account. The proprietor's Capital account is to be credited with the net profit, and his Personal account is to be closed into his Capital account.

J. M. Warren
Trial Balance, December 31, 19—

Cash	2460 20	
Inventory	3647 19	
Notes Receivable	2214 45	
Accounts Receivable	3114 34	
Real Estate Investment	5215 90	
Furniture and Fixtures Investment	322 40	
Notes Payable		4629 45
Accounts Payable		3514 26
J. M. Warren, Capital		8246 51
J. M. Warren, Personal	19 16	
Purchases	10725 04	
Freight In	578 82	
Warehouse Expense	1621 93	
Sales		15746 21
General Expense	2225 42	
Real Estate Expense	328 72	
Real Estate Income		447 60
Interest Expense	129 67	
Interest Income		19 21
	32603 24	32603 24

The following additional figures are required in preparing the Income and Profit and Loss Statement.

Inventory, January 1	$ 2,378.82	Gross Sales	$16,246.53
Returned Purchases	113.26	Returned Sales	328.42
Rebates and Allowances		Sales Rebates	
on Purchases	212.63	and Allowances	171.90
Total Purchases	12,319.30		

Exercise 39

Prepare statements and a compound journal entry to close from the following trial balance and other data. The net profit or loss is to be recorded in the proprietor's Personal account, the balance of which is not to be closed into the Capital account because the proprietor intends to withdraw whatever sum stands to his credit in his Personal account after the final results are determined.

F. B. Clarke
Trial Balance, December 31, 19—

Cash	1454 24	
Accounts Receivable	2515 20	
Notes Receivable	2312 62	
Merchandise Inventory	3225 06	
Store and Lot Investment	6245 —	
Green Spring Farm Investment	2092 60	
Furniture and Fixtures Investment	529 70	
Accounts Payable		2191 26
Notes Payable		2793 14
Mortgage Payable		3000 —
F. B. Clarke, Capital		10296 50
F. B. Clarke, Personal		250 —
Sales		16672 95
Purchases	12593 55	
Freight In	628 31	
Warehouse Expense	1428 19	
General Expense	2526 30	
Store Expense	225 62	
Interest Income		33 78
Store Income		540 —
Farm Income		875 15
Farm Expense	750 59	
Interest Expense	125 80	
	36652 78	36652 78

Additional Data

Inventory, January 1	$ 1,972.80	Gross Sales	$16,894.36
Total Purchases	14,134.77	Returned Sales	125.19
Returned Purchases	173.14	Sales Rebates	
Purchase Rebates		and Allowances	96.22
and Allowances	90.22		
Goods donated to charity			
at invoice cost	25.60		

Review Exercises

Exercises 40 to 47 inclusive, which follow, provide a test of the student's knowledge of the principles underlying the classification of the accounts which have been presented up to this point. A double sheet of journal paper and a double sheet of ledger paper will be required. Allow twenty-two lines for the Cash account, eight lines for the Purchases account, and six lines each for all other accounts—one line for the heading and five lines for the entries.

R. E. Wood began business as a hardware merchant on November 1. He did not keep a regular set of books. All the records of the business he transacted to December 31 are in the form of memorandums he made from time to time, invoices he received for purchases of merchandise and bills for expense items, memorandum charges to customers for merchandise sold, and his checkbook stubs showing the records of all cash deposits and payments. On December 31 it is necessary for him to ascertain what his profit or loss has been for the two months that he has been in business, so that he can prepare his income tax return. He also wishes to determine the financial condition of his business on this date, because he intends to open a set of books at the beginning of business for the new year.

You have just been employed as his bookkeeper. It is first necessary to set up accounts which will properly record Mr. Wood's transactions for November and December, from which to prepare a Profit and Loss Statement and a Balance Sheet as of December 31. As it will be somewhat difficult to record his transactions in chronological order, all entries are to be journalized and entered under date of December 31, and are then to be posted to the ledger.

Exercise 40

Mr. Wood reports that when he began business on November 1 he invested $10,000 in cash, a stock of merchandise he had purchased at auction on October 20 which cost him $2,750, office and store furniture, fixtures, and equipment which were also purchased at the same auction sale at a price of $700, and a new automobile truck which cost $1,500, and which was delivered to him on October 29. On that date he issued a check for $1,200 to apply on the purchase price. This payment, however, was not made out of the funds he invested in his business, but from other money he had in his possession at that time. On November 1 he issued a 60-day note for $300, dated November 1, with interest at 6% payable at maturity, for the balance of the purchase price of this delivery equipment, the note to be paid from the funds of his business when it matured.

Prepare a journal entry to record the assets invested. Then prepare another entry to record any claims against these assets. Next, open the ledger accounts required and post the entries.

Exercise 41

Mr. Wood closed a deal on October 20 for the purchase of a business property located at the corner of Main and Oak Streets. It is known as 32 Main Street. The property consists of a lot having a frontage of 40 feet on Main Street and a depth of 100 feet on Oak Street, improved by a two-story brick store and warehouse building 40 feet wide and 70 feet deep. The purchase price of the building was $7,000 and of the lot, $4,000.

Mr. Wood did not take title to the property until November 1, on which date he issued a check for $5,000 on the checking account of his business to apply on the purchase price, and executed a mortgage, dated November 1, in the amount of $6,000, bearing interest at the rate of 6% per annum, for the balance. The former owner of the property had already paid the taxes for the current year, which amounted to $261.18. Mr. Wood accordingly issued his check to him for $43.53, which amount was one-sixth of the year's taxes applicable to the months of November and December. He also issued a check for $142.52 to pay the bill for examining the title, recording the deed, arranging for the mortgage, and other expenses incurred on the property prior to the time he began to use it for business purposes.

Exercise 42

Among the furniture and fixtures which Mr. Wood purchased at auction was a second-hand typewriter for which he paid $28. On November 3, he traded in this machine on the purchase of a new machine, the price of which was $87.50. He was allowed $20 for the old machine and issued his check to the typewriter company for the difference, $67.50.

Note: Losses similar to the loss between the cost price of the old typewriter and the price received when it was disposed of are *unusual* or non-operating losses in the sense that they result from transactions outside of those from which the regular or operating income of the business is derived. They are referred to as *incidental* or *miscellaneous* losses; consequently, they should be accounted for in a separate account under the title of "Miscellaneous Losses." The losses charged to this account should be listed separately in the Profit and Loss Statement with the other "deductions from income." Likewise, unusual or non-operating profits, such as the profit on the sale of real estate reported in the next transaction, are not operating profits. They are *incidental* or *miscellaneous* profits, and should be accounted for in a separate account under the title of "Miscellaneous Profits." They should be listed separately in the statement with the other "additions to income."

On November 15, Mr. Wood sold the rear part of his lot for $1,500, accepting at the time that the transaction was consummated, a check for $500 and two notes for $500 each.   Both notes were dated November 15, one payable in 30 days and the other in 60 days, with interest at 6%, payable at maturity.   The cost of the part of the lot disposed of was $1,200.   The purchaser intends to erect a building in which to conduct a drug store.

On October 21, Mr. Wood employed a contractor to build a partition on the second floor so as to make a room for a photographer's studio. Mr. Wood leased the space and the tenant took possession on November 1.   The cost of this partition and of other alterations and repairs about the building required to put it in first-class condition was $280, for which Mr. Wood issued his check to the contractor on November 5.

Exercise 43

An analysis of Mr. Wood's merchandising transactions for the two months he has been in business discloses the following facts and figures:

The bills for merchandise purchased amount to $2,147.16.   All this merchandise was bought on open account.   For one reason or another he returned for credit merchandise included in these purchases amounting to $72.26, and received rebates and allowances amounting to $13.52.   He also took from his stock of merchandise tools and other articles for use in the store and warehouse which cost $32.90.

Note: Open an Accounts Receivable account and an Accounts Payable account in which to record all debits and credits to trade debtors and trade creditors, respectively.

Mr. Wood billed all goods sold to customers on open account in duplicate, and retained the duplicate copies as his records of the transactions. As his customers paid him, he marked the carbon copies "Paid."   His sales, as shown by these carbon copies, total $2,714.88.   His customers returned goods amounting to $15.80, for which he allowed credit.   He also rebated on sales to his customers various sums amounting to $22.37.

His inventory of unsold merchandise on hand on December 31, taken at invoice cost, amounts to $3,267.28.

Exercise 44

Since he began business on November 1, Mr. Wood has deposited all cash received.   He classified his deposits when entering them on the stub of his checkbook so as to show the amounts received in settlement of accounts receivable, the proceeds from cash sales, the income from rentals, etc. An analysis of these deposits shows that he received in settlement of customers' accounts the sum of $1,842.55. Included in this amount was an item of $1.36 for interest on a past due account. The deposits of receipts from cash sales amounted to $312.18.

In drawing a check in payment of one of his bills for merchandise purchased, he transposed the figures on the bill from $123.50 to $132.50. His creditor refunded the overpayment by a check for $9, which was deposited. He also made two deposits of $35 each for the checks received in payment of the rent of the studio for November and December. He received a check for $5.44 from the railroad company for an overpayment on a freight bill on goods purchased, because of a mistake in the rate assessed on the shipment. This check was also deposited.

On December 15 he received a check for $502.50 in payment of the first note he accepted from the purchaser of the rear part of his lot. This check included the interest on the note for 30 days. This check was deposited, also.

Exercise 45

An analysis of Mr. Wood's cash payments, exclusive of those previously reported, as prepared from the stubs in his checkbook discloses the following data:

During November and December his payments in settlement of sums owed to his creditors amounted to $928.47. On December 30 he issued a check for $303 in payment of the note he gave on November 1 for the balance of the purchase price of his truck. The check included the interest on the note for 60 days. During the period he paid freight bills amounting to $97.84 on goods purchased. He issued two checks in favor of himself for $125 each for his salary for November and December.

On November 3 he issued a check for $75 in payment of a bill for repairing, painting, and varnishing the furniture and fixtures he purchased at auction. These permanent improvements were necessary to put the equipment in good condition. The work was completed prior to the time he began to transact business. His bills for boxing, packing, and shipping materials and for store and warehouse supplies paid during the two months amount to $52.60. On November 8 he issued a check for $43.25 in payment of a bill for repairing the plumbing and installing new plumbing and fixtures in the building. These were permanent improvements required to put the plumbing in first-class condition.

Mr. Wood employs a warehouseman and truck driver whose time is fully occupied in handling incoming and outgoing stock in the warehouse.

His wages for the two months were $180. He also employs a sales clerk to wait on customers in the store and to assist him in the general conduct of the business. The clerk's salary was $162 for the period. On December 20 a carpenter's bill for $5.80 for minor repairs to various parts of the building was paid by check. In filling an order, the clerk dropped a hammer and broke a plate glass top in a show case. The cost of replacing the plate glass top was $11.50, which was paid by check. On November 2 Mr. Wood insured the building against fire, the face value of the policy being $7,000. He issued a check for $32.90 in payment of the premium on the policy. He paid bills amounting to $123.84 for office supplies and stationery, electric light, coal, license fees for the truck, gasoline, oils, and similar expenses.

On December 31 he made a payment of $1,000 on the mortgage covering his real estate, to retire a part of the principal. He included in his check the accrued interest from November 1 to December 31 on the full amount of the mortgage, his check amounting to $1,060. The balance of cash shown by the checkbook is $4381.92.

Exercise 46

In addition to the foregoing transactions, Mr. Wood also had the following transactions during the period. On November 22 he accepted a draft drawn on him by a creditor at 60 days after sight dated November 20 for $224.58, the amount of a bill of merchandise purchased. He intends to pay this draft at maturity.

One of his cutomers who owed him $103.95 for a bill which matured on December 15 could not pay the bill at that time, and Mr. Wood accepted his 30-day note dated December 15 with interest at 6% for the amount of the bill.

Exercise 47

After all the transactions in Exercises 40 to 46, inclusive, have been entered and posted, take a trial balance, prepare a Work Sheet, and make a Profit and Loss Statement. Then close the profit and loss accounts into the Profit and Loss Summary account.

Mr. Wood states that he wants to use the profit which he made on the sale of the lot, plus such other part of his profit from other sources credited to his Capital account as will make an investment of an even $15,000, to start business at the beginning of the new year. The remainder of his profits is to be credited to his Personal account subject to withdrawal whenever he may wish to draw it. Make the entries to record this distribution of profits and post them to the ledger.

Prepare a Balance Sheet as of December 31, showing in the capital section the distribution of profit which has been ordered.

Next, prepare a trial balance from the ledger as it stands after the profit and loss accounts have been closed. Such a trial balance is called a *post-closing* trial balance. It includes only the asset, liability, and capital accounts. Its purpose is to make certain that the ledger is in balance after it has been closed for a fiscal period and before any entries for the next fiscal period have been posted.

On January 1, Mr. Wood drew a check in his favor for that part of his profit that was credited to his Personal account. Make the journal entry to adjust.

Mr. Wood has purchased a complete set of books in which to keep the accounts of his business for the ensuing year. Set up the journal entry that would be required to open his new books and ledger at the beginning of business on January 1. Then make the adjusting entry for the inventory of merchandise of December 31.

Note to Teacher: Accruals are not to be taken into consideration in working Exercises 40 to 47 inclusive.

Chapter 23—Complementary Exercises in Statements

The following exercises, aside from providing additional practice material, are intended to test the student's ability to classify accounts and prepare statements in proper form, and to give him an opportunity to exercise his judgment on business affairs.

Exercise 48

From the following trial balance prepare the statements required to show Mr. Morgan's profits and losses for the business transacted during October, as well as his financial condition on October 31. Then draft the journal entries to close the ledger. Close the net profit or loss into the proprietor's Personal account.

A. C. Morgan

Trial Balance, October 31, 19—

Cash	1847 04	
Accounts Receivable	2865 49	
Notes Receivable	1828 80	
Merchandise Inventory	884 36	
Accounts Payable		920 16
Notes Payable		924 14
A. C. Morgan, Capital		5124 86
Sales		7714 90
Purchases	6816 80	
Freight In	49 72	
General Expense	231 22	
Store Expense	68 80	
Taxes and Insurance	17 20	
Interest Paid	12 13	
Interest Received		37 50
Bad Debt Losses	100 —	
	14721 56	14721 56

Additional Data

Sales Returned	$14.80	Purchases Rebates	$19.45
Sales Rebates	26.72	Goods taken from stock at	
Purchases Returned	21.56	cost by owner	7.50
Inventory, October 1	925.40		

Exercise 49

H. A. Fallon Co.
Trial Balance, December 31, 19—

Cash	12600 —	
Accounts Receivable	11000 —	
Notes Receivable	8000 —	
Merchandise Inventory	12000 —	
Store Building Investment	18000 —	
Store Land Investment	6000 —	
Fairmount Ave. Real Estate	4000 —	
Store Furniture and Equipment	8500 —	
Accounts Payable		15300 —
Notes Payable		7000 —
Mortgages Payable		13000 —
H. A. Fallon, Capital		32800 —
H. A. Fallon, Private	1000 —	
Sales		111400 —
Purchases	72000 —	
Freight and Express In	2900 —	
General Expense	3500 —	
Store Salaries and Wages	11500 —	
Warehouse Supplies	2700 —	
Warehouse Salaries and Wages	5200 —	
Building Expense	1800 —	
Building Income		1560 —
Fairmount Ave. Real Estate Expense	180 —	
Fairmount Ave. Real Estate Income		700 —
Interest Expense	160 —	
Interest Income		240 —
Interest on Mortgages	640 —	
Bad Debt Losses	320 —	
	182000 —	182000 —

Additional Data

Gross Sales	$112,670	Total Purchased	$74,660
Returned Sales	380	Purchases Returned	1,120
Sales Rebates	890	Purchase Rebates and	
Inventory, January 1	11,200	Allowances	740

Lots No. 2, 4, 6, 8, 10, and 12 on Fairmount Ave. were purchased as an investment by Mr. Fallon personally for $1,000 each. Lot No. 2 was sold for $1,400, and Lot No. 8 for $1,300. The money to buy the lots and to pay taxes and other expenses was supplied from the company's funds, and the proceeds from the sales were deposited to the company's credit. As the new bookkeeper for the Fallon Company, you have pointed out to Mr. Fallon that these transactions should not have been entered on the company's books, but in his personal books. He has instructed you to make the necessary entries to eliminate these items from the books of the company.

Set up in journal form the entries required, and then adjust the trial balance accordingly. Next prepare the statements which will show Mr. Fallon the results of the year's business. Then draft the journal entries required to close the ledger.

Credit the proprietor's Personal account with that part of the net profit required to close it, and carry the remainder to his Capital account.

Exercise 50

Your father, wishing to purchase a going lumber business and having $10,000 to invest, is offered two businesses which are for sale—the James Lumber Company and the State Lumber Company. The assets and liabilities as shown by the books of these concerns are as follows:

James Lumber Company		State Lumber Company	
Cash	$1,250.00	Cash	1,100.00
Accounts Payable	3,000.00	Accounts Receivable	6,600.00
Office Building	3,500.00	Notes Payable	2,250.00
Lumber Yard Land	7,000.00	Office Equipment	850.00
Lumber Inventory	3,000.00	Stock in Trade Inventory	6,000.00
Accounts Receivable	3,500.00	Notes Receivable	750.00
Furniture and Fixtures	700.00	Accounts Payable	2,300.00
Notes Payable	2,750.00		
Notes Receivable	1,000.00		
Mortgage Payable	3,600.00		

Your father has verified the cash balances, notes receivable, accounts receivable, notes payable, and accounts payable of both concerns. He finds, however, that about 5% of the accounts receivable of the James Lumber Company and about 10% of those of the State Lumber Company are doubtful of collection. He has come to the conclusion that the inventories of both concerns contain about $1,000 worth of lumber that will have to be sacrificed at about 20¢ on the dollar to get rid of it. He also found that the James Lumber Company is the endorser on a 60-day note for $200 made by James A. Clarke, a builder, to the Third National Bank, which was discounted by Mr. Clarke to raise money. The note has not yet become due, but Clarke's ability to pay it at its maturity is problematical, and it is practically certain the indorser will be held liable on it.

Your father wishes you to set up Balance Sheets for the two concerns to show their net assets after taking into consideration the facts above reported.

Keep in mind that your father is willing to allow $1,000 for good will in case he purchases either business; that the State Lumber Company pays $125 rent a month for its lumber yard; that both businesses are in a run-down condition and will require energetic effort to build them up, with the possibility of an advertising expenditure of $400 or $500 being required; that the liabilities of both concerns mature within 60 days, except the mortgage on the office building and land of the James Lumber Company, which has three years to run, with the next annual payment of $1,000 due six months hence; and that in paying $10,000 for either business he is investing all his cash and must depend on the income of the business to meet the living expenses of his family.

Which business would you advise him to purchase?   Write as many reasons to support your judgment as you can.

Exercise 51

John A. Marchant, a wholesale dealer in plumbers' supplies, started in business nearly two years ago.   He did not make an income tax return at the end of the first year he was in business, thinking that because he had conducted his business at a loss no return was necessary.   The Collector of Internal Revenue for his district has just notified him that he has violated the law in not making a return for last year, and on Mr. Marchant's making affidavit to the fact that he did not neglect to make a return through any intention to evade the income tax law but from ignorance of its provisions, the Collector has taken his case under advisement, after accepting a deposit of $50 as an offer of compromise in lieu of the assessment of the penalty prescribed by law against those who fail to make returns.   The Collector also called on Mr. Marchant to furnish his office with statements of his profits and losses, and of his assets and liabilities at the date of closing for the two years he has been in business.   These statements cannot be found in the files, and must be prepared from the trial balances taken on December 31 of the first and second year, respectively.   The trial balances appear on page 160.

The balance of $100 in the Profit and Loss account is the difference between a debit of $175 for the loss on the sale of second-hand office furniture and equipment, and a credit of $75 for a commission received for assisting a firm of plumbers in securing a contract.   As Mr. Marchant did not include explanations in posting to his Purchases and Sales accounts, and cannot find the original vouchers giving the amounts of goods returned, rebates and allowances on purchases and sales, etc., this detail cannot be shown in the statements.

1. Prepare the statements Mr. Marchant should submit to the Collector. Set up the miscellaneous profits and losses under separate headings.

2. Prepare for Mr. Marchant a tabulation showing the increase or decrease in the accounts included in the two income statements, and reconcile the net increase or net decrease of income with the difference between the final results shown by the two statements.

3. Prepare a similar tabulation of increases and decreases in the amounts of the various assets and liabilities, and reconcile the net increase or decrease of assets with the increase or decrease in invested capital.

4. Draft the journal entries to close the ledger for this year. Credit the net profit to the Capital account.

John A. Marchant

Trial Balances, December 31, 19—

Accounts	Last Year		This Year	
Mortgage Payable		4000 —		3000 —
Cash	2200 —		4140 —	
Notes Receivable	1300 —		1800 —	
Inventory	4500 —		4200 —	
Notes Payable		2000 —		1500 —
Building, 106 Howard St.	7000 —		7250 —	
Land, 106 Howard St.	3500 —		3500 —	
Accounts Receivable	1900 —		3100 —	
Purchases	18000 —		23600 —	
Warehouse Expense	1650 —		1920 —	
Accounts Payable		3000 —		3500 —
Salaries and Wages	5000 —		5300 —	
Real Estate Expense	720 —		690 —	
Sales		28000 —		39600 —
General Expense	2300 —		2100 —	
Real Estate Income		960 —		960 —
Interest Cost	140 —		270 —	
Losses on Bad Debts	90 —		120 —	
Interest Income		40 —		50 —
John A. Marchant, Capital		14100 —		13800 —
Freight Inward	1400 —		1600 —	
Warehouse Fixtures and Equipment	1800 —		1800 —	
John A. Marchant, Personal		100 —		
Office Furniture and Fixtures	700 —		920 —	
Profit and Loss			100 —	
	52200 —	52200 —	62410 —	62410 —

Review

Accounts. From the books of original entry—that is, the purchases book, the sales book, the cash book, and any other book of record in which entries have been made the first time—we post to the ledger or book of final entry.

Debit items are posted to the left-hand side of an account; credit items, to the right-hand side. When the left-hand side of an account is the larger, there is a debit balance; when the right-hand side is the larger, there is a credit balance.

The ledger, if correctly posted, contains a record of all transactions.

In double-entry bookkeeping, every transaction is entered in two accounts; therefore, debits and credits always balance, if the work is correct.

The Purchases account shows—

(1) Amount of merchandise purchased;

(2) Amount of merchandise returned or for which rebates or allowances have been made;

(3) Inventories, if necessary, to show the amount of merchandise on hand at the beginning and at the close of the accounting period.

When we purchase a bill of goods, we credit the person from whom we purchased it and debit Purchases account (included in the purchases book total).

The Sales account shows—

(1) Amount of goods sold;

(2) Amount of goods returned or rebates and allowances allowed.

When we sell merchandise to a customer, we debit his account and credit Sales account (included in the sales book total).

The Cash account is debited when cash is received; the person from whom the money is received is credited. The Cash account is credited when money is paid out; the person who receives the money is debited.

Assets, Liabilities, and Capital. Any value that is owned is an asset. Any debt or obligation that is owed is a liability. The owner's interest in a business is his capital.

Every business transaction affects the assets, liabilities, or capital of the business. For instance, a purchase for cash increases the asset *merchandise*, and decreases the asset *cash*. A charge purchase increases the asset *merchandise* and increases the liability *accounts payable*.

A sale for cash increases the asset *cash* and increases the *sales income account*.

A charge sale increases the asset *accounts receivable* and increases the *income sales account*.

When cash is received from a debtor, the asset *cash* is increased and the asset *accounts receivable* is decreased. When cash is paid to a creditor, the asset *cash* is decreased and the liability *accounts payable* is decreased.

When money is invested in the business, the *Capital account* is increased and the asset *cash* is increased.

	Increases			Decreases		
	Asset	Liability	Capital	Asset	Liability	Capital
(1)	$6,000		$6,000			
(2)	800	$800				
(3)	1,200			$1,200		
(4)	250			250		
(5)				300	$300	

(1) Invested $6,000.
(2) Purchase on account, $800.
(3) Purchase for cash, $1,200.
(4) Cash received on account, $250.
(5) Cash paid on account, $300.

Questions

1. Of what value are financial statements to the proprietor?
2. Why are financial statements of banks published?
3. What is the purpose of the Profit and Loss Statement?
4. Give several reasons for keeping books.
5. What does a checkmark in the folio column indicate?
6. Name several kinds of entries that are recorded in the general journal.
7. Discuss correction entries. Why are erasures on records never permissible?
8. Name the parties to a check.
9. What is meant by "acceptance" of a draft?
10. When is a note "protested"? Who pays the protest fees?
11. What are trading accounts?
12. What is meant by the expression, "f. o. b. point of shipment"?
13. What is forgery, and what precautions should be taken to prevent it?
14. What is meant by reconciling your bank balance?
15. Why are books closed?
16. Why are schedules of accounts receivable and accounts payable prepared?
17. What is *good will*? How is the value of *good will* determined?

Part Two
Partnership Accounting

220. The accounts required by commercial enterprises conducting wholesale businesses appropriate for the partnership or corporate form of organization, except the accounts that are peculiar to corporation accounting, are presented in Part Two. Corporation accounts are treated in Appendix A, page 283.

The material in Part Two correlates with Practice Set Two.

ASSETS, LIABILITY, AND CAPITAL ACCOUNTS

ASSETS

Current Assets:

    Cash

    Merchandise inventory

    Notes receivable

    Trade acceptances receivable

    Stock and bond investments

    Accounts receivable

    Advances to employees

    Accrued assets

Fixed Assets:

    Buildings

    Land

    Office furniture and equipment

    Store fixtures and equipment

    Delivery equipment

    Mortgages receivable

Deferred Debit Items:

    Insurance prepaid

    Interest prepaid

    Materials and supplies on hand

Other Assets:

    Doubtful assets

    Good will

LIABILITIES

Current Liabilities:

    Accrued liabilities

    Notes payable

    Trade acceptances payable

    Accounts payable

Fixed Liabilities:

    Mortgages payable

Deferred Credit Items:

    Rentals received in advance

    Interest collected in advance

Reserves for Depreciation

Capital

    Partners' capital accounts

    Partners' personal accounts

PROFIT AND LOSS ACCOUNTS

Cost of Goods Sold Group:

Purchases
Purchases returned
Purchases rebates and allowances
Freight and cartage inward
Duties and storage
Warehouse salaries and labor

Operating Expense Group:

Purchasing expense
Selling expense
Shipping materials and supplies
General expense
Administrative expense

Deductions from Income Group:

Interest expense
Interest on mortgaged debt
Bad debt losses
Miscellaneous losses

Income from Sales Group:

Sales
Sales returned
Sales rebates and allowances
Freight and cartage outward
Delivery expense*
Sales discounts

Additions to Income Group:

Real estate income
Interest income
Interest on bank deposits
Interest on mortgages receivable
Purchases discounts
Miscellaneous profits

* This account may be classified as a deduction from sales or as an operating expense.

Chapter 24—Partnership

221. In the preceding work in this text, we have studied the sole proprietorship form of business organization. Business organizations are also conducted under partnership agreements. A partnership may be said to exist when two or more persons contribute their money, services, or skill, or all of them, to be employed jointly in some lawful commerce or business, the profits or losses to be divided in certain agreed proportions. In a sole proprietorship business one owner furnishes the capital and usually manages the business. In a partnership there may be two or more owners, each supplying, as a rule, a certain amount of capital and having certain duties to perform in the management of the enterprise. There are two principal classes of partnerships—general partnerships and limited partnerships.

The Partnership Form of Business Organization Enables Two or More Individuals to Pool Their Capital and Experience in a Single Enterprise.

222. General partnerships. A general partnership is one in which all the partners are *real or ostensible* partners; that is, their names are made known, and they appear to the world as partners and in reality are such. In a general partnership *each* partner as a *joint owner* has the power to act for *all* the other partners as *their agent* in transacting the business of the partnership. *Each* member of a general partnership shares with his associates the liabilities for the debts of the partnership incurred

ARTICLES OF COPARTNERSHIP

This AGREEMENT made April 1, 19—, between JAMES CROWE
of 65 Broadway, Borough of Manhattan, New York City, WILLIAM
MASON of 1300 Adams Street, Hoboken, New Jersey, and HENRY
ADAMS of 2000 Bushwick Avenue, Brooklyn, New York,

WITNESSETH:

1. In consideration of the mutual covenants herein contained, and subject to the terms and conditions herein set
forth, the parties hereto agree as partners to engage in the
manufacture, distribution, and sale, at wholesale and retail,
of chemicals and chemical products for textile and similar
industries.

2. The name of the partnership shall be CROWE, MASON &
ADAMS.

3. The principal place of business of the partnership
shall be located at 65 Broadway, Borough of Manhattan, City of
New York, and the factory thereof shall be located at 1300
Adams Street, Hoboken, New Jersey. The firm may establish
such other branch places of business as may be unanimously
agreed by the parties hereto.

4. Purchases of raw materials and sales of products shall
be made wherever most advantageous.

5. The term of the partnership shall be five years,
beginning simultaneously with the execution hereof, and shall
end on the 31st day of March, 19—.

6. The capital of the firm shall be the sum of $90,000.
Each party shall contribute thereto contemporaneously with the
execution hereof the sum of $30,000 in cash. It is understood
and agreed that said contributions to capital shall bear no
interest.

7. Said capital and all other moneys of the firm, as
well as all instruments for the payment of moneys to the firm,
shall be deposited in the name of the firm with the Cosmo-
politan National Bank, of the Borough of Manhattan, City of
New York. All moneys credited in said bank to the partnership
shall be subject to withdrawal only by check in the name of
the partnership and signed jointly by any two of the parties
hereto.

8. No further advances of capital or moneys are to be
made to the partnership by any parties hereto without the
consent of the other parties, and in case such advances are
made with the consent of the parties hereto, the same shall
bear interest at the rate of 6% per annum.

9. Except as hereinafter otherwise provided, no advances
or loans shall be made by the partnership to any of the parties
hereto, save by unanimous consent of the parties hereto; and
in such event, the indebtedness shall bear interest at the
rate of 6% per annum.

10. Each party shall be entitled to draw from the funds
of the firm $150 a week for his living expenses. Such sums so
drawn shall be charged to him and, at the annual accounting,
debited against his share of the profits; and if, at such
annual accounting, the share of the profits of any of the
parties hereto shall not equal the sum or sums so drawn by
him, he shall at once pay the deficiency into the said firm,
which deficiency is to draw interest at 6% per annum until
paid.

11. Each party shall devote all his time and attention
to the business of the firm and shall not, during the term of
this agreement, either directly or indirectly, engage in any
other business, whether such business is competitive or
otherwise.

12. Neither party shall, without the consent of the others, and on behalf of the firm, make, execute, deliver, indorse, or guarantee any commercial paper, nor agree to answer for or indemnify against any act, debt, default, or misconduct of any person, corporation, or partnership (other than that of the parties hereto); nor shall any of the parties hereto, without the consent of the others, compromise or release debts owing the firm, except on full payment thereof; nor engage in any transaction or make any contract on account of the partnership involving more than $1,000.

13. Except as hereinafter otherwise provided, all differences as to the management of the business shall be decided by a majority of the parties hereto, which shall be binding on all parties and the firm.

14. Full and accurate accounts of the transactions of the partnership shall be kept in proper books at the principal place of business of the firm, and shall be open at all times to the inspection of any partner. Each party shall cause to be entered on said partnership books a full and accurate account of all his transactions in behalf of the firm.

15. At the end of each calendar year a full and accurate inventory shall be prepared, and the assets, liabilities, and income, both gross and net, shall be ascertained, and the net profits or net loss of the partnership shall be fixed and determined. The net profits or net loss shall be divided equally among the parties hereto, and the account of each shall be credited or debited, as the case may be, with his proportionate share thereof.

16. At the termination of this partnership, by the expiration of its term or for any other cause, a full and accurate inventory shall be prepared, and the assets, liabilities, and income, both gross and net, shall be ascertained; the debts of the partnership shall be discharged; and all moneys and other assets of the partnership then remaining shall be divided in specie among the parties, share and share alike.

17. Should the firm be dissolved by reason of the death, withdrawal, or other act of any partner before the expiration of said term, the remaining partners may, if they so desire, continue the business, and they shall have the right to purchase the interest of such partner in the business, assets, and good will by paying to such partner or his lawful representative or representatives, the value of such interest, as determined by the last annual inventory and accounting, together with 6% interest on such value since such inventory. On such payment, the retiring partner or his representatives shall execute and deliver to the remaining partners all necessary instruments conveying such interest. The continuing partners shall assume all existing firm obligations, hold the seller or sellers harmless from all liability thereon, and may use the firm name thereof, or any similar name, provided the same does not contain the name of the retiring partner.

IN WITNESS WHEREOF the parties have hereunto set their hands and seals the day and year first above written.

James Crowe   L. S.

Wm. Mason   L. S.

Henry Adams   L. S.

Illustration 67
ARTICLES OF COPARTNERSHIP

through the acts of *any* partner. The most important characteristic of a general partnership is the liability at common law placed on *each partner* for the *full amount of the partnership debts*. In other words, if a general partnership becomes insolvent, each partner's personal wealth and property are subject to seizure to pay the partnership debts.

223. Limited partnerships. A limited partnership is one in which *certain* partners are *denied the power to act as agents* of the other partners or to have any voice whatever in the management of the partnership business. On the other hand, the *liability* of the partners on partnership debts *is limited to the amount of capital contributed by them*. Such partners are called *special* partners. In a limited partnership, however, there *must be at least one general partner* who is liable for any deficiency in the assets available to liquidate partnership debts. Special partners must contribute *capital in cash or lawful money of the United States* in order to become partners.

Special Characteristics of Partnerships

The distinctive features of partnerships may be stated briefly as follows:

1. A partnership, whether general or limited, is founded upon a voluntary contract of mutual agency, generally referred to as "Articles of Copartnership," which should contain the following provisions:

(a) Date of the partnership contract.
(b) Names of the partners.
(c) Statement that they are to be partners in either a general or a limited partnership.
(d) Scope of the partnership enterprise.
(e) Duration of the partnership.
(f) Name of the firm and its principal office.
(g) Amount of the capital invested and each partner's investment.
(h) Stipulations governing the expenditure of partnership funds.
(i) Stipulations regarding the distribution of profits and the sharing of losses.
(j) Rights of the partners to withdraw money for personal use.
(k) Stipulations as to how the books of account shall be kept.
(l) Duties and responsibilities of the several partners.
(m) Special provisions and stipulations.
(n) Provision for the dissolution of the partnership.
(o) Method of dividing partnership assets on dissolution.

It should be clearly understood that partners must transact partnership business strictly within the provisions of the articles of copartnership.

The drawing of a partnership agreement, because of the liabilities of each partner to third parties and to his copartners, is a matter of such importance that it should always be entrusted to competent attorneys.

2. The liability of the individual partners for partnership debts as already discussed.

3. The joint ownership of partnership assets and profits, and the joint responsibility for partnership liabilities and losses. Each partner's interest in the assets, his share in the profits, his responsibility for liabilities, and the proportion of the losses he must assume must be clearly set forth in the partnership contract. In the absence of a contract, these questions must be decided by mutual consent or be adjudicated by the courts.

4. Partnerships have a limited life. The partnership contract should specify how long the partnership is to exist. In the absence of such a stipulation, the partnership continues at the will and mutual consent of the partners. A partnership may be terminated, however, by—

(a) insolvency and bankruptcy;
(b) the expiration of the term for which it was to exist;
(c) mutual consent of the partners;
(d) the death of one of the partners;
(e) the sale by one partner of his interest to a third party who is not a partner;
(f) the contemplated admission of a new partner who is not satisfactory to all the other partners; and
(g) the retirement of one of the partners.

On the dissolution of a partnership, the available assets must first be applied to liquidate all existing partnership liabilities. The remainder of the assets are then distributed to the several partners in proportion to their respective interests as stipulated in the partnership contract.

Partnership Accounts

224. The accounting of a partnership is conducted in the same manner as the accounting of a single proprietorship business except that each partner has a Capital account and a Personal account in the books of the partnership. Each partner's Capital account should be under his name, followed by the word "Capital" or "Partner." His Personal account should be under his name, followed by the word "Personal," or "Private," or "Drawing." The Capital and Personal accounts of partners are kept in accordance with the same principles which govern the keeping of a sole proprietor's Capital and Personal accounts.

Exercise 52

H. B. Gordon has been conducting a wholesale hardware business for several years. He has the opportunity to take on new lines of goods and to expand his business, but has not sufficient capital to do so. He is a careful financier, a shrewd buyer, and an efficient manager. However, he is not a good salesman. He finds it necessary, in order to have a well-balanced organization, to secure the services of a thoroughly experienced hardware man who is a competent salesman, and who has some capital to invest. He makes a proposal to C. M. Long, who meets his requirements, to become his partner. Mr. Gordon's invested capital at present is $20,000. Mr. Long is to invest $10,000 in cash and is to devote his full time and services to the partnership business. The contract of co-partnership stipulates that he is to have a one-third interest in the business. Mr. Long accepts Mr. Gordon's proposal, and their attorneys draw up a partnership agreement under which the partners are to conduct the business under the firm name of Gordon & Long. This agreement stipulates that they are to share in the profits and losses of the business in proportion to their capital investments.

Mr. Gordon's assets and liabilities at the time the partnership is formed are as follows:

Cash	3,000.00
Merchandise	12,000.00
Accounts Receivable	2,000.00
Delivery Equipment	1,000.00
Building Investment	8,000.00
Land Investment	2,000.00
Mortgage Payable	4,000.00
Notes Payable	1,000.00
Accounts Payable	3,000.00

1. In the books of the partnership, draft the journal entry required to record Mr. Gordon's investment.

2. Draft the entry to record Mr. Long's investment.

3. At the end of the first year's business, Gordon & Long's books show that the firm has made a net profit of $6,000, which stands to the credit of the Profit and Loss Summary account. The partners have decided to allow the net profit to remain in the business as an addition to the invested capital. Draft the journal entry to distribute the profit in accordance with this decision.

Exercise 53

R. L. Glade and C. J. Bronson have been conducting competing grocery stores in Forest Park, a suburb of Baltimore, for several years. They have decided to join forces, organize a partnership, and admit a third partner, Raymond Blake. The business is to be located in the store building owned by Mr. Glade. They will conduct the partnership business under the firm name, "Forest Park Grocery Company." Their attorneys have drawn up a partnership contract which has been duly executed. The assets and liabilities taken over by the Forest Park Grocery Company from the individuals composing the firm are as follows:

R. L. Glade		C. J. Bronson		Raymond Blake	
Cash	1200.00	Merchandise	6400.00	Cash	4000.00
Accounts Receivable	400.00	Notes Payable	1000.00	Notes Receivable	2000.00
Delivery Equipment	1200.00	Accounts Receivable	300.00		
Building Investment	12000.00	Delivery Equipment	1500.00		
Accounts Payable	2000.00	Accounts Payable	1600.00		
Land Investment	3000.00	Cash	400.00		
Merchandise	2200.00				
Mortgage Payable	6000.00				

1. Draft the opening entries for the books of the Forest Park Grocery Company.

2. Prepare a Balance Sheet of the partnership after the books are opened.

Exercise 54

At the close of the first year's business, Mr. Blake, who has been in charge of the accounting of the firm, submitted the following Balance Sheet to his partners, prepared before any adjustment of profits and losses had been made.

Forest Park Grocery Co.
Balance Sheet, December 31, 19—

Assets		Liabilities	
Cash	7,200.00	Notes Payable	500.00
Accounts Receivable	900.00	Accounts Payable	3,237.00
Notes Receivable	500.00	Mortgage Payable	4,500.00
Building Investment	14,000.00	Reserve for Building Depreciation	280.00
Land Investment	3,000.00	Reserve for Delivery Equipment	
Merchandise	9,675.00	Depreciation	675.00
Delivery Equipment	2,700.00	R. L. Glade, Capital	12,000.00
C. J. Bronson, Private	125.00	C. J. Bronson, Capital	6,000.00
		Raymond Blake, Capital	6,000.00
		Profit and Loss	4,908.00
Total Assets	38,100.00	Total Liabilities and Capital	38,100.00

1. During the year each partner drew a monthly salary of $200. These salaries were charged to the Salaries and Wages account, and credited to Cash as paid. Mr. Bronson drew $125 in excess of his salary, which was charged to his Personal account. This amount is to be taken out of his share of the profits.

2. The partners have decided to credit $3,200 of the net profit to their Capital accounts in the proper proportions, as it is their desire to retain this part of the profit in the business as working capital. The balance of the net profit is to be credited to their Personal accounts in the proper proportions, and then checks are to be issued immediately to the partners to close out their personal accounts.

3. Draft the journal entries required to record this distribution of profits, and make the entry in journal form required for the checks issued to the partners.

4. Prepare a Balance Sheet for the partnership after the books have been finally adjusted, making such changes in the amounts and in the arrangement of the items as set up in Mr. Blake's Balance Sheet as are necessary to exhibit the financial condition of the enterprise in proper form.

5. Can you suggest a reason for the increase of $2,000 shown by the Building Investment account?

Exercise 55

At the end of the second year's business, the firm had a net loss because of a fire which damaged the building and the stock in trade, not sufficient insurance having been carried. The amount of the net loss as shown by the Profit and Loss Statement was $1,200, which stands charged to the Profit and Loss Summary account. The partners closed out the loss against their Capital accounts.

1. Draft the journal entry required.

2. Prepare the partners' Capital accounts as they appear when closed at the end of the second year's business.

Exercise 56

Mr. Blake has had several disagreements with Mr. Glade and Mr. Bronson on matters of business policy. He has accordingly decided to retire from the firm at this time. The articles of copartnership stipulate that upon the retirement of any partner he is to receive payment for his interest as it may appear on the books of the firm on the date of with-drawal.   Mr. Glade and Mr. Bronson have agreed to pay Mr. Blake $4,000 out of the funds of the firm, and he is to accept the firm's note for the remainder of his interest, payable six months from December 31 with interest at 6%.   To carry out this arrangement, the check and note have been issued to Mr. Blake.

1. Draft in journal form the entries required to record the settlement made with Mr. Blake.

2. What actions should Mr. Glade and Mr. Bronson take immediately in continuing to do business as partners in the Forest Park Grocery Company?

Chapter 25—Control Accounts

225. A control account is a general ledger account that contains aggregate debits and credits which comprise the sum of the corresponding individual debits and credits in the books of original entry or in a group of accounts. In other words, it is a summary account.

When books of original entry—purchases book, cash payments book, and journal—are ruled with special columns in which to enter accounts payable items, the Accounts Payable account has the function of a control account. When the sales book, cash receipts book, and journal are ruled with special columns in which to enter accounts receivable items, the Accounts Receivable account has the function of a control account.

Self-Proving Special-Column Books of Original Entry

226. When separate accounts receivable and accounts payable ledgers are kept, it is necessary to have special columns in the books of original entry in which to make entries of the debits and credits to be posted to these ledgers. Books of original entry can also be designed in such manner as to make it possible to prove the equality of the debits and credits entered in each book. When a purchases book is ruled with two or more special columns, it is called a *columnar purchases* book.

To illustrate, the following purchases book is a form commonly used:

Purchases Book

Date		L. P.	Accounts credited	Date of invoice	Terms	Purchases Dr.		Freight Inward Dr.		Accounts Payable Cr.	
19–											
Jan.	3		Koehring & Co.	Dec. 31	30 days	200	—			200	—
	8		Mason & Bridge	Jan. 2	2/10 n/30	320	—	36	13	356	13
	17		J. B. Carson & Co.	Jan. 12	2/10 n/30	318	90			318	90
	25		Easton Canning Co.	Jan. 19	2/10 n/30	586	90	44	23	631	13
	29		Koehring & Co.	Jan. 24	30 days	711	47			711	47
						2137	27	80	36	2217	63

Illustration 68

The first entry in Illustration 68 records an invoice received from Koehring & Company for goods purchased, the invoice cost of which was $200. Observe that this amount is entered in the Purchases Dr. column and in the Accounts Payable Cr. column, and is the equivalent of an ordinary journal entry. Notice also that the invoice was entered on January 3, but was dated December 31, terms 30 days.

The second entry records a purchase of merchandise from Mason & Bridge amounting to $320, to which were added freight charges prepaid amounting to $36.13, making the total of the invoice $356.13. The invoice cost of the merchandise is entered in the Purchases Dr. column, the freight in the Freight Inward Dr. column, and the total amount of the invoice in the Accounts Payable Cr. column. The sum of the two entries in the debit columns is thus equal to the entry in the credit column. It follows, therefore, that if all entries are made correctly, the sum of the footings of the debit columns will equal the footing of the credit column. When the totals are posted to the ledger accounts, the debit of $2,137.27 to the Purchases account plus the debit to Freight Inward account of $80.36, a total of $2,217.63, will equal the amount credited to the Accounts Payable account.

Exercise 57

1. Rule paper similar to the rulings shown in Illustration 68, write the headings, and enter the following purchases of J. M. Snowden:

Sept. 3 Turner & Son, 8/31, 30 days, $600.00 Freight In $44.50
4 T. J. Franklin, 9/1, 2/10 n/30 728.40
5 A. W. Johnson, 9/3, 2/10 n/30 255.00 Freight In 25.00
7 Turner & Son, 9/5, 30 days 370.00
10 Watson Company, 9/7, 2/10 n/30 465.00 Freight In 72.16
11 Jones & Dewers, 9/10, 30 days 820.00 Freight In 17.83
12 A. W. Johnson, 9/11, 2/10 n/30 116.00

2. Show proof that the footings of Accounts Payable credit equal the Purchases debit plus the Freight Inward debit.

3. Prepare a general journal entry to show how the totals of the purchases book show both debits and credits.

4. How much would Mr. Snowden save if he paid invoices on which he was allowed 2% discount within the discount period?

227. The sales book may be ruled in a similar manner, as shown in the following illustration:

Sales Book

Date	L. P.	Accounts debited	Order No.	Terms	Accounts Receivable Dr.		Sales Cr.		Freight Out Cr.	
19—										
Jan. 5		Walter A. Hodge	1	2/10 n/30	509	50	509	50		
8		Barton & Co.	2	2/10 n/30	314	22	294	14	20	08
15		L. C. Fowler	3	30 days	414	26	381	49	32	77
17		O. C. Johnston & Son	4	2/10 n/30	678	53	678	53		
22		Walter A. Hodge	5	2/10 n/30	375	42	359	14	16	28
28		Barton & Co.	6	30 days	429	50	429	50		
					2721	43	2652	30	69	13

Illustration 69

In the first entry the selling price of the goods sold to Walter A. Hodge is $509.50; consequently, Accounts Receivable account is debited and Sales account is credited for this amount in the first two columns.   In the second entry, however, the selling price of the goods is $294.14; but as freight prepaid amounting to $20.08 is added to the invoice, the customer is charged for the total, or $314.22.   The entry of $314.22 in the Accounts Receivable Dr. column is equal to the sum of $294.14 and $20.08 entered in the Sales Cr. and Freight Out Cr. columns, respectively.   It follows, therefore, that when the sales book is footed at the close of the month, the sum of the footings of the credit columns will be equal to the footing of the debit column.

Observe that the Freight Out account is credited for the amount of freight charged on bills rendered to customers for goods sold.   These credits offset or cancel the debits to the Freight Out account entered in the cash book for the cash paid out to prepay the charges on shipments to customers.   In other words, if $100 had been paid out during January for freight on outgoing shipments, of which amount $69.13 was chargeable to customers, the Freight Out account would have been charged from the cash book for $100, and would have been credited from the sales book for $69.13, leaving a debit balance of $30.87 in the Freight Out account. This amount represents the expense for freight out incurred by the seller for shipping goods to customers f. o. b. delivery point.

Instead of keeping a sales book similar to the one shown in Illustration 69, many concerns prepare invoices for goods sold on printed sales invoice forms made out in duplicate.   The forms are numbered consecutively. The original copies are mailed to customers.   The duplicate copies serve a twofold purpose: (1) The charges to customer's accounts are posted from them to the accounts in the sales ledger.   They thus serve as a looseleaf sales book.   Under this plan, order numbers are posted to customers' accounts so that whenever it is necessary to look up details of a sale, the order can be readily located in the sales binder by reference to the customer's account for the order number.   (2) At the end of the month the total sales are ascertained by listing on a sales abstract sheet the number and amounts of all sales invoices written during the month.   This sheet contains columns for accounts receivable debits, sales credits, and freight out credits, and is used as a posting medium in posting totals to the general ledger.

Exercise 58

1. Rule paper similar to the rulings in the sales book shown in Illustration 69, print in headings, and enter the following sales of J. M. Snowden:

Order
No.

1	Sept.	2 McDonald Bros., 2/10 n/30	$245.60	Freight Out $24.40
2		5 T. M. Sloan, 2/10 n/30	402.88	Freight Out 16.25
3		8 J. B. Carson, 30 days	325.00	Freight Out 16.25
4		15 Mason & Company, 2/10 n/30	480.00	Freight Out 72.40
5		17 Silver & Grant, 30 days	640.28	
6		23 T. M. Sloan, 2/10 n/30	462.48	
7		29 J. B. Carson, 30 days	680.00	

2. Show proof that the footings of the Accounts Receivable debit equal the Sales credit plus the Freight Outward credit.

3. Prepare a general journal entry to show how the totals of the sales book show both debits and credits.

4. How much money would Mr. Snowden actually receive if his debtors paid within the discount period?

228. The special-column cash book illustrated below is used extensively by wholesale and mercantile concerns.

Cash Receipts

Date	L. P.	Account Credited	Explanation		Cash Dr.	Sales Discounts Dr.	Accounts Receivable Cr.	General Ledger Cr.
19–								
Jan. 1	1	Balance		679.50				
4		Notes Payable	60-day loan at bank		1000 —			1000 —
7		Burnside Grocery	Bill Dec. 6		128 45		128 45	
10		Walter A. Hodge	Bill Jan. 5		499 31	10 19	509 50	
14		Freight Inward	Rebate on frt. bill		13 62			13 62
21		O. C. Johnston & Son	Bill Jan. 17		664 96	13 57	678 53	
24		Sales	Cash Sales		209 42			209 42
29		Notes Receivable	F. A. Blair's note		100 —			100 —
29		Interest Income	60 days' int. on note		1 —			1 —
31		Total Cash Receipts			2616 76			
31		Balance Jan. 1			679 50			
					3296 26	23 76	1316 48	1324 04
Feb. 1		Balance		971.42				

Illustration 70

Observe that the cash balance at the beginning of the month is noted in the explanation column so that the footing of the Cash Dr. column will show the total receipts for the month. The Cash Cr. column shows the total cash payments. To balance the book at the close of the month, the balance on January 1 is added to the total receipts to get the footing of $3,296.26, which represents the sum of the balance at the beginning of the month plus the receipts during the month. From this amount the total payments are deducted, and the difference of $971.42, which represents the balance at the close of the month, is added to the payments to get the proof footing of $3,296.26. The balance is then brought down under date of February 1, the amount being entered in the explanation column.

Cash Payments

Date		L. P.	Account Debited	Explanation	Cash Cr.		Purchase Discounts Cr.		Accounts Payable Dr.		General Ledger Dr.	
19—												
Jan.	1		General Expense	Jan. rent	175	—					175	—
	2		F. A. Meyer & Co.	Bill Dec. 4	228	40			228	40		
	4		Interest Expense	60 days discount on note	10	—					10	—
	10		Mason & Bridge	Bill Jan. 2	349	73	6	40	356	13		
	15		Selling Expense	Advertising	35	40					35	40
	18		Freight Inward	P.R.R. bill Jan. 17	21	29					21	29
	20		J. B. Carson & Co.	Bill Jan. 12	312	52	6	38	318	90		
	26		Notes Payable	Note due today	500	—					500	00
	26		Interest Expense	30 days' int. on note	2	50					2	50
	31		General Expense	Salaries	240	—					240	—
	31		Warehouse Expense	Wages	125	—					125	—
	31		Administrative Exp.	Salaries	325	—					325	—
	31		Total Cash Payments		2324	84						
	31		Balance Jan. 31		971	42						
					3296	26	12	78	903	43	1434	19

Illustration 71

This arrangement of the cash book makes it possible to prove the equality of debit and credit items on each side of the book, as follows:

Proof of Cash Book Footings

Receipts Side			Payments Side		
Cash Dr.	2616.76		Accounts Payable Dr.	903.43	
Sales Discounts Dr.	23.76		General Ledger Dr.	1434.19	
Total Debits		2640.52	Total Debits		2337.62
Accounts Receivable Cr.	1316.48		Cash Cr.	2324.84	
General Ledger Cr.	1324.04		Purchase Discounts Cr.	12.78	
Total Credits		2640.52	Total Credits		2337.62

Proof of Cash Balance

Balance Jan. 31, per checkbook stub	921.42
On hand in petty cash drawer	50.00
Balance Jan. 31, per cash book	971.42

Study the entries in the cash book. Observe that on January 4 a note for $1,000 was discounted at bank, the discount amounting to $10. On the receipts side, cash is debited for the face of the note by the entry of $1,000 in the Cash Dr. column, and the Notes Payable account is credited by the entry in the General Ledger Cr. column, the Notes Payable account being a general ledger account. On the payments side, Interest Expense is debited for $10 by the entry in the General Ledger Dr. column, the Interest Expense account being a general ledger account, while cash is credited by the entry in the Cash Cr. column. The difference between the debit of $1,000 and the credit of $10 to the Cash account represents the proceeds of the note, $990, which would be entered on the checkbook stub as a deposit. Thus, in every entry on either side of this cash book, both the debit and credit items are entered.

On January 7 Burnside Grocery paid an invoice amounting to $128.45, on which no cash discount was taken. Observe that the debit to cash is entered in the Cash Dr. column and the credit to the customer in the Accounts Receivable Cr. column, the Burnside Grocery account being a sales, or customers', ledger account. Notice, however, that when Walter A. Hodge paid his invoice of $509.50, he deducted a cash discount of $10.19, the amount of his check being $499.31. The actual cash received is entered in the Cash Dr. column, the amount of the cash discount is entered in the Sales Discounts Dr. column, and the amount of the invoice, representing the sum of the cash received and the discount, is entered in the Accounts Receivable Cr. column, Mr. Hodge's account being a sales ledger account.

The rent of $175 for January was paid on January 1. Observe that the credit to cash is entered in the Cash Cr. column, and the debit to General Expense in the General Ledger Dr. column, that account being a general ledger account. On January 2 a payment of $228.40 was made to F. A. Meyer & Company in payment of an invoice for goods purchased, no cash discount being taken. The payment is entered in the Cash Cr. column and in the Accounts Payable Dr. column, Meyer & Company's account being a creditors' ledger account. On January 10 Mason & Bridge were paid $349.73 in full for an invoice owed to them amounting to $356.13, on which a cash discount of $6.40 was deducted. Cash is credited for the cash actually paid, the discount is entered in the Purchase Discounts Cr. column, and the amount charged to Mason & Bridge is entered in the Accounts Payable Dr. column, the account being a creditors' ledger account. Study the other entries in the cash book and determine why the entries shown were made.

229. Illustration 72 shows a standard form of journal used when a purchase ledger and a sales ledger are kept in addition to the general ledger.

Journal, January 5, 19—

L. P.	Explanation	General Ledger		Accounts Receivable		Accounts Payable	
		Dr.	Cr.	Dr.	Cr.	Dr.	Cr.
	Koehring & Co.					12 50	
	Purchases Returned		12 50				
	Goods returned for credit on their bill of Dec. 31						
	12						
	Notes Receivable	314 22					
	Barton & Co.				314 22		
	Received their 30-day note dated Jan. 8 for bill of same date						
	25						
	Easton Canning Co.					19 20	
	Purchases Reb. & Allow.		19 20				
	Overcharge due to error on their bill of Jan. 19						
	26						
	Sales Rebates & Allowances	5 42					
	Walter A. Hodge				5 42		
	Credit allowed for defective goods billed on Jan. 22						
	31						
	Freight Inward	41 65					
	Koehring & Co.						41 65
	Debit memo. for freight prepaid on bill of Jan. 24						
	31						
	Barton & Co.			10 —			
	Delivery Expense		10 —				
	Hauling charges on goods billed on Jan. 28						
		361 29	41 70	10 —	319 64	31 70	41 65

Illustration 72

Observe that all entries to be posted to sales ledger accounts are entered in the debit and credit columns for accounts receivable, all entries to be posted to accounts in the purchase ledger are entered in the accounts payable columns, and all entries to be posted to general ledger accounts are entered in the general ledger columns. The equality of debits and credits in this journal can be proved by comparing the sum of the footings of the debit and credit columns, as follows:

Debit Footings	Credit Footings
361.29	41.70
10.00	319.64
31.70	41.65
402.99	402.99

230. In view of the foregoing discussion of special rulings in the books of original entry, it is apparent that special columns are used for three principal purposes:

(1) To segregate in a special column numerous debits or credits to a given account so that the total of such items may be posted monthly instead of posting individual entries daily, thus saving time and labor;

(2) To segregate in special columns debit and credit items affecting accounts kept in subsidiary ledgers so that the totals of these columns may be posted monthly to control accounts in the general ledger; and

(3) To classify the debit and credit items recorded in the several books of original entry in such a way that the equality of the total debit items and the total credit items may be readily determined before postings to the general ledger are made, thus preventing errors in general ledger accounts and in trial balances.

Chapter 26—Current Assets

231. Generally speaking, the current assets of a trading business are its cash, stock in trade, and "receivables." The stock in trade and receivables are constantly in process of being converted into cash. The cash assets and credit of a concern are employed to purchase stocks of merchandise. These investments are converted into notes and accounts receivable as the goods are sold. As the receivables are collected they are converted into cash, thus completing the "trading cycle."

Current assets are frequently referred to as the *quick, liquid, floating,* or *working* assets, to express the idea that they are constantly fluctuating in amount as they are employed in carrying on the operations and processes of the business. It is partly from this conversion of assets from one form to another that profits are made or losses are incurred.

Cash Account

232. The Cash account is debited for all cash received and credited for all cash paid. Its balance shows the amount of cash which should be on hand, whether in bank or in the cash drawer. The entries in this account are the postings of the total receipts and total payments from the cash book. The cash book is thus used as a *posting medium* to transfer the receipts and expenditures to the cash account.

The balance shown by the Cash account at the end of any month should be proved, or "reconciled," with the sum of the cash in bank and on hand at that time. Because it provides for such reconciliation, the Cash account may be called a "control" account. A control account is a general ledger account that contains the *aggregate debits and credits* which comprise the *sum of the corresponding individual debits and credits* in the books of original entry, or in a group of accounts. In other words, it is a *summary* account. For instance, if the balance of cash on hand at the beginning of a month is $500, and there have been receipts of $100, $200, $300, and $400 entered during the month in the cash receipts book, the amount of the posting for the total cash receipts to the Cash account must be $1,000, and the debit footing of the Cash account must be the sum of the balance and the total receipts, or $1,500. Similarly, if all cash received is deposited, the total deposits during the month must be equal to the difference between the debit footing of the Cash account at the close of the month and the balance at the beginning of the month.

Likewise, if the payments were $100, $200, and $300, the posting of the total payments to the credit of Cash account must be the sum of the individual payments, or $600. Further, if all payments were made by check, the sum of the checks paid by the bank would likewise be $600, or an amount equal to the credit footing of the Cash account. The balance at the end of the month is therefore the difference between the debit and credit footings of the Cash account, or $900. The balance may be proved by adding to the previous balance of $500 the receipts of $1,000, and subtracting the payments of $600.

Accounts Receivable Account

233. The accounts receivable previously considered have consisted of the amounts owed by customers and trade debtors for goods sold to them. Accounts receivable may also include charges to patrons for services rendered. For instance, the sums owed by patients for services rendered are the accounts receivable of a physician, and the sums owed to public utility corporations for electric light, gas, and telephone services are accounts receivable to such concerns.

234. Function of Accounts Receivable as a control account. In the previous work of this course all accounts, including those with customers and trade debtors, have been kept in one ledger. The ledger which contains the asset, liability, capital, income, and profit and loss accounts is referred to as the general ledger. As a separate account must be kept with each customer, it is obvious that in most businesses the general ledger would quickly become filled with accounts receivable. For this reason businesses with large numbers of customers find it convenient to keep customers' accounts in a separate ledger.

When a separate class or group of accounts is segregated in a separate ledger, a summary account must be kept in the general ledger to represent them. Such a summary account is called a *control account*, because it is debited and credited for the total amounts of all charges and credits to the group of accounts it replaces. The ledger containing the segregated accounts is referred to as a subsidiary ledger. The ledger containing the segregated accounts of trade debtors is variously designated as the customers' ledger, the sales ledger, or the accounts receivable ledger.

The sales book of John Walker & Company for January is reproduced on page 184. It is obvious that the sales which were made required the opening of the accounts which appear opposite the sales book, if all accounts are kept in the general ledger.

Book of Original Entry Sales Book, January 2, 19—		General Ledger W. C. Archer	
W. C. Archer	$100 —	100.00	
5		400.00	
H. M. Carter & Co.	200 —	H. M. Carter & Co.	
11		200.00	
Wm. Martin Sons Co.	300 —	Wm. Martin Sons Co.	
18		300.00	
W. C. Archer	400 —	500.00	
23		A. B. Phelps Co.	
Wm. Martin Sons Co.	500	600.00	
29		Sales	
A. B. Phelps Co.	600 —		2100.00
Total Sales	2100 —		

Observe that the amounts of the sales are posted to the Personal accounts of the several customers, and that the Sales account is credited for the total sales. When customers' accounts are segregated in a sales ledger, thus removing them from the general ledger, it is necessary to open the Accounts Receivable account in the general ledger to take their place. Accordingly, at the close of each month the Accounts Receivable account is debited for the total sales at the same time that the Sales Account is credited. In other words, the total of the sales for each month is debited to Accounts Receivable and credited to Sales. If the accounting work is done accurately, the total of the charges to customers for goods sold as thus recorded in the general ledger must be equal to the sum of the charges for goods sold posted from the sales book to customers' accounts in the sales ledger. Thus, the general ledger account is said to *control* the sales ledger accounts. If the customers' accounts referred to above are segregated in the sales ledger, the general ledger and sales ledger accounts will appear as follows:

Sales Ledger W. C. Archer		General Ledger Accounts Receivable	
100.00		2100.00	
400.00		Sales	
H. M. Carter & Co.			2100.00
200.00			
Wm. Martin Sons Co.			
300.00			
500.00			
A. B. Phelps Co.			
600.00			

Observe that the sum of the debits posted to the sales ledger accounts is equal to the amount posted to the debit of the Accounts Receivable account in the general ledger.

During January the cash receipts book of John Walker & Company, including sums received from customers on account as well as other receipts, shows the following items. As the customers' accounts are kept separate in the sales ledger, it follows that the receipts from customers to apply on their accounts must be segregated or separated in the cash receipts book by entering them in a separate, or special, column in order to ascertain at the end of the month the total to be posted to the credit of the accounts receivable in the general ledger. This total thus controls the items credited to customers' accounts in the sales ledger from the cash book.

Cash Receipts Book

Date	Accounts	Accounts Receivable Cr.	Cash Dr.
19–			
Jan. 8	Cash Sales		60 —
15	H. M. Carter & Co.	200 —	200 —
18	Real Estate Income		100 —
27	W. C. Archer	300 —	300 —
29	Cash Sales		40 —
30	Wm. Martin Sons Co.	300 —	300 —
		800 —	1000 —

Sales Ledger

W. C. Archer

100.00	300.00
400.00	

H. M. Carter & Co.

200.00	200.00

Wm. Martin Sons Co.

300.00	300.00
500.00	

A. B. Phelps Co.

600.00	

General Ledger

Accounts Receivable

2100.00	800.00

Sales

	2100.00
	60.00
	40.00

Real Estate Income

	100.00

Cash

1000.00	

The schedule of open accounts in the sales ledger, and the trial balance of the general ledger, now show the following results:

Schedule of Accounts Receivable of Sales Ledger		Trial Balance General Ledger		
W. C. Archer	200.00	Accounts Receivable	1300.00	
Wm. Martin Sons Co.	500.00	Sales		2200.00
A. B. Phelps Co.	600.00	Real Estate Income		100.00
		Cash	1000.00	
Total Accounts Receivable	1300.00		2300.00	2300.00

Observe that the sum of the balances of the customers' accounts in the sales ledger is equal to the balance of the Accounts Receivable account in the general ledger. In other words, the balance of the latter account controls the sum of the balances in the sales ledger.

The principal purposes of segregating personal accounts receivable in the sales ledger and setting up a control account for them in the general ledger are—

(1) To reduce the clerical work of the general bookkeeper, as assistant bookkeepers can be assigned the task of keeping sales ledger accounts.

(2) To expedite the taking of trial balances of the general ledger, because the control account for accounts receivable in the general ledger takes the place of hundreds and even thousands of customers' accounts. An error in the sales ledger consequently does not hold up the taking of the general ledger trial balance until the mistake is found.

(3) The general bookkeeper is enabled to maintain a check or proof on the accuracy of the sales ledger clerks.

(4) The general ledger is relieved of all personal accounts with trade debtors.

A similar system of maintaining a general ledger control over accounts with trade creditors can be established by keeping the Accounts Payable account as a summary account in the same manner. The control of Accounts Payable, which are kept in the purchase ledger or creditors' ledger, will be discussed in connection with accounts payable. In large businesses it is sometimes necessary to have several sales ledgers, such as Sales Ledger A-F, Sales Ledger G-K, Sales Ledger L-Q, and Sales Ledger R-Z.

235. At least once a year the sales ledgers should be reviewed thoroughly by the general bookkeeper for the purpose of listing "doubtful" accounts and "uncollectible" accounts. A doubtful account is one which is some time past due and which has not been collected after resorting to the usual methods employed in collecting delinquent accounts. The total of doubtful accounts should be deducted from the total accounts receivable, and should be set up as a separate item under the caption "Other Assets" in preparing a balance sheet. It is evident that as doubtful accounts receivable are past-due accounts, the collection of which is uncertain, they should not be included as current assets with the other current assets receivable not yet due.

Bad accounts receivable are accounts considered to be uncollectible; consequently, they become *losses*. At least once a year such accounts should be listed and charged off the books by debiting Bad Debt Losses account and crediting Accounts Receivable. Losses from bad debts result from selling on credit to customers who subsequently become financially embarrassed or fail in business, and to dishonest people who will not pay their just debts. Such losses are incurred by practically all businesses and cannot be entirely avoided.

Exercise 59

May   1 Sold goods to McCormick & Co., $211.42.
    3 Sold merchandise to Forbes & Keck, $309.22.
    8 Sold Niles Barton & Co. on account, $475.
   11 Received check from McCormick & Co. on account, $175.
   14 Sold merchandise to John B. Austin, $328.48.
   22 Sold goods to State Electric Co., $121.42.
   28 Received check from Niles Barton & Co. for invoice May 8, $475.
June 2 Sold goods to McCormick & Co., $41.80.
    8 Received check from Forbes & Keck for invoice May 3, $309.22.
   17 Sold Niles Barton & Co. goods amounting to $144.20.
   23 Sold merchandise to State Electric Co., $89.19.
   27 Received check from John B. Austin on account, $200.
   29 Received check from State Electric Co. for invoice June 23, $89.19.

1. Set up the sales book and cash book entries to record these transactions.

2. Open sales ledger accounts for the customers and post the entries.

3. Set up general ledger accounts to record the status of the transactions as of May 31, and again as of June 30, including a control account for the sales ledger.

4. Reconcile the schedule of accounts receivable with the balance of the control account as of May 31 and June 30.

Questions

1. Show that the Accounts Receivable account has the function of a control account.

2. What four advantages are gained by segregating personal accounts receivable and setting up a control account for them in the general ledger?

3. What are "doubtful" accounts?

4. How should "doubtful" accounts be listed in the balance sheet?

5. How are "uncollectible accounts" handled?

Chapter 27—Accounts Payable Account

236. The obligations included in the Accounts Payable account of a trading concern are the debts owed to trade creditors for merchandise purchased on account. This account functions as a control account in the same manner that the Accounts Receivable account controls debtors' accounts in the customers' ledger. In order to remove the personal accounts with individual creditors from the general ledger, they are segregated in a separate ledger, which is referred to as the *purchase* or *creditors'* ledger.

237. Function of Accounts Payable account as a control account. When the Accounts Payable account is conducted as a control account, the books of original entry must be ruled with special columns in which to enter accounts payable items. To illustrate, the following transactions are recorded properly in the accompanying cash payments book, purchases book, and journal.

Jan. 4 Purchased merchandise from C. A. Blake & Sons, $100.
      8 Bought merchandise from Bowen & King, $200.
    15 Returned goods to C. A. Blake & Sons for credit, $20.
    16 Bought merchandise from Armstrong Clothing Co., $300.
    18 Received a debit memorandum from Bowen & King for undercharge on invoice of goods entered on January 8, $70.
    20 Paid balance due on C. A. Blake & Sons' invoice entered January 4, $80.
    22 Bought merchandise from Bowen & King, $400.
    23 Paid Armstrong Clothing Co. on account, $150.
    27 Received rebate from Armstrong Clothing Co. for overcharge, $10.
    28 Paid Bowen & King for invoice entered January 8, $270.
    30 Bought merchandise from C. A. Blake & Sons, $500.
    30 Credited C. A. Blake & Sons for freight prepaid by them on invoice of goods entered on this date, $40.

Purchases Book, January 4, 19—

C. A. Blake & Sons	100 —
8	
Bowen & King	200 —
16	
Armstrong Clothing Co.	300 —
22	
Bowen & King	400 —
30	
C. A. Blake & Sons	500 —
Total Purchases	1500 —

Cash Payments Book

Date	Accounts	Accounts Payable Dr.	Cash Cr.
19–			
Jan. 20	C. A. Blake & Sons	80 —	80 —
23	Armstrong Clothing Co.	150 —	150 —
28	Bowen & King	270 —	270 —
		500 —	500 —

189

Journal, January 1, 19—

		General Ledger		Accounts Payable	
		Dr.	Cr.	Dr.	Cr.
	15				
C. A. Blake & Sons				20 —	
Purchases			20 —		
	18				
Purchases		70 —			
Bowen & King					70 —
	27				
Armstrong Clothing Co.				10 —	
Purchases			10 —		
	30				
Freight In		40 —			
C. A. Blake & Sons					40 —
		110 —	30 —	30 —	110 —

When the foregoing entries and totals are posted, the accounts in the creditors' ledger and in the general ledger will appear as follows:

Purchase Ledger

C. A. Blake & Sons

Jan. 15	20.00	Jan. 4	100.00
20	80.00	30	500.00
		30	40.00

Bowen & King

Jan. 28	270.00	Jan. 8	200.00
		18	70.00
		22	400.00

Armstrong Clothing Co.

Jan. 23	150.00	Jan. 16	300.00
27	10.00		

General Ledger

Purchases

Jan. 18	70.00	Jan. 15	20.00
30	1500.00	27	10.00

Freight In

Jan. 30	40.00	

Accounts Payable

Jan. 31	500.00	Jan. 31	1500.00
Jan. 31	30.00	Jan. 31	110.00

Cash

		Jan. 31	500.00

Trace all postings from the books of original entry to the ledgers. Observe that all postings to the purchase ledger accounts are for items entered in special columns. The one money column in the purchases book is the equivalent of a special column, because its total is posted to the debit of the Purchases account and to the credit of the Accounts Payable account in the general ledger. In other words, in every instance in which a creditor's account is debited or credited, the Accounts Payable account is likewise debited or credited, because the totals of all special columns for purchase ledger items are posted at the close of the month to that account.

Observe also that the credit balance of the Accounts Payable account is equal to the sum of the credit balances of the creditors' accounts in the purchase ledger.

Exercise 60

Record the following transactions in a purchases book, sales book, cash receipts and payments books with double money columns, and in a special-column journal containing debit and credit columns for general ledger accounts, sales ledger accounts, and purchase ledger accounts.

Jan. 2 Bought merchandise from Walter Williams & Co., $300.
  2 Sold merchandise to J. H. Broome, $100.
  3 Bought merchandise from Carter & Clarke, $400.
  5 Sold merchandise to Boyce & Richards, $200.
  6 Received debit memo. for prepaid freight on purchase from Walter Williams & Co. entered on January 2, $45.
  7 Sold goods to Manning & Sons, $300.
  8 Allowed credit to J. H. Broome for goods returned for credit, $20.
  9 Sold goods to Boyce & Richards, $400.
  10 Allowed Manning & Sons credit for damaged goods sold them on January 7, $15.
  12 Sold goods to Fletcher Bros. Co., $150.
  13 Purchased merchandise from Merchants Supply Co., $500.
  14 Sent debit memorandum to Walter Williams & Co. for defective goods returned for credit, $18.
  15 Sold merchandise to J. H. Broome, $250.
  16 Purchased goods from Carter & Clarke, $600.
  17 Received cash from Boyce & Richards in full of account, $600.
  19 Received check from J. H. Broome on account, $200.
  20 Received credit from Merchants Supply Co. for overcharge on invoice entered on January 13, $30.
  21 Sold goods to Fletcher Bros. Co., $350.
  22 Issued check to Walter Williams & Co. on account, $150.
  23 Issued check to Carter & Clarke for invoice entered January 3, $400.
  24 Fletcher Bros. Co. returned merchandise for credit, $40.
  26 Sold goods to Boyce & Richards, $450.
  27 Received cash from Manning & Sons for balance of invoice of January 7, $285.
  28 Sold goods to J. H. Broome, $75.
  29 Sold goods to Manning & Sons, $100.
  30 Issued check to Merchants Supply Co. on account, $100.
  31 Received check from Fletcher Bros. Co. on account, $300.

1. Open accounts for debtors and creditors in the sales ledger and purchase ledger, respectively. Also open the general ledger accounts required. Post all daily entries. Then foot the books of original entry and post the totals.

2. Take trial balances of each ledger and reconcile the purchases and sales ledger balances with the respective control accounts.

Questions

1. What account in the general ledger controls the accounts in the purchases ledger?

2. Explain the function of the accounts payable account as a control account.

3. What accounts are included in the creditors' ledger?

Chapter 28—Merchandise Inventory Account

238. The inventory account is debited at the close of a fiscal period for the inventory value of the stock in trade on hand at that time. It should be credited on the first day of the succeeding fiscal period for the same amount. The purpose of the inventory account is to set up on the books as an asset the inventory on hand at the close of a period, and to clear the amount of the inventory from the purchases account, since it is not a part of the cost of goods sold for the period for which profits are being computed.

Exercise 61

R. L. Johnson's inventory of merchandise at the end of last year was $5,678.40.

Give the journal entry for December 31 of last year, and for January 1 of the present year.

Valuation of the Merchandise Inventory

239. From the time accounting was developed on a scientific basis, the prevailing practice in calculating inventories has been to price the goods on hand at their cost price, or at their market price in case it was lower than cost price.

For example, let us suppose that a shoe dealer includes in his inventory 100 pairs of shoes which originally cost $3 a pair. However, the market price at the time of the taking of inventory is $3.50. Shall the merchant inventory these shoes at $3 or $3.50?

240. When market is above cost. Inventorying at the market price will result in making the total inventory $50 greater than if the cost of $300 were taken as the inventory figure. This increase in the inventory will result in a corresponding decrease of $50 in the cost of goods sold for the period, which in turn will result in increasing the gross trading income by $50 when the total cost of goods sold is deducted from the net income from sales in finding the gross trading income.

241. When market is below cost. Now let us assume that the market price of the shoes in question is $2.50. Shall the merchant inventory them at $300, their cost price, or at $250, their market price? The prevailing practice has been to inventory at the market price, in case it is lower than cost, for the reason that it is conservative and the part of wisdom to anticipate the loss of $50, should circumstances compel the sale of the shoes at the market price, or 50¢ a pair less than their cost.

242. When cost is used. Let us now assume that in inventorying the shoes the actual cost of $300 is used. This amount is the actual sum invested by the dealer in the goods in cash or its equivalent. Regardless of a higher or a lower market price or any other consideration, the merchant has neither gained nor lost on his investment of $300 in shoes at the time of taking the inventory. On the contrary, he merely has an asset in the form of stock on hand which cost him $300 instead of having $300 in cash or some other asset. When he sells the goods, *then*, and not until then, will he gain or lose. In either event, his profit or loss will be measured by how much more or less he receives for the goods than their cost of $300.

The following exercises are designed to illustrate the difference in results when the various rules for inventorying goods on hand are applied, and to emphasize the principles discussed above.

Exercise 62

1. The yearly sales of a hardware merchant were $60,000. His purchases during the year were $50,000. His inventory at the close of the year, taken at invoice cost, was $10,000. There was no inventory at the beginning of the year. What was the gross trading income?

2. Assuming that at the time of taking the inventory at the close of the year the market prices of the stock on hand averaged 20% below cost prices, and that the inventory was taken at market prices, what would have been the gross trading income?

3. Assuming, on the other hand, that the market prices were 20% above cost, what would have been the gross trading income?

4. Under which conditions are profits and assets overstated? understated?

Exercise 63

1. On January 1 a dealer in automobile accessories had an inventory, taken at invoice cost, of $5,000. His purchases during the year were $30,000, and his sales were $40,000. His inventory on December 31, taken at invoice cost, was $10,000. What was his gross trading profit?

2. Assuming that the inventories were based on market prices, and that they were 20% higher than cost on January 1, and that they were 20% lower on December 31, what would have been the gross trading profit?

3. Assuming, on the other hand, that market prices were 20% lower than cost on January 1, and 20% higher on December 31, what would have been the gross trading income?

4. Under which conditions are profits and assets overstated? understated?

Exercise 64

1. If we use the same figures and percentages given for Exercise 63, and assume that the inventory of January 1 was taken at cost and the inventory of December 31 at market (20% above and again at 20% below cost), what would have been the gross trading profits under both conditions?

2. Assuming that the inventory of January 1 was taken at market (20% above and again at 20% below cost) and that the inventory of December 31 was taken at cost, what would have been the gross trading profits under these conditions?

3. Under which conditions are profits and assets overstated? understated?

Supplies Inventory

243. Supplies of materials used in conducting a business are purchased in quantities. At the end of the fiscal period, the supplies on hand are inventoried as a basis of further purchases and as a means of ascertaining their value as an asset. Such an inventory is called a "Supplies Inventory."

Perpetual or Going Inventory

244. Supplies of materials used in the manufacture of articles such as parts for engines, or requisitioned for use for consumption, as food in the hotel business, are usually recorded daily. Such an inventory, if kept, is called a "perpetual" or "going" inventory. This daily inventory may be kept in a "Stores Ledger" or on cards. The perpetual inventory gives the following information:

(1) Supplies on hand.

(2) Supplies bought.

(3) Supplies requisitioned.

(4) Supplies on hand at end of day.

Chapter 29—Notes Receivable

245. A note receivable is generally considered to be a better asset than an open book account. The principal legal difference between them is that the former acknowledges liability for the exact amount of the debt it represents, but in the case of an open account all the items must be proved legally by an action at law. A promissory note is *prima facie* evidence of value received. An open account is evidence of a debt that is subject to reduction under certain circumstances and contingencies. Neither, however, is a preferred claim over the other in cases of bankruptcy or liquidation.

On the other hand, in the case of a note that has been given by a customer in settlement of his account, it is apparent that he has entered into a second contract more binding upon him than the contract of sale on which he became liable for the goods sold to him on credit. He has substituted a written promise to pay an exact sum of money unconditionally at a definitely specified date for an oral or implied promise to pay an open account within a period more or less indefinite. Under the terms of the contract of sale, he could reduce his debt by claims for rebates and by returning part of the goods sold to him. Nothing, however, except the payment of the face value of the note, with interest, if any, will satisfy the second contract.

Bills of Exchange

246. Care should be taken to distinguish promissory notes from "bills of exchange." A bill of exchange is a written request by one party to a second party asking him to pay a third party a certain sum of money at a specified time. A bill of exchange is really a three-party draft, and is now used principally in foreign trade to effect settlements of accounts. For instance, a merchant at Bordeaux, France, indebted to a Chicago manufacturer, can draw a bill of exchange in favor of the manufacturer on the merchant in New York who buys goods from the French merchant. The bill of exchange effects a settlement, in whole or in part, of the Bordeaux merchant's account with the manufacturer and of the New York merchant's account with the Bordeaux merchant, without any cash actually being transferred from one to the other, or any expense being incurred by any of the parties in the form of exchange rates representing the difference in the value of American and French currency.

When a bill of exchange, payable at some future time, is accepted by the party on whom it is drawn, it becomes in effect a promissory note although it does not usually bear interest.

Illustration 73 shows a bill of exchange issued by Dodwell & Company, Foochow, China, in favor of The H. M. Rowe Company on the Chartered Bank of India, Australia, and China, which has branches, among other places, at Foochow and New York City. Notice that it reads, "On demand pay this second of exchange (first being unpaid) etc."

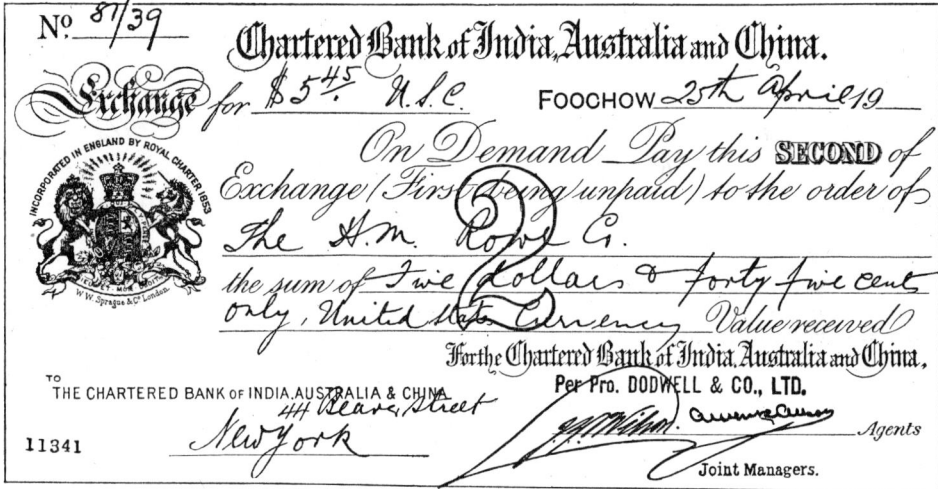

Illustration 73
BILL OF EXCHANGE

Foreign bills of exchange are usually issued in duplicate to provide against the possibility of one or the other being lost in transit. They are mailed on different dates, so as to be carried by different ships. The original copy of this bill of exchange, which read, "On demand pay this first of exchange," reached The H. M. Rowe Company first and was deposited by it for collection. Upon the collection of one copy of a bill of exchange, the other copy becomes null and void.

Judgment Notes

247. A *judgment note* is a promissory note in which the maker gives the payee or holder a power of attorney, authorizing the holder to appear in court and obtain a judgment against the maker for the face of the note and accrued interest, if any, in the event it is not paid at maturity. A judgment note is a severe form of contract, and should, if possible, be avoided under all circumstances by debtors. The effect of securing a

$ 1000.00 Baltimore, Md., April 10, --------------------, 19

----------------Sixty days-------------------- after date -----I---- promise to pay to the

order of John A. Miller & Co. ---

One Thousand ---Dollars,

with interest, at their office, 612 W. Baltimore St., Baltimore, Md., -----------

----------- hereby waiving all exemption laws of Maryland or any other State, and authorizing any attorney of record to appear for ---me---- in any Court and confess judgment for the amount of this note and 10 per cent. attorney's fees, waiving all right of appeal or stay of Execution.

Witness my-------- Hand --- and Seal this 10th day of April, 19 .

Witness: Roland B. Jackson (SEAL)

R. R. Gantt (SEAL)

Illustration 74
JUDGMENT NOTE

judgment against one who defaults in the payment of a debt is to establish legally the fact that the debt exists and remains unsatisfied. Furthermore, it gives the creditor the right to dispose by process of law of the debtor's property or assets to satisfy the debt.

Trade Acceptances

248. A *trade acceptance* is an *accepted draft* drawn after date or after sight, usually for the amount of a particular bill of goods sold, so as to mature on the same date the bill would mature. It may be a two-party or a three-party paper. It represents an obligation arising out of a

TRADE ACCEPTANCE

NO. 45 San Francisco, Calif., (CITY OF DRAWER) December 10, 19 (DATE)

TO - - - - James Morrow - - - - - (NAME OF DRAWEE) Dallas, Texas (ADDRESS OF DRAWEE)

ON February 10, 19 (DATE OF MATURITY) PAY TO THE ORDER OF Ourselves - - - - - - - - - - (NAME OF PAYEE)

Five Hundred and no/100 - - - - - - - - - - - - - DOLLARS, ($500.00)

THE OBLIGATION OF THE ACCEPTOR HEREOF ARISES OUT OF THE PURCHASE OF GOODS FROM THE DRAWER. THE DRAWEE MAY ACCEPT THIS BILL PAYABLE AT ANY BANK, BANKER OR TRUST COMPANY IN THE UNITED STATES WHICH HE MAY DESIGNATE.

ACCEPTED AT Dallas, Texas (CITY) ON Dec. 15 (DATE) 19 Arthur Banton (SIGNATURE OF DRAWER)

PAYABLE AT First National Bank (NAME OF BANK)

LOCATION Main and State Streets

James Morrow (SIGNATURE OF ACCEPTOR) BY John Brown

Illustration 75
TRADE ACCEPTANCE

current transaction involving a purchase of goods by the drawee from the drawer. It is drawn by the seller on the buyer, and is accepted by the buyer. It is usually drawn in favor of either the seller or the seller's bank, but may be drawn in favor of a third party, or bearer.

Collateral Notes

249. A *collateral note* is a promissory note which provides security for the payment of the debt represented by the note, in addition to the principal security. The principal security is the bare promise of the maker to pay the sum named; collateral security may consist of stocks, bonds, negotiable warehouse receipts, or other tangible property given to the holder of the note to support the principal security. A collateral note gives the holder the right to sell the collateral in case the note is not paid at maturity. The stocks, bonds, or other securities pledged on a collateral

$1000.00 XXX

Baltimore, Md. April 10, 19

Sixty days after date,

for VALUE RECEIVED, I promise to pay to the Traders National Bank of Baltimore, Md. or order, One Thousand & no/100 Dollars, with interest at 6% having deposited with said Traders National Bank as collateral security for the payment of this note 200 shares of Capital Stock of the Jackson Manufacturing Company, Curtis Bay, Baltimore, Md., the present value of which is Fifteen Hundred Dollars, ($1500.00)

with such additional collateral as may, from time to time, be required by the said payee, and which additional collaterals I hereby promise to give at any time on demand. If these additional collaterals be not so given when demanded, then this note to be due; and rebate of interest taken, shall be allowed on payment prior to maturity. And I hereby give to said payee, the Traders National Bank of Baltimore, full power and authority to sell and assign and deliver the whole or any part of said collateral, or any substitutes therefor, or any additions thereto, at any Broker's Board, or elsewhere at public or private sale, at the option of said payee, on the non-performance of the above premises, or any of them, or at any time thereafter and without advertising or giving to me any notice, or making any demand of payment.

IT IS ALSO AGREED, that said collaterals may, from time to time, by mutual consent, be exchanged for others, which shall also be held by said Traders National Bank of Baltimore on the terms above set forth; and that if I shall come under any other liability, or enter into any other engagement with said Traders National Bank of Baltimore, while it is the holder of this obligation, that the net proceeds of sale of the above securities may be applied either on this note, or on any other of my liabilities or engagements held by the Traders National Bank as it may elect.

Roland B. Jackson

Illustration 76

COLLATERAL NOTE

note, however, are not the property of the party who lent the money or who holds the note and must not, under any circumstances, be used or disposed of by him except in default of payment.   The collateral is pledged only to make the loan secure; and when the note is paid, the collateral must be returned to the maker.   The nominal value of the collateral usually exceeds the amount of the note, because at a forced sale the collateral might not bring a sum equal to the amount of the debt. Illustration 76 shows a collateral note.

Summary

1. A promissory note is a promise by one party to another to pay a specified sum of money at a specified date, with or without interest.   For what purposes is it used principally?

2. A bill of exchange is a general name for two-party and three-party drafts and acceptances, drawn usually to effect a settlement of accounts without a transfer of funds, and without interest.   For what purpose are bills of exchange now most generally used?

3. A judgment note is a promissory note in which the maker confesses judgment as to the legality of the debt and its amount.

4. A collateral note is a promissory note which provides security for its payment at maturity in the form of collateral in addition to the principal security.

5. A commercial draft is usually a two-party draft drawn without interest to secure payment for a shipment of merchandise before its delivery to the purchaser, or to secure the collection of a past-due book account.

6. A trade acceptance is usually a two-party draft drawn without interest for the invoice price of a certain lot of goods sold, to mature at the expiration of the term of credit, in order to give the seller an opportunity to liquidate the proceeds of the sale immediately by discounting the acceptance.

Notes Receivable Account

250. The **Notes Receivable account** is debited for the face value of all notes, including bills of exchange, collateral notes, and judgment notes, made or indorsed in our favor by others. It is credited for the face value of such notes when paid, transferred by indorsement to others, or discounted. The balance represents the total face value of all unpaid notes receivable on hand. As this balance can be reconciled with the total of the unpaid notes on hand, the Notes Receivable account is to that extent a control account.

The **Trade Acceptances Receivable account** is conducted in precisely the same manner in which the Notes Receivable account is kept.

Exercise 65

Jan. 12 Brown Brothers sold an invoice of goods to Watson & Co., terms note at 60 days without interest, amounting to $500.

15 Brown Brothers received Watson & Co.'s 60-day note, dated January 12, for $500 in settlement of the invoice.

16 Brown Brothers discounted the note at bank and received credit for the proceeds, the discount rate being 6%.

March 13 The note being due at the bank on this date, Watson & Co. issued a check to pay it.

1. Make the entries in journal form required for such of these transactions as should be recorded on Brown Brothers' books.

2. Post the entries to accounts, rule out balancing items, and take a trial balance.

3. Assume that instead of giving a note to Brown Brothers, Watson & Company had accepted a trade acceptance drawn on them by Brown Brothers dated January 12 for 60 days, and that Brown Brothers on January 16 discounted the acceptance at bank at the rate of $5\frac{1}{2}\%$. Set up in ledger account form the entries which should have been made on Brown Brothers' books.

4. Take a trial balance of these accounts after ruling out balancing items.

5. In what respect do the two trial balances differ?

Review Questions

1. Of what do the current assets of a business consist? What are receivables? What other terms are used to designate current assets?

2. What is a control account? To what extent is the Cash account a control account? the Notes Receivable account?

3. What kind of assets are notes receivable?   Does a note acknowledge liability for the debt it represents, or not?   What is a bill of exchange?   a judgment note?   a collateral note?   a trade acceptance?

4. How are trade acceptances used, and what are the advantages to be gained by using them?   How are notes used as credit instruments?   For what purpose are commercial drafts usually drawn?

Interest and Discount on Notes and Acceptances

251. An interest-bearing note is obviously worth at maturity the sum of its face value and the interest.   If it is discounted or transferred by indorsement before maturity, it is worth, at the date of discount or transfer, its face value plus the interest to maturity minus the discount from the discount date to the date of maturity.   Notes are discounted for the purpose of converting them into ready cash.   They are transferred to others to effect settlement of accounts.   The discounting or transferring of a note constitutes in effect a conditional sale of an asset.   The thing sold is the promise of the maker of the note to pay it on a specified future date.   Such a sale differs from an ordinary sale of property only in case the note is not paid by its maker at maturity.   In such an event, the party who discounted or transferred it is compelled to redeem the promise by paying the note himself, because he sold it for what it was represented on its face to be worth.   He is in effect compelled to buy back that which he previously sold, because it was not of the value it was represented to be.   It is for these reasons that financial institutions which discount notes and acceptances are said to be "dealers in commercial paper."   An understanding of the following terms is therefore essential in the study of negotiable instruments:

(a) The *principal* of a note or acceptance is its face value.

(b) The *amount* is the sum of the principal and the interest to maturity. In the case of a 60-day note for $600 with interest at 6%, the amount is $606.

(c) The *proceeds* is the amount minus the discount.   If the note referred to above were discounted 30 days before its maturity date, the discount would be the interest computed on $606 for 30 days at 6%, or $3.03, making the proceeds, $602.97.

(d) The *discount* is the interest computed on the amount for the term of discount.   It should be clearly understood that discount is always computed on the amount of interest-bearing notes—not on the face value.

(e) The *date of maturity* is the date on which the paper is due.   A note dated March 1 and drawn for a period of two months is due on

May 1—the corresponding day in the second month following its
date. A 60-day note dated March 1 is due on April 30. Being
dated March 1, it has 30 days to run in March and 30 days in April,
making the total of 60 days. A note dated March 12 to run 90
days is due on June 10—19 days in March, 30 days in April, 31 days
in May, and 10 days in June, making the total of 90 days.

(f) The *term of discount* is the time from the date of discount to the date
of maturity. In the case of a 60-day note dated March 1 that is
discounted on March 20, the term of discount is the time from
March 20, the date of discount, to April 30, the date of maturity,
or 41 days—11 days in March and 30 days in April.

Renewals of Notes Receivable

252. It sometimes happens that the maker of a note cannot pay it when
it matures. Under such circumstances, he is usually required to pay the
interest on the note to date, and to give a new note for the principal sum of
the old note. Aside from the entry for the interest received, many accountants make no other entry because the Notes Receivable account and the
debtor's account have already been debited and credited, respectively, for
the face value of the original note, which has simply been replaced by a
second note of the same amount. A memorandum of the renewal should
nevertheless be made in the explanation column of the Notes Receivable
account.

Theoretically, however, the maker of the note should be debited and
Notes Receivable credited to record the debtor's failure to pay the first
note and to close it out of the Notes Receivable account, because it is
canceled by the new note and is now void and of no effect. Notes
Receivable should then be charged for the new note and the debtor
credited.

Assuming that C. O. Bacon is the maker of a note for $100, which was
renewed in full upon the payment of the interest accrued of $1, we have
the following entries:

Cash	60 days on C. A. Bacon's note	1.00	
Interest Income	renewed today		1.00
C. A. Bacon	C. A. Bacon renewed note due today	100.00	
Notes Receivable	in full by new note		100.00
Notes Receivable	New note received today to take up	100.00	
C. A. Bacon	C. A. Bacon's original note		100.00

Observe that the debits and credits in the second and third entries offset
each other; hence, the Notes Receivable account will still show the same
debit balance of $100 after these entries are made and posted.

It frequently happens that the maker of a note cannot pay it in full when it matures, but can make a partial payment.   In fact, most holders of notes insist on a partial payment in case the obligation cannot be paid in full.   The accounting for a renewed note requires special attention. The best practice is illustrated in the following example.

On March 1, Black & Co. gave Poe & Dunn a note dated on that date in the amount of $300, payable in 60 days without interest, for the amount of a bill of goods purchased.   On April 30, the due date, Black & Co. paid $200 on the note and gave Poe & Dunn a new note dated April 30 for $100, the balance of the principal sum of the first note.   The first entry on Poe & Dunn's books required to record the renewal of the note is:

| Black & Co. | Face value of 60-day note dated | 300.00 | |
| Notes Receivable | March 1 renewed | | 300.00 |

This entry charges back to the personal account of Black & Co. the original debt for which the note was given, and credits the note out of the Notes Receivable account, because the original note is to be considered as paid and canceled by the cash and the new note received in place of it. A second entry, to record the cash received and to pass credit for the amount of the original debt now paid in cash to Black & Co.'s personal account is required, as follows:

| Cash | Cash paid on face value of note of | 200.00 | |
| Black & Co. | March 1 when renewed | | 200.00 |

A third entry is required to record the new note received, as follows:

| Notes Receivable | New note for remainder of face value | 100.00 | |
| Black & Co. | of note March 1 when renewed | | 100.00 |

The ledger accounts of Poe & Dunn, showing the entries for the sale of the goods, the receipt of the original note, and its renewal, would appear as follows:

Black & Co.		Sales		Notes Receivable		Cash	
300.00	300.00		300.00	300.00	300.00	200.00	
300.00	200.00			100.00			
	100.00						

The debit to Notes Receivable of $100 now standing on the books records the balance of the debt owed by Black & Co., which is evidenced by the note which Poe & Dunn now hold.   Observe that the sum of the debits to Notes Receivable and Cash is equal to the credit balance of the Sales account.

Assuming that the note of March 1 bore interest at 6%, and that the accrued interest was paid at the time of the renewal, the same entries would be required, with the addition in the second entry of the debit to Cash and the credit to Interest Income for the amount of the interest, as follows:

Cash	Principal and interest received on Black	203.00
Black & Co.	& Co.'s note of March 1	200.00
Interest Income		3.00

Exercise 66

April 5 Mason & Co. sold an invoice of goods to J. B. Horne, amounting to $600. Mason & Co.'s usual term of credit is 30 days. In consideration of receiving 90 days' time on his purchase, Mr. Horne agreed to give Mason & Co. a 90-day note, dated April 5, with interest at 6%.

      9 Mason & Co. received Mr. Horne's note for $600 according to terms.

July 5 The note was due on July 4, but payable on July 5, as July 4 is a holiday. The maker could not pay it in full, but paid $400 of it in cash, plus the accrued interest, and gave Mason & Co. a new note dated July 4 for 30 days with interest for the balance of the principal sum of the first note.

Aug. 3 Mr. Horne paid his note of July 4 with interest to date.

1. Draft the journal entries which should have been made in Mason & Co.'s books, and post them to ledger accounts. Rule out balancing items as they are entered. Then take a trial balance of the open accounts.

2. In the trial balance, which account shows the income from the goods sold? Should this income be a debit or a credit?

3. Which account shows the income received as interest on the notes? Should this income be a debit or a credit?

4. Which account shows the assets finally realized from the proceeds of the sale of goods and the interest received? In what form was this income finally realized? Should the assets realized be debits or credits?

Review Questions

1. What is an interest-bearing note worth at maturity? What is it worth on the date it is discounted?

2. What is the face of a note? its amount? its proceeds? How is the maturity date usually determined? the term of discount? How is the interest computed? the discount?

3. What entry should the payee of a note make if the maker renews it and pays only the interest on the old note? What entry should he make if the interest and a part of the principal of the old note are paid, and a new note given for the balance? What entry is required on the payee's books if the maker renews a note which the payee has discounted for a partial amount of the principal?

206 ROWE BOOKKEEPING AND ACCOUNTING PRACTICE

Renewals of Discounted Notes Receivable

253. In case it is desired to renew a note which has been discounted at bank, it is usually necessary for the maker to secure the consent of the payee, the indorser or indorsers, if any, and the bank. If the maker has a good credit, permission to renew is usually granted readily. If the credit of the maker is questionable, full payment of the note may be demanded, and he will be forced to liquidate some of his assets to pay the note. In some instances the renewal can be secured by having the renewal note indorsed by responsible parties known to the payee and the bank, thus guaranteeing its payment at maturity in case the maker fails to make settlement.

On March 1, Black & Co. gave Poe & Dunn a note dated on that date in the amount of $300, payable in 60 days with interest at 6%. On March 10, Poe & Dunn had the note discounted at the First National Bank and received credit for the proceeds. The bank thus became the holder, or owner, of the note. The bank bought it from Poe & Dunn, and in effect became the payee in place of them. On April 30, when the note was due, Black & Co. paid the bank $200 on the note plus the interest to date, and gave Poe & Dunn a new note dated April 30 for $100 with interest at 6%, which was immediately indorsed over to the bank. The entries on Poe & Dunn's books required to record the receipt of the note, its discounting, and its renewal are:

| Notes Receivable | Received from them 60-day note dated | 300.00 | |
| Black & Co. | March 1 with interest at 6% | | 300.00 |

This entry records the receipt of the note on March 1. When the note was discounted on March 10, the following entry was required:

Cash	Proceeds of Black & Co's note	$300.42	
Interest Expense	discounted today	2.58	
Notes Receivable			300.00
Interest Income			3.00

No entry is required on Poe & Dunn's books for the $200 in cash paid on the original note, or for the renewal note of $100, because the cash was paid to the bank and the new note became the property of the bank when Poe & Dunn indorsed it over. Consequently, the entries for the cash received and the new note, including the interest and discount on it, would be recorded on the books of the bank. The transaction was closed, as far as Poe & Dunn's books were concerned, when the foregoing entry for the discounting of the original note was made, provided Black & Co. took up the renewal note when it became due, or made some further disposition of it with the bank. Black & Co. might have made its check for the $200 payable to Poe & Dunn, in which event the latter would simply have indorsed it to the bank, no entry being required.

Exercise 67

Aug. 8 Butler Brothers sold an invoice of goods to Hopkins & Brownley, amounting to $682.40, terms note for 90 days, with interest at 6%.

   11 Butler Brothers received Hopkins & Brownley's note for the amount of the sale, the note being dated August 8.

   27 Butler Brothers' bank discounted the note and gave them credit for the proceeds.

Nov. 6 By arrangement with Butler Brothers and their bank, Hopkins & Brownley paid the bank $400 on the principal of the note plus the accrued interest, and issued to Butler Brothers a new note for the balance of the principal of the old note, which was indorsed by them to the bank and discounted. This note was for 30 days with interest at 6%.

Dec. 6 Hopkins & Brownley paid the bank for the second note with interest in full.

1. Set up in ledger account form the entries for such of these transactions as should be accounted for on Butler Brothers' books.

2. Take a trial balance of the open accounts after all canceling items have been ruled out.

3. What accounts reflect the income from the sale of the goods, the income for interest, the expense of discounting the note, and the assets realized from the transaction?

Dishonored Notes

254. Let us assume in Exercise 67 that Hopkins & Brownley defaulted on the payment of the original note of $682.40 when it was due on November 6. In order to secure the right to demand payment from the indorsers, Butler Brothers, the bank would protest the note for non-payment by making an affidavit before a notary public that Hopkins & Brownley had failed to pay the note after due demand on them had been made. Butler Brothers sold the note to the bank when it was discounted and received a valuable consideration in the form of the proceeds. Butler Brothers are legally obligated to reimburse the bank because the subsequent failure of the makers to pay the note invalidated or rendered defective the title to the property which they transferred to the bank by indorsing the note when it was discounted. Butler Brothers would therefore have to issue their check to the bank for a sum equal to the face of the note, the interest, and the protest fees. Assuming the latter item to be $2.72, the following entry on Butler Brothers' books would be required:

Hopkins & Brownley	Face, interest, and protest fees on their	695.36	
Cash	note of Aug. 8 dishonored at bank on		695.36
	Nov. 6		

The effect of this entry is to charge back to Hopkins & Brownley's personal account on Butler Brothers' books the amount of the original debt, and the expense for interest and protest fees incurred by Butler Brothers because of the makers' failure to pay the note. The debt thus again takes the status of an open book account. If Hopkins & Brownley subsequently pay the debt, Cash is debited and their account credited, thus closing the transaction. If they do not pay voluntarily, Butler Brothers can sue Hopkins & Brownley to enforce payment.

Exercise 68

July 17 Corning & Co. sold an invoice of goods to R. J. Stevenson & Co. amounting to $672.41, terms 90-day trade acceptance without interest.

22 Corning & Co. received the accepted draft, the acceptance being dated on the day the goods were purchased by Stevenson & Co.

26 Corning & Co. had the acceptance discounted by the National Exchange Bank and received credit for the proceeds, the discount rate being 5½%.

Oct. 15 Stevenson & Co. could not pay the acceptance in full on its due date, but by arrangement with Corning & Co. and the bank, the debtor issued a check to the bank in the amount of $400, and gave a 30-day note, dated October 15, with interest at 6%, payable to Corning & Co., for the balance of the principal sum still due on the trade acceptance. This note was indorsed by Corning & Co. to the National Exchange Bank.

Nov. 14 When the note became due, Stevenson & Co. could make only a partial payment on it; but the bank refused to carry the paper any longer and demanded payment in full, first from Stevenson & Co., and then from Corning & Co., the indorser of the note. Corning & Co. in turn accepted a check from Stevenson & Co. for $100 plus the accrued interest on the note, issued its check to the bank in full settlement of the note held by it, and charged the unpaid balance of the debt back to Stevenson & Co.'s account on its books.

1. Make the journal entries required to record properly such of these transactions as should appear on Corning & Co.'s books.

2. Post the entries to the proper ledger accounts, rule out balancing items, and take a trial balance.

3. What were the income from sales, the expense for discount, and the net cash proceeds as shown by Corning & Co.'s books as of November 14?

4. Assuming that Stevenson & Co. failed in business, and were unable to pay anything on the balance of the debt due, what entry should Corning & Co. make on its books?

5. Assuming that Stevenson & Co. had failed, but in liquidating its business the receiver was able to pay 10¢ on the dollar to all creditors, and Corning & Co. had received its pro rata share in cash in final settlement of its account, what entry should be made on Corning & Co.'s books?

Chapter 30—Notes Payable

255. The **Notes Payable account** is credited for the face value of all notes issued to others, including bills of exchange, collateral notes, and judgment notes. The account is debited for the face value of such notes when paid. Its balance represents the liability on notes outstanding and unpaid at any date, which is a current liability that should be included in the Balance Sheet. As the balance of this account can be reconciled with the total of the unpaid notes as shown by the stub of the notes payable book, it is to that extent a control account.

A **Trade Acceptance payable** is similar to a note payable, and of course is the opposite of a trade acceptance receivable. The Trade Acceptances Payable account is kept in accordance with the principles which govern the keeping of the Notes Payable account. In many instances notes and trade acceptances payable are recorded in one account under the title, "Notes and Acceptances Payable." The balance represents the unpaid obligations on notes and trade acceptances, which should be included as a current liability in the Balance Sheet.

Exercise 69

Jan.   12 Watson & Co. purchased an invoice of goods from Brown Brothers, terms note at 60 days without interest, amounting to $500.

15 Watson & Co. issued to Brown Brothers a 60-day note in their favor dated January 12, for $500 in settlement of the bill.

March 7 Watson & Co. received notice from the City National Bank that the note was held by the bank and would be due and payable on March 13. Brown Brothers had discounted the note at this bank on January 16.

13 Watson & Co. issued its check to the City National Bank in payment of the face of the note.

1. Make the entries, in journal form, required for such of these transactions as should be recorded on Watson & Co.'s books.

2. Post the entries to accounts, rule out balancing items, and take a trial balance.

3. Assume that instead of issuing a note, Watson & Co. had accepted Brown Brothers' trade acceptance drawn on them dated January 12 for 60 days. Set up in ledger account form the entries which should have been made on Watson & Co.'s books.

4. Take a trial balance of these accounts after ruling out balancing items.

5. In what respect do the two trial balances differ?

Renewals of Notes Payable

256. When the maker of a note payable cannot pay it at maturity, he can sometimes, with the permission of his creditor, renew it by paying the interest to date and giving a new note in place of the old note. Aside from the entry for the interest paid, no other entry except a notation of the renewal in the Notes Payable account is required. The Notes Payable account already has been credited for the face value of the original note, which has simply been replaced by a second note of the same amount.

When, however, the maker of a note pays the interest and a part of the principal sum at maturity, an adjustment of the Notes Payable account is required. The best practice is illustrated in the following example. On March 1, Black & Co. gave Poe & Dunn a note dated on that date in the amount of $300, payable in 60 days with interest at 6%. On April 30, when it was due, Black & Co. paid $200 on the note plus the accrued interest, and gave Poe & Dunn a new note dated April 30 for $100, the balance of the principal sum of the first note. The first entry on Black & Co.'s books required to record the renewal of the old note, in journal form is—

Notes Payable	Partial payment of principal and interest on	200.00	
Interest Expense	note of March 1 in favor of Poe & Dunn	3.00	
Cash			203.00

A second entry to close out the old note and record the new note in the Notes Payable account would be required as follows:

Notes Payable	Renewal of $100 on principal of note of	100.00	
Notes Payable	March 1 in favor of Poe & Dunn by new		100.00
	note dated April 30		

After all entries for the original note and the renewal were posted to the Notes Payable account, it would appear thus:

April 30	200.00	March 1	300.00	
April 30	100.00			
		April 30	100.00	

Observe that the Notes Payable account now stands with a credit of $100, representing the liability under the new note.

Exercise 70

April 5 Mason & Co. sold an invoice of goods to J. B. Horne, amounting to $600. In consideration of receiving 90 days' time on his purchase, Mr. Horne agreed to give Mason & Co. a 90-day note, dated April 5, with interest at 6%.

April 9 Mason & Co. received Mr. Horne's note for $600 according to terms.
July 5 The note was due on July 4, but payable on July 5, as July 4 is a holiday. The maker could not pay it in full, but paid $400 on it in cash, plus the accrued interest, and gave Mason & Co. a new note dated July 4 for 30 days with interest for the balance of the principal sum of the first note.
Aug. 3 Mr. Horne paid his note of July 4 with interest to date.

1. Draft the journal entries which should have been made in Mr. Horne's books, and post them to ledger accounts. Rule out balancing items, and take a trial balance.

2. Which accounts show the cost of the goods purchased, the expense for interest paid, and the expenditures required in financing the transactions?

3. Assume that Mr. Horne accepted Mason & Co.'s trade acceptance instead of giving them his note. On the date of the renewal of the trade acceptance it was replaced with the 30-day note mentioned. Make the required entries, take a trial balance, and compare it with the first trial balance.

Renewals of Discounted Notes Payable

257. In case it is desired to renew a note which has been discounted at bank by the payee, the maker must secure the consent of the payee, the indorser or indorsers, if any, and the bank. The accounting procedure is similar to that required when the payee accepts a renewal. For instance, on March 1, Black & Co. gave Poe & Dunn their note dated on that date in the amount of $300, payable in 60 days, with interest at 6%. On March 10, Poe & Dunn had the note discounted at the First National Bank and received credit for the proceeds. On April 30, when the note was due, Black & Co. paid the bank $200 on the note plus the interest to date, and gave Poe & Dunn a new note dated April 30 for $100 with interest at 6%, which was immediately indorsed by them over to the bank for discounting. The entries on Black & Co.'s books required to record the transaction are:

Notes Payable	Partial payment on principal and interest on	200.00	
Interest Expense	note of March 1 in favor of Poe & Dunn	3.00	
Cash			203.00
Notes Payable	Renewal of $100 on principal of note of	100.00	
Notes Payable	March 1 in favor of Poe & Dunn by new note dated April 30.		100.00

Black & Co. would issue its check in favor of the bank for the $200 on the first note. If, however, the check had been drawn to the order of

Poe & Dunn, they would have indorsed it to the bank, or would have deposited Black & Co.'s check and issued their check in turn to the bank. Poe & Dunn would have to pay the bank the amount of the discount on the new note.

Exercise 71

Aug. 8 Butler Brothers sold an invoice of goods to Hopkins & Brownley amounting to $682.40, terms note for 90 days, with interest at 6%.

      11 Butler Brothers received Hopkins & Brownley's note for the amount of the sale, the note being dated August 8.

      27 Butler Brothers' bank discounted the note and gave them credit for the proceeds.

Nov. 6 By arrangement with Butler Brothers and their bank, Hopkins & Brownley paid the bank $400 on the principal of the note plus the accrued interest, and issued to Butler Brothers a new note for the balance of the principal of the old note, which was indorsed by them to the bank and discounted. This note was for 30 days with interest at 6%.

Dec. 6 Hopkins & Brownley paid the bank for the second note with interest.

1. Set up in ledger account form the entries required on Hopkins & Brownley's books for these transactions. Rule out balancing items.

2. Take a trial balance of the open accounts.

3. Which accounts reflect the cost of the merchandise purchased, the expense for interest, and the funds expended in financing the transactions?

Sometimes partial payments are made on notes receivable or payable before they are due. In such cases, the proper entry is to debit cash and credit Notes Receivable, or to debit Notes Payable and credit Cash for the amount paid on the note, as the case may be. The partial payment should be indorsed on the back of the note, which indorsement serves as a receipt for the amount paid on the principal. The balance due on a note partly prepaid would therefore be shown in the Notes Receivable or Notes Payable account by the difference between the debit and credit entries for that particular note.

Chapter 31—Advances To Employees

258. Concerns that employ traveling salesmen or other agents through whom their business is transacted are frequently required to advance funds to pay the expenses for railroad fares, hotel bills, and other traveling expenses. Frequently money is advanced to employees whose income may have been stopped or reduced on account of illness or injury. All such sums are accounts receivable to the employing concern, and should be set up as an asset in the Balance Sheet under the caption, "Advances to Employees." Such accounts receivable should not be confused with the accounts of trade debtors.

An account may be opened in the general ledger with each employee to whom money is advanced, under such titles as "William A. Blake, Salesman," "Loan to J. M. Butler, Engineer," etc. A better practice is to open one account under the title, "Advances to Employees," which is charged with all sums advanced to employees, and credited when such advances are returned. For example, if William A. Blake is employed as a salesman and is given a traveling expense fund of $100, Advances to Salesmen account should be charged, Mr. Blake's name being entered in the explanation column in the ledger account. If Mr. Blake should submit an expense report of $35 for traveling expenses for the first week, a check should be issued to him and charged to the proper expense account, thus replenishing his expense money fund to $100. The salesman thus owes his employer the amount charged to the Advances to Employees account, which, when returned in the event he resigned, would be credited to that account. Advances to employees of this character, and money lent to be paid back out of salaries or wages, should be treated in the Balance Sheet as current assets. Advances to employees payable at a more or less distant future date, or the collection of which is doubtful, should be included with the group, "Other Assets."

Exercise 72

The New England Belting Company had the following transactions with its employees from August 1 to December 31.

Aug. 1 M. C. Little was employed as a traveling salesman in the New England territory. A check was issued to him for $150 for expense money.

31 Mr. Little submitted an expense report showing total expenditures for August of $102.50. A check was issued to him for this amount, Selling Expense being debited.

Sept. 10 The home of Walter Wilson, the factory superintendent, was destroyed by fire, and the company advanced $500 to him with which to make the first payment on new furniture and household equipment, under an agreement that $50 was to be deducted from his salary check at the end of each month.

Sept. 30 Mr. Little's expense report showed payments of $115.95, for which he was reimbursed by check.

Sept. 30 $50 was deducted from the factory superintendent's salary and credited against the money advanced to him. Instead of receiving a check for $250, which was chargeable against Factory Salaries and Labor account, he received a check for $200, which was charged to that account.

Oct. 14 The Secretary of the company was authorized to make a special trip through New England, stopping at the principal cities, for the purpose of appointing local sales agents for the products of the company. He was advanced $600 with which to pay his expenses.

Oct. 31 Mr. Little's expense report for $98.20 was received, and a check was issued in his favor for the amount.

31 Another deduction of $50 was made from the factory superintendent's salary.

Nov. 5 The Secretary returned from his trip and submitted an expense report of $580.25, which was charged to Selling Expense. He returned the balance of his expense money to the company.

30 Mr. Little's expense report for this month amounted to $106.50, for which he received a check.

30 At his request, the company did not deduct the $50 from Mr. Wilson's salary this month, because he needed his full salary to pay the extra bills resulting from the loss of his home.

Dec. 31 Mr. Little submitted an expense report for $85.30, and received a check for it.

1. Draft and post the journal entries required to record the foregoing transactions. Open one account for all advances.

2. How much money was owed to the company by each of these employees on December 31?

Chapter 32—Accrued Assets

259. During a fiscal period it is customary to record incomes *either as they are earned* or *as they are collected*. For instance, the income from sales of merchandise on account is *recorded as earned* by charging customers and by crediting Sales as goods are sold. Such income is earned and recorded, *but not collected*. Uncollected income recorded, therefore, stands on the books as a receivable until it is collected. On the other hand, income that is *not recorded as earned* is recorded *when it is collected*. For instance, incomes from rent and interest are not customarily charged against the parties from whom they are to be received, but are recorded only as received, Cash being debited and the proper income accounts being credited.

Income is collected in the form of assets of one kind or another—usually in cash or its equivalent. Income may be received in the form of personal property. For instance, the cash value of a load of farm products, accepted by a doctor for services rendered to a farmer, is income to the physician. It is an expense to the farmer. When earned or collected, income is always recorded by debiting some asset account and crediting some income account.

At the time of closing books, there may be certain items of income which have been earned during the period but which do not as yet appear on the books because they have not been collected. For example, if books are closed on December 31, the interest on a note receivable for $1000, dated November 1, having three months to run, which consequently is not due or payable until February 1, has nevertheless been earned for the months of November and December. This interest is an asset just as the note itself is an asset, and at closing time should appear as such on the books. The note on December 31 is worth $1010—its face value plus two months' interest. The income which this interest represents is likewise a proper credit to the Interest Income account for the two months it has accrued.

Unpaid rents due from tenants for periods of time prior to the date of closing are likewise income for the year during which the rented space was occupied. For instance, a tenant paying $50 a month who has paid his rent to November 30 would be indebted to his landlord for one month's rent on December 31. The landlord's claim against the tenant is one of his assets on the date stated, and the income it represents should properly be credited to real estate income for the year ending December 31. It follows that, in order to state correctly in the accounts all assets as of the date of closing, it is necessary to accrue such items by recording all un-collected income. This object is accomplished by debits to Accrued Assets account and credits to the proper income accounts.

Accrued assets may therefore consist of earned or accrued income not yet due, or such income which is due but has not been collected. The interest mentioned above is income not yet due. The rent is income due but not received. Other examples of accrued assets are interest accrued but not received on investments, commissions earned but not received for selling goods for or rendering services to others, dividends declared but not received on stocks owned, and royalties due but uncollected under copyright and patent right privileges.

Accounting for Accrued Assets

260. The Accrued Assets account is kept in exactly the same manner in which the Merchandise Inventory account is kept. A list of accrued assets at closing time is really an inventory of accrued income. The rules are—

Accrued Assets

Debit at the end of any fiscal period for all accrued assets representing earned income not recorded or collected.	Credit for the same items at the beginning of the next fiscal period.

If we take the interest and rent referred to in Section 259 as examples, the journal entry required to set up the accrued assets on December 31 would be—

Accrued Assets	60.00	
Interest Income		10.00
Real Estate Income		50.00

The ledger accounts affected by these accrued incomes are shown below. In order to simplify the illustrations, it is assumed that no other items have been entered in these accounts. Observe that the accrued assets now appear in the ledger, and the income they represent is credited to the proper income accounts, which will be included in the Income and Profit and Loss Statement in finding the net profit for the period ending December 31.

Accrued Assets		Interest Income		Real Estate Income	
10.00			10.00		50.00
50.00					

Statements would next be prepared and the ledger closed. In the closing process, the Interest Income and Real Estate Income accounts would be closed into the Profit and Loss Summary account, and that account in turn would be closed into the Capital account. The income accounts would thus be balanced. If we eliminate other items in the Capital account in order to simplify the illustrations, the ledger would then show the following data:

Accrued Assets		Interest Income		Real Estate Income		Capital	
60.00		10.00	10.00	50.00	50.00		60.00

At the beginning of business on January 1 next, the above journal entry would be reversed, thus:

Interest Income	$10.00	
Real Estate Income	50.00	
Accrued Assets		$60.00

The Accrued Assets account would thus be closed, and the ledger would then appear as follows:

Accrued Assets		Interest Income		Real Estate Income		Capital	
60.00	60.00	10.00	10.00	50.00	50.00		60.00
		10.00		50.00			

Now if we assume that on February 1 the interest on the note for three months, $15, and the rent for December and January, $100, were received in cash, the accounts would show the following results on that date:

Cash		Interest Income		Real Estate Income		Capital	
115.00		10.00	10.00	50.00	50.00		60.00
		10.00	15.00	50.00	100.00		

The Accrued Assets account does not appear in this showing of the accounts because it was balanced and closed on January 1. Observe that the balance now standing to the credit of the Interest Income account is the interest earned on the note for the month of January; also that the credit balance of the Real Estate Income account is likewise the rent earned during January.

Exercise 73

The City Trading Company inventoried its accrued income on December 31 as follows:

(a) Interest at 6% on a 90-day note receivable for $2,000 dated October 28.
(b) A dividend of 7% on 10 shares of stock of the Fourth National Bank payable December 31, par value $100 a share.
(c) A commission of 5% uncollected for selling $500 worth of goods for the Morton & Brown Co.
(d) Interest accrued for six months on a $1,000 U. S. Government Bond, annual interest at $4\frac{1}{2}\%$.
(e) A tenant occupying an office on the second floor of the company's building has not paid nor been charged with the November and December rent, amounting to $30.

1. Draft and post the journal entries required to accrue these items.

2. Set up and post the journal entry required to close the income accounts.

3. Draft and post the journal entries required to close the accrued assets account as of January 1 in the next period.

4. Assume that on January 26 all income accrued on December 31, including all interest on the note due today, was collected in cash. Draft the entry required in journal form and post it.

5. What was the total accrued income for which the old period was given credit? How much of the income collected on January 26 was earned in the new period?

Questions

1. Of what do advances to employees consist? How should they be classified in the Balance Sheet?
2. What are accrued assets? When and how are they accounted for? Is the Accrued Assets account a fiscal or a running account?

Chapter 33—Fixed Assets

261. Fixed assets are the permanent investments in the various kinds of tangible real and personal property and equipment required to house a business and to conduct its operations. In Part One, investments in real estate and furniture and fixtures were treated as typical assets of this group. Fixed assets will now be considered in greater detail.

Building and Land Investments

262. Real estate includes land and the structures erected on it. The costs of land and buildings and other permanent improvements are usually included in the Real Estate Investment account. It is the best practice, however, in setting up accounts for real estate investments, to open one account for the land and a separate account for the improvements. Land tends to increase in value as the population increases and commerce and industry expand; in other words, the land *appreciates* in value. Buildings gradually decrease in value from deterioration due to the passage of time and wear and tear from use; that is, they *depreciate* in value. For these reasons land and buildings require different treatment in accounting for their respective valuations. Capital assets which depreciate from wear and tear, or from obsolescence, are called "wasting" assets.

Building Investment Account

263. The purchase price of a building, including the cost of agents' commissions for buying, title examination fees, and all other expenses incurred up to the time the property becomes productive or is placed in use, should be charged to the Building Investment account. The contract price of a building erected by a contractor, plus expenses for building permits, fees, and similar expenses incurred until the property is turned over to the owner, are likewise capital investments properly chargeable to the Building Investment account. When there is a group of buildings, as in the case of a manufacturing plant, the cost of the group is usually carried in one account, under the title, "Plant Buildings."

The costs of additions to buildings and permanent improvements and betterments are also properly chargeable to the Building Investment account as capital investments. After the original investment and the cost of improvements, as determined by purchase or construction costs, have been charged to the Investment account, the asset value thus set up on the books remains unchanged except when—

1. Depreciation is charged off annually;
2. The asset is disposed of in whole or in part;
3. The reorganization of the business or changes in ownership justify or require a revaluation by appraisal, as a result of material increases or decreases in property values;
4. The property is fully depreciated on the books.

Valuation of Fixed Assets

264. The *book value* of a capital asset at any time is its original cost as shown by the Investment account less the depreciation charged off to date. Depreciation is charged off by debiting Depreciation account and crediting Reserve for Depreciation account annually at the close of the fiscal period for the yearly depreciation. The debit balance of the Depreciation account is an operating expense for the period. The credit balance of the Reserve for Depreciation account represents profits withheld from distribution and retained in the working capital with which to pay for repairs and renewals, and eventually for the replacement of the property when it becomes obsolete. The difference between the debit balance of the Investment account for a capital asset and the credit balance of its Reserve for Depreciation account is the book value of the asset; that is, the value at which it is carried on the books.

Accounting for Sale of Capital Assets

265. When the whole or any part of a capital asset is sold, the Investment account should be credited for the original cost price of the portion disposed of. In ascertaining the profit or loss on the sale, the depreciation charged off to date should first be deducted from the original cost to determine the book value of the property sold. The book value, when compared with the proceeds of the sale, will give the profit or loss, which should be accounted for in the Profit and Loss account, or in a special account set up to receive it. Appreciation in the value of capital assets, unlike depreciation, is not recorded on the books, except in unusual circumstances to be explained later, on the theory that such appreciation is not an earning of invested capital, and cannot be realized as profit unless the property is sold.

When a capital asset is sold, the best procedure in recording the transaction is as follows:

1. Close the balance of the Reserve for Depreciation account, if any, into the asset Investment account.

2. Debit the proper asset account for the proceeds of the sale, debit profit and loss for the loss on the sale, if any, and credit the asset Investment account for the total, which will be the book value of the asset sold, or;

3. Debit the proper asset account for the proceeds of the sale, credit the asset Investment account for the book value of the asset sold, and credit profit and loss for the profit on the sale, if any.

To illustrate this procedure, suppose that a building and the lot on which it was erected were purchased five years ago for $12,000 and $4,000, respectively, the total purchase price being $16,000. Depreciation at the rate of 2% per annum has been charged off on the building for five years. The property was sold today for $13,500, the sale prices being $9,000 for the building and $4,500 for the lot. Before the sale of the property is recorded, the accounts would appear as follows:

Building Investment	Land Investment	Reserve for Building Depreciation
12,000.00	4,000.00	1,200.00

The following entries, in journal form, record the sale of the property.

Reserve for Building Depreciation	$1,200.00	
Building Investment		$1,200.00
Cash	9,000.00	
Profit and Loss	1,800.00	
Building Investment		10,800.00
Cash	4,500.00	
Land Investment		4,000.00
Profit and Loss		500.00

After the above entries are posted, the accounts show the following results:

Building Investment		Land Investment		Reserve for Building Depreciation	
12,000.00	1,200.00	4,000.00	4,000.00	1,200.00	1,200.00
	10,800.00				
12,000.00	12,000.00				

Cash		Profit and Loss	
9,000.00		1,800.00	500.00
4 500.00			

Observe that all the accounts except the Cash and Profit and Loss accounts are now closed. The Cash account shows the proceeds of the sale, and the Profit and Loss account balance of $1,300 is the net loss on the entire transaction.

Exercise 74

Jan. 3 The General Stores Co. purchased two lots at the corner of Sixth and Pine Sts., improved by two store buildings. The purchase price of the corner property was $12,000, the building being valued at $9,000 and the lot at $3,000. The purchase price of the property next to the corner lot was $10,000, the building being valued at $8,000 and the lot at $2,000. The purchase price was paid in cash.

 5 Checks were issued for the commission of the agent who negotiated the transaction, for examining the title and recording the deeds, in the amount of $1,100. These expenses were pro-rated over the two buildings and the two lots in the proportions which their purchase prices were to the total purchase price.

Feb. 8 Checks were issued to pay contractors' bills for making permanent improvements and alterations to the buildings, amounting to $900, of which $500 applied on the corner building and $400 on the other.

Dec. 31 Depreciation on both buildings was charged off at the rate of 2% of their costs, as charged to the Building Investment account.

Dec. 31 At the end of the second year a similar charge for depreciation was made.

Dec. 31 At the end of the third year another charge for depreciation was made.

Jan. 10 Three years after the property was acquired, the property next to the corner was sold for $10,750. Before accepting the offer made by the purchaser, the General Stores Co. had the property appraised. The appraisers fixed the market value of the building at $7,500 and the lot at $3,250.

1. Draft the journal entries required for these transactions and depreciation charges, and post them to ledger accounts.

2. What was the book value of the land and of the buildings on December 31 of the year the property was purchased? at the end of the second year? at the end of the third year?

3. What was the profit or loss on the land sold and on the building sold?

Chapter 34—Revaluation of Capital Assets

266. When a business has been conducted for a considerable term of years, or when its ownership changes hands, or other investors purchase an interest in it, a revaluation of capital assets is in most instances required in order to determine true and correct realizable asset values, or *equities*. In the course of time wasting assets may have been depreciated on the books at amounts less than the actual depreciation. On the other hand, they may have been depreciated at a rate greater than the actual depreciation. *The true measure of the equity in wasting assets at any time is the sum which can be realized for them if they are offered for sale as part of the invested capital of a going concern.* These sums may be more or less than book values, because depreciation, being based on estimates of how rapidly capital assets will deteriorate from use and the passage of time, cannot result in book values that agree exactly with their actual marketable worth as investments.

Accounting for Revaluation of Capital Assets

267. When capital assets are revalued, the best procedure in adjusting the accounts is as follows:

1. The balance of each Reserve for Depreciation account should be closed into its corresponding asset Investment account.

2. The asset Investment accounts should then be closed into the Capital account.

3. The appraised values of the capital assets, constituting the new values at which they are to be carried on the books, are charged to the asset Investment accounts and credited to the Capital account, or to surplus in the case of a corporation.

To apply this procedure to a specific case, let us assume that John Martin has been conducting a dry goods business for the past twenty-five years. His Building Investment account is charged with the cost of his store building purchased twenty years ago, $17,000. His Land Investment account is charged with $5,000. His Reserve for Depreciation account has a credit balance of $6,000, representing the sum of annual depreciation charges at the rate of $300 annually, for twenty years. His other assets amount to $20,000. He has no liabilities. His accounts therefore appear as follows:

Building Investment	Land Investment	Reserve for Depreciation
17,000.00	5,000.00	6,000.00

Other Assets	John Martin, Capital
20,000.00	36,000.00

He has agreed to sell a one-third interest in his business to his store manager, L. C. Minor. As his books stand, a one-third interest in the business is worth $12,000, or one-third of the credit balance of Mr. Martin's Capital account. The question has been raised by Mr. Minor as to whether the assets with which Mr. Martin has himself credited are *now* actually worth $36,000. A firm of appraisers employed by them to appraise Mr. Martin's real estate has valued his building at $7,000 and the land at $6,000. These valuations have been accepted by Mr. Martin and Mr. Minor. The valuations of the other assets as carried on Mr. Martin's books are accepted as correct. The entries required to adjust the revaluation of the real estate on Mr. Martin's books, in order to determine the amount of his present true invested capital, are as follows:

Reserve for Depreciation	$6,000.00	
Building Investment		$6,000.00
John Martin, Capital	16,000.00	
Building Investment		11,000.00
Land Investment		5,000.00
Building Investment	7,000.00	
Land Investment	6,000.00	
John Martin, Capital		13,000.00

After the foregoing entries are posted, the accounts would show the following results:

Building Investment		Land Investment		Reserve for Depreciation	
17,000.00	6,000.00	5,000.00	5,000.00	6,000.00	6,000.00
	11,000.00	6,000.00			
7,000.00					

Other Assets		John Martin, Capital	
20,000.00		16,000.00	36,000.00
		Net Cap. 33,000.00	13,000.00
		49,000.00	49,000.00
			33,000.00 Net Cap.

After the true investment value of the real estate, based on an appraisal, is taken into account, Mr. Martin's books show that a one-third interest in his business is worth $11,000 instead of $12,000. As a result of the appraisal, the proprietor's Capital account and the asset accounts show a reduction in invested capital of $4,000 on the building and an increase of $1,000 on the land.

The student of accounting should clearly understand that—

1. The proceeds of the sale of a capital asset in excess of its book value represent a profit, which must be set up on the books as such.   It is a profit which is subject to taxation as income.

2. When the proceeds of the sale of a capital asset are less than its book value, the difference is a loss, which should be accounted for as such.

3. The excess of the appraised value of a capital asset over its book value, when taken up on the books, is not profit, but *unearned increment;* that is, it is an increase in the value of invested property which results from appreciation and not from earned profits.   This unearned increment must be credited to Capital to offset the increase in assets recorded on the other side of the ledger.

4. When the appraised value of a capital asset is less than its book value, the difference represents the amount of the depreciation in value in excess of the depreciation actually charged off.   As this excess of depreciation has not been included in operating expenses from year to year, it should be charged directly to Capital when it is accounted for on the books to offset the decrease in assets recorded on the credit side of capital asset investment accounts.

Ignorance of the principles underlying the valuation of capital assets has caused financial embarrassment to many business concerns.   The showing of "paper profits" by crediting profit and loss for the unearned increment on capital assets results in overstating the amount of profit actually earned from operations, and received in cash or other assets convertible into cash.   Distributions of profits based on such inaccurate accounting result in capital being withdrawn under the misapprehension that profits are being distributed.

Exercise 75

F. M. Kay has been conducting a real estate brokerage business for the past thirty years.   He now wishes to sell to each of his sons, Walter and Harry, who have been employed by him for several years, a one-fourth interest in his business.   They are to pay their father out of profits as they are earned and determined from year to year until their interests are paid for in full.   Mr. Kay's assets and liabilities on the date of this transaction are as follows:

Cash	$4,000.00
Accounts Payable	300.00
Real Estate Investment	24,000.00
Reserve for Building Depreciation	4,860.00
Accounts Receivable (all collectible)	700.00
F. M. Kay, Capital	23,540.00

Mr. Kay's real estate consists of a small office building and lot. When he purchased the property eighteen years ago, the building was valued at $18,000, and the land at $6,000. He has depreciated the building at the rate of 1½% per annum. In ascertaining a fair price to charge his sons for their interests, Mr. Kay has appraised the building at $10,000 and the land at $7,200. These valuations are based on present real estate values in the section in which the property is located.

1. Set up the ledger accounts showing Mr. Kay's assets and liabilities before the appraisal, segregating his Real Estate investment of $24,000 in separate accounts.

2. Draft the journal entries required to give effect on the books to the values determined by the appraisal, and post the entries.

3. How much will Walter and Harry Kay have to pay their father to buy their respective one-fourth interests?

Accounting for Valuation of Fixed Capital Assets When They Are Fully Depreciated

268. When a fixed capital asset has been fully depreciated, which means that the Reserve for Depreciation account shows a credit balance equal to the debit balance shown by the asset Investment account, no more depreciation should be written off. The two accounts should be allowed to stand as open accounts in the ledger in order to show that the asset is still owned and on hand but has been fully depreciated, the debit balance of the one offsetting the credit balance of the other.

Other Investments in Fixed Capital Assets

269. In practically every business enterprise a certain part of the invested capital must be reinvested in equipment of various kinds in order to carry on its operations and functions. These investments include the purchase of such property as—

1. Office furniture, fixtures, and equipment, such as desks, chairs, bookcases, typewriters, adding machines, filing cabinets, safes, and office devices;

2. Store fixtures and equipment, such as show cases, display counters and tables, shelves, cash registers, and similar equipment;

3. Warehouse fixtures, tools, and implements, such as bins, shelves, trucks, scales, packing tables, etc.; and

4. Delivery equipment, such as automobile trucks and motorcycles.

Office, store, and warehouse equipment is usually depreciated at the rate of about 5%, the rate being based on an average useful life of twenty years. This depreciation, as in the case of depreciation on buildings, is an operating expense that should be set up on the books annually at the end of each period by a charge to the proper Expense account and a credit to Reserve for Depreciation.

Motor-driven delivery equipment depreciates much more rapidly than office and store equipment. For this reason the accounting process is simplified by setting up a separate investment account for it. Automobile trucks wear out and must be replaced in about five years; therefore, they are usually depreciated at the rate of from 20% to 25% per annum. This depreciation likewise must be charged as an operating expense annually and credited to Reserve for Depreciation.

The investment accounts for the furniture and equipment described above are kept in accordance with the principles underlying the capitalization of all other fixed assets. The same rules apply that govern the keeping of the "Furniture and Fixtures" account treated in Part One of this text (page 120). They are debited for the cost price of all equipment purchased or the price at which they are invested as assets. The accounts are credited for the original cost price or investment price of the whole or any part of the equipment disposed of which previously has been charged to the accounts. Their balances at any time represent the original cost price of the different kinds of equipment on hand.

Chapter 35—Treatment of Capital Asset Investment Accounts

270. In the ledger the investment accounts for capital assets owned show debit balances, representing the original cost price or investment price of the assets. The reserve for depreciation accounts kept in conjunction with the investment accounts show credit balances, representing the amount of depreciation written off on the capital assets to date. The book value of any capital asset, or the asset value at which it is carried on the books, is therefore reflected by the difference between the balance of its Investment account and the balance of its Reserve for Depreciation account. The credit balance of the Reserve account is in fact a subtraction in the ledger from the debit balance of the Investment account. As the Balance Sheet should show the book value at which capital assets are being carried at any given date, each capital asset should be stated at its full cost or investment value less the reserve for depreciation written off, the difference being the book value. In other words, the reserve accounts are treated in the Balance Sheet as deductions from assets, and not as liabilities, thus:

Fixed Assets:		
Building Investment	20,000.00	
Deduct—Reserve for Building Depreciation	1,000.00	19,000.00
Furniture and Equipment Investment	3,000.00	
Deduct—Reserve for F. and E. Depreciation	360.00	2,640.00
Total Fixed Capital Assets		21,640.00

The reserves for depreciation of capital assets are in no sense liabilities; they represent that part of the profits not distributed to the owners, but retained in the business as a part of its working capital with which to pay for repairs to and replacement of capital assets, as the need arises.

Exercise 76

Jan. 1 Walter R. Porter began business as a clothing merchant. He paid $700 for fully equipping his office. His store fixtures, show cases, counters, shelves, etc., required an investment of $2,000. He purchased for $900 a light delivery truck for delivering goods sold to customers.

Dec. 31 At the end of the first year he depreciated the office equipment at the rate of 4%, the store equipment at the rate of 5%, and the delivery equipment at the rate of 25%.

Jan. 21 About one year after purchasing a certain show case, which cost him $200, he replaced it with another case which cost $250. He was allowed a credit of $120 on the second-hand case and paid in cash $130 in full payment for the new case.

Dec. 31 At the end of the second year he charged off depreciation at the same rates as for the first year.

Feb. 1 About two years after it was purchased, he traded in a typewriter on a new machine, the price of which was $95. The first machine cost $75, and the second-hand value allowed for it was $35. He paid the difference on the new machine in cash.

Dec. 31 At the end of the third year he charged off depreciation at the usual rates.

1. Draft in journal form the entries required to record these transactions. Post the entries to ledger accounts.

2. What was the original cost, the depreciation, and the book value of each class of equipment at the end of the first year? at the end of the second year? at the end of the third year?

3. What was his loss on the sale of capital assets at the end of the first, second, and third years?

4. What was the increase in his investment in these assets at the end of the first, the second, and the third year?

5. Set up in proper form that section of his Statement of Assets, Liabilities, and Capital which should include these investments.

Review Questions

1. What are fixed assets?

2. Of what does real estate consist? Should investments in land and improvements be kept in the same or in separate accounts?

3. What do you understand to be the meaning of the term *appreciation? depreciation?* What capital assets have a tendency to appreciate? Which ones generally depreciate? What are the causes of appreciation? of depreciation?

4. What expenditures are properly chargeable to the capital asset Investment account? Of what does the purchase price or construction cost of a building consist? What is the book value of a capital asset? At what value should it be carried on the books and in the Balance Sheet? What entries should be made in case a capital asset is sold?

5. Name some fixed assets besides buildings and land. How should capital asset investment accounts and their reserve for depreciation accounts be treated in the Balance Sheet? Are reserves for depreciation of capital assets debits or credits in the ledger? Are they to be considered as assets or liabilities?

Chapter 36—Mortgages

271. A mortgage is a *provisional conveyance or transfer* of the *title or equity* in the ownership of real or personal property to a creditor to secure the payment of a debt representing money lent or contracted to be paid, the mortgage to become void on the payment of the debt. Until it is paid, a mortgage is a *lien* against the property on which the mortgage loan was made. The instrument representing a mortgage on real estate is called a *mortgage deed*. A mortgage on movable personal property is referred to as a *chattel mortgage*. The party who borrows money on a mortgage is the *mortgagor*. The party who lends the money is the *mortgagee*.

To illustrate, suppose the J. K. Horner Company, being the owner of real estate worth $20,000, wishes to borrow $5,000 with which to make permanent improvements, or to finance current or new operations. By offering to give a mortgage on its property for the sum needed and to pay interest at an agreed rate, the company can induce a lender of funds to make the loan as an investment. A mortgage executed for such a loan would provisionally convey a $5,000 equity in the company's title to its property to the party who made the loan; the title to revert back to the borrowing company when the loan is paid off. The mortgage contract would stipulate the date on which the mortgagee was to be repaid and the dates on which the accrued interest was to be paid.

A mortgage may be redeemed by the payment of the full amount of the loan with interest at a certain date, or by the payment of the principal sum in installments at stated dates with interest. The non-payment of the principal or interest at any interest period as called for in the mortgage empowers the mortgagee to foreclose it. *Foreclosure* is a legal procedure which makes *permanent* the temporary transfer of title under the mortgage, and grants to the mortgagee the right to possess and take over the full ownership of the mortgaged property for liquidation, any proceeds from its sale in excess of the mortgagee's claim to be paid to the mortgagor.

A mortgage is similar to a promissory note in that it is a contract to pay a specified sum of money on a specified date or dates. Mortgages, however, are long-time obligations; that is, they usually run for a period of years. A mortgage is similar to a collateral note because definitely specified property is pledged as security for its payment. It differs from such notes because it vests title to the debtor's property for the amount of the debt in the creditor until the debt is paid. A mortgage given to secure money borrowed from another is a *mortgage payable*. A mortgage received for money lent to another is a *mortgage receivable*.

231

Millions of dollars are borrowed annually by business enterprises on mortgages to raise working capital. The extractive, agricultural, manufacturing, transportation, and public utility industries, in particular, are large borrowers of funds secured by mortgaging fixed assets. In many instances, funds for development and expansion are borrowed on mortgage bonds. A mortgage bond is a bond the payment of which is secured by a mortgage on capital assets.

Mortgages Receivable Account

272. The Mortgages Receivable account is conducted precisely in accordance with the principles which govern the keeping of the Notes Receivable account. It is debited for the principal sum of all mortgages owned and held on the property of others. It is credited for the principal sum or sums when and as paid to redeem the mortgages, whether they are retired in one settlement or in installments at stated intervals. The balance of the account represents the sum due on Mortgages Receivable at any time.

Exercise 77

Feb.   8   Mallory & Taylor, having outgrown their former quarters, purchased a new property and removed their business. Their former business property, consisting of a building and lot at Fort and Water Streets, for which they paid $33,742.85, was sold today to the Greer Bros. Co. for $30,000, terms $20,000 cash, and a mortgage for $10,000 to run five years, redeemable in installments of $2,000 each on the 8th day of February in each succeeding year after the sale, with interest at 6%. Mallory & Taylor's books show that the cost of the building was $25,492.85, and the cost of the lot was $8,250. The appraised prices at the date of the sale were $20,000 for the building and $10,000 for the lot. On this date the Reserve for Building Depreciation account on their books showed a credit balance of $2,468.28.

Feb.   8   At the end of the first year Mallory & Taylor received a check from the Greer Bros. Co. for $2,600, representing the first payment of $2,000 on the principal and the interest on the full amount of the mortgage for one year at 6%.

Feb.   8   At the end of the second year, they received another check for $2,480, representing a second installment on the principal and the interest on $8,000 for one year.

Aug.   8   On the following August 8, being in need of funds, Mallory & Taylor sold the mortgage to the Commonwealth Mortgage Finance Co. for $6,000 plus the accrued interest to date, and received a check for $6,055, the Finance Co. having deducted $125 for the cost of searching the title. (Debit Miscellaneous Losses for this charge.)

1. Draft the journal entries required to set up the accounts as they appeared in Mallory & Taylor's ledger before the vacated property was sold. Post these entries.

2. Draft and post the journal entries required for the other transactions.

3. Analyze the profits and losses on the sale of the property, and the incomes and expenses in connection with the mortgage.

Mortgages Payable Account

273. The Mortgages Payable account is kept in accordance with the principles which govern the keeping of the Notes Payable account. It is credited for the principal amount of mortgages executed and placed on property purchased, or when loans are secured on them. The account is debited for the amounts paid from time to time in redeeming the principal of the mortgaged debt. The balance of the account represents at any time the liability owed on outstanding mortgages, which is a fixed liability that should be included in the Balance Sheet.

Exercise 78

Feb. 8 The Greer Bros. Co. purchased from Mallory & Taylor their former quarters, consisting of a building and lot, situated at the corner of Fort and Water Sts. The consideration was $30,000, based on appraised values of $20,000 for the building and $10,000 for the lot. The terms of the transaction provided that $20,000 was to be paid in cash, and that a mortgage was to be taken by Mallory & Taylor for the balance of the purchase price, $10,000, the mortgage to run 5 years and to be redeemable in installments of $2,000 each on the 8th day of February in each succeeding year after the sale, with interest at 6%. The transaction was completed according to these terms. Greer Bros. Co. also issued checks in the amount of $1,728.50 to pay the agent's commission for buying the property, searching the title, and having the deed recorded.

Feb. 8 At the end of the first year the Greer Bros. Co. issued a check for $2,600 in favor of Mallory & Taylor, which included the first payment of $2,000 on the principal and the interest on the full amount of the mortgage for one year at 6%, or $600.

Feb. 8 At the end of the second year another payment of $2,000 on the principal of the mortgage was made, the check including the interest on $8,000 for one year, or $480.

Feb. 8 At the end of the third year the Greer Bros. Co. issued its check for $2,360 on account of principal and interest to the Commonwealth Mortgage Finance Co. This company had purchased the mortgage from Mallory & Taylor the preceding August 8.

1. Draft the journal entries required to record these transactions in the books of Greer Bros. Co.   Post to ledger accounts.

2. What was the original cost of the property?   How much did the purchasers still owe on it at the end of the third year?   How much had they paid during the three years for the use of the capital borrowed?

Chapter 37—Stock and Bond Investment Account

274. Investments in stocks, bonds, and other securities may be kept in one account under the title, "Stock and Bond Investments"; or a separate account may be opened for each class or kind of security purchased, such as "Mechanics National Bank Stock" or "United States Government Bonds." The stock and bond investment accounts are kept according to the principles which govern the keeping of other capital investment accounts. They should be charged with the original cost of securities purchased, plus the fees required by law or custom, and the charges for services rendered by agents or brokers in acquiring the securities. In other words, such accounts should be charged with the total expenditures of cash or its equivalent required to secure ownership of what is purchased. The account should be credited for the cost price of the whole or any part of the securities sold. The balance of the account will thus at any time represent the investment cost of the securities owned.

275. Stock is issued by corporations in consideration for the capital invested by the stockholders, or owners. It is, therefore, referred to as capital stock. The stock is in the form of a certificate showing that the holder is the owner of a certain number of shares of the total capital stock. The book value, or net worth, of the stock of a corporation is measured by the book value of its net assets. The stock of a corporation which has issued 1,000 shares, and whose net assets are $100,000, is worth $100 a share. If the net assets are $80,000, the stock is worth $80 a share at book value.

Stock is said to be "at par" when it is selling for the amount stated in the incorporation papers; "above par" or "below par" when it is selling above or below this stated price.

Dividends on *preferred stock* earnings can be distributed.

The commission for buying and selling stock is called *brokerage*.

276. Bonds and mortgage notes are similar to ordinary notes payable in that they are obligations to pay a definite sum of money on a definitely specified date or dates, with interest. They are issued for the purpose of raising or borrowing money. The bonds and mortgage notes of business enterprises differ from ordinary notes in that their payment is secured by pledging property which can be sold in case of default in the payment of principal or interest. In this respect, bonds and mortgage notes are similar to collateral notes. The payment of Government bonds and certificates of indebtedness is secured by reserving funds from moneys collected by taxation with which to pay principal and interest when due. The funds so reserved are referred to as *sinking funds*. The payment of the principal and interest cancels the indebtedness represented by such securities as have been described, and the obligation is then said to have been "retired."

Coupon bonds are printed with interest coupons attached, which are to be presented for payment when the interest is due.

Registered bonds are registered by corporations or government units, the amount of dividend being sent by check.

Exercise 79

Sept. 12 J. B. Dunn & Co. purchased 50 shares of Baltimore & Ohio Railroad Co. stock at 53, and issued a check to the brokers for $2,658.50 in payment of the stock, the brokers' commission, and other charges.

Nov. 20 The market price having advanced and the need for funds having arisen, Dunn & Co. instructed its brokers to sell 25 shares of the stock. The brokers sold the shares for 59¾ a share, and after deducting a commission of $3.13, paid Dunn & Co. as the proceeds $1,490.62.

Dec. 31 The market quotation on the stock on this date was 55.

1. Set up in journal form the entries required to record these transactions properly. Then post to ledger accounts. Charge the Profit and Loss account for expenses incurred in selling the securities, and also carry any profits or losses to that account.

2. What was the inventory value of the stock on hand on December 31, and what entries, if any, were required to record it as an asset?

3. What was the net profit or loss on the transactions as of December 31?

Exercise 80

Feb.   10 John H. Bacon purchased 100 shares of Philadelphia & Reading Railroad stock, par value $50, at 47. His check for the stock plus his broker's commission and other fees amounted to $4,732.50.

March 20 He purchased two $500 Government bonds at 98 from a friend who was in need of funds, and issued his check for $980.

July   1 He cashed the interest coupons on his bonds and received $21.25 in interest, which was at the rate of 4¼% for one-half year.

July   10 He received a check for $150 for a semi-annual dividend at 3% on the Philadelphia & Reading stock.

Oct.   18 Mr. Bacon instructed his broker to sell 25 shares of Philadelphia & Reading stock at 52, the market price on this date. He received a check from his broker for the proceeds of $1,293.75.

Oct.   20 He purchased 100 shares of People's Gas Co.'s stock at par of $10 and issued his check in payment in the amount of $1,001.25, which included the broker's commission.

Dec.   12 As he needed funds, Mr. Bacon instructed his broker to sell 60 shares of his People's Gas stock at the current price, 9½, and received a check for the proceeds amounting to $568.75.

Dec.   31 He received a dividend check on his Philadelphia & Reading stock amounting to $112.50, and cashed his interest coupons on his bonds and received $21.25. No dividends were declared on the People's Gas stock.

1. Set up in ledger account form the entries required to record his transactions in stocks and bonds. Open a separate account for each kind of security.

2. At what sum should he inventory these securities on December 31, if Philadelphia & Reading was quoted at 55, the Government bonds at 99, and People's Gas at 8¼?

3. What was his net income from interest and dividends?

4. What was his net profit or loss on all the transactions as of December 31?

Chapter 38—Deferred Debit Items

277. It is customary to charge expense bills to the various expense accounts *as the bills are paid* during an accounting period. At the time of closing the books, these accounts may therefore contain charges for expense items of which the full benefit has not been received during the period in which the bills were paid. In other words, that part of the expenses paid *but not actually incurred* during the period in which they are recorded is properly chargeable to the *succeeding period or periods*.

For instance, suppose an insurance premium on a policy to run three years and amounting to $300 has been paid during the current period. It is apparent that the expense for this premium has been prepaid for the second and third years which the policy has to run. Of the $300 paid, $200 represents *unconsumed expense* at the end of the current period. Unless one-third of the expense for the premium is carried over to each of the second and third years, the expense account for the current year will be *overcharged* in the amount of $200 above the actual expense incurred. On the other hand, the expense account for each of the following two years would be *undercharged* in the amount of $100.

It is thus apparent that the cost of unconsumed or prepaid expense items should be adjusted and allocated to the succeeding fiscal period or periods during which the benefit from the expenditure will be secured, and to which they therefore properly apply. It would manifestly be unfair to charge the current period with any portion of expenses which were not actually incurred until a subsequent period, because the net profit would be understated or the net loss overstated for the current period; and, on the other hand, the net profit would be overstated or the net loss understated in subsequent periods.

Suppose that warehouse supplies amounting to $600 have been purchased and charged to the Warehouse Expense account, $150 worth of which were on hand at the date of closing. The actual expense incurred for the current year is therefore $450. It is plain that the Warehouse Expense account should be adjusted in such manner as to show a debit balance of $450 for the current period, which will require that the charge for the $150 representing the cost of the unconsumed supplies be carried over, or *deferred*, to the next period. Of the interest prepaid on a note payable for $1,000, dated November 1 to run for three months, $10 is applicable to the current period, and $5 to the following period.

In order to state profits and losses accurately, it is therefore necessary to defer the charges for prepaid or unconsumed expense items to the period which will be benefited by the expenditures they represent. As they are to be applied to a later period, and as expenses are always debits, such charges are referred to as *deferred debit items*. They are sometimes called deferred charges to operations, but this term is not broad enough to include the entire group because they are not all operating expenses. Interest, for instance, is a deduction from income and not an operating expense.

Accounting for Deferred Debit Items

278. The adjustment of the accounts containing prepaid expense items is accomplished by opening the Deferred Debit Items account at the close of the fiscal period as a *temporary asset account*. It is debited for the amounts of the various prepaid expenses, the accounts to which they were charged when paid being credited. The effect of this entry is to set up the prepaid expenses as an asset at the date of closing, and to reduce the charges in the various expense accounts to an amount equal to the cost of the consumed or incurred expenses for the current period. Although prepaid and unconsumed expense items are not assets of the kind that can be sold or converted into cash or its equivalent, it is obvious that their prepayment has reduced the amount of the cash assets on the date of closing. In other words, their prepayment during the current period will have the effect of reducing the outlays of cash for expense bills during the next fiscal period. These considerations therefore justify their treatment as assets at the date of closing. In other words, prepaid expenses are *temporarily capitalized* when the books are closed in order to secure an accurate statement of expenses incurred during the current period.

After the books are closed, the journal entry already described is reversed. On the first day of the next period the proper expense accounts should be debited for the prepaid expense items, Deferred Debit Items account being credited. The effect of this entry is to close the latter account, and to charge back again to the expense accounts the items for which the previous period was given credit, because they properly apply to the new period. If we take the transactions cited above as examples and eliminate all other items, the expense accounts before the books were closed would appear as follows:

Insurance Expense	Warehouse Expense	Interest Expense
300.00	600.00	15.00

The entry required to adjust the amounts of the prepaid portions of these expenses would be:

Deferred Debit Items	$355.00	
Insurance Expense		$200.00
Warehouse Expense		150.00
Interest Expense		5.00

When this entry is posted, the accounts at the time the Income and Profit and Loss Statement and the Balance Sheet are prepared will therefore show the following results:

Insurance Expense		Warehouse Expense		Interest Expense		Deferred Debit Items	
300.00	200.00	600.00	150.00	15.00	5.00	355.00	

The Income and Profit and Loss Statement would show insurance expense for the current period of $100, warehouse expense of $450, and interest expense of $10. The deferred debit items amounting to $355 would be included in the Balance Sheet as a temporary asset. After the books were closed and the expense accounts were balanced, the above journal entry would be reversed, thus:

Insurance Expense	200.00	
Warehouse Expense	150.00	
Interest Expense	5.00	
Deferred Debit Items		355.00

When this entry is posted, the accounts would finally appear as follows:

Insurance Expense		Warehouse Expense		Interest Expense		Deferred Debit Items	
300.00	200.00	600.00	150.00	15.00	5.00	355.00	355.00
	100.00		450.00		10.00		
300.00	300.00	600.00	600.00	15.00	15.00		
200.00		150.00		5.00			

It will thus be observed that at the beginning of the following period the expense accounts will stand charged with the amounts of the expenses already paid but applicable to the new period, and the Deferred Debit Items account will be closed out. This account consequently functions as an inventory account for prepaid expense items. It is opened at the end of one fiscal period, and closed at the beginning of the next period. The total of the prepaid expenses for which it is debited and credited is in fact an inventory of deferred expenses.

Exercise 81

The expense accounts of H. A. Hartman & Company at the close of a fiscal period, December 31, show the following balances, which include charges for certain prepaid and unconsumed expense items: general expense, $3,300; taxes and insurance, $1,800; interest expense, $130; warehouse expense, $2,900; and delivery expense, $1,100.   An analysis of these accounts develops the following facts:

(a) During the year the company paid taxes on its real estate amounting to $340 for the year beginning July 1 and ending the following June 30, six months after the date the books were closed.

(b) On December 28 a check was issued for $75 for the January rent of a small warehouse.

(c) There are warehouse supplies and equipment on hand which cost $120.

(d) The office supplies and stationery on hand cost $50.

(e) On December 1 the company paid in advance the interest on its three months' note dated December 1 for $2,000.

1. Set up the ledger accounts with the balances given before the deferred debit items are entered.   Draft the journal entry required to record the deferred debit items at the date of closing.

2. Post this entry to the accounts, and close out the amounts of the several expenses for the current period.

3. Make the entry which should be made on January 1, and post it to the accounts.

4. What was the total of the deferred debit items, how much was the actual expense incurred for the current period under each classification, and how much of the expense charged to the accounts during the current period should be carried over to the next period?

Questions

1. What is a mortgage?   What are the objects of mortgaging property?   What is meant by the retirement of a mortgage?   What is a bond?   For what purpose are bonds issued?   How are they retired?

2. On what kind of assets are mortgages usually placed?   What is a chattel mortgage?   What kind of liabilities are mortgages payable?   What kind of assets are mortgages receivable?   What effect does the placing of a mortgage have on the equity of the owner in the mortgaged property?   Does the securing of a loan on a collateral note, or on a judgment note, have the same effect on the owner's equity in the property put up as security?

3. Assuming a mortgage has been placed, state which party is the mortgagor. Which party is the mortgagee? Under what circumstances can the mortgage be foreclosed? Which party would foreclose it? Of what do the foreclosure proceedings consist? How much of the proceeds of the sale of a property under foreclosure reverts back to the debtor?

4. What are deferred credit items? What is the purpose in setting them up on the books? Explain the procedure in accounting for them. Are deferred credit items liabilities which must be paid off in cash?

5. Of what do advances to employees consist? How should they be classified in the Balance Sheet?

6. What are accrued assets? When and how are they accounted for? Is the Accrued Assets account a fiscal or a running account?

Chapter 39—Other Assets

279. The Balance Sheet of a trading or mercantile business should show under the caption, "Other Assets," any assets on the books which are not properly included under current or fixed assets. Such assets consist of doubtful accounts receivable, the collection of which is problematical because they are some time past due; advances to employees collectible in the distant future, or the collection of which is doubtful; and the book value of stocks and bonds owned that are not readily salable at prices approximating their purchase price, or the actual value of which is doubtful. The asset "Good Will" should also be listed under this heading if it appears on the books.

280. All the assets previously considered are *tangible* assets; that is to say, they consist of physical property, real and personal, and receivables —all of which represent intrinsic or realizable values. Good will, on the other hand, is an *intangible* asset. In other words, it has no intrinsic property value. The value of the good will of a business is the sum which can be realized for it over and above the amount of its net assets if the business is sold. In other words, good will may be defined as the value placed on the disposition or inclination of the public to patronize a particular business because of the good reputation it has established as a going concern. It represents the estimated value of a business in excess of its actual net assets because of its having an established current trade. Stated in another way, it is the value placed on the future profits of a business that are assured from the patronage already established.

The Good Will account should never be opened except when a business is purchased at a price greater than the actual net assets taken over by the new management. The Good Will account under such circumstances is charged for the difference between the purchase price and the net assets purchased. For instance, suppose that a business having total assets of $11,000 and liabilities of $3,000 is purchased for the sum of $10,000, all the assets and liabilities to be taken over by the new owner. It is evident that when the purchaser sets up the accounts of the business, the actual value of the net assets purchased will be the difference between the total assets and liabilities, or $8,000. His investment, however, is $10,000, the amount he paid the former owner. The difference of $2,000 represents the cost of the good will purchased along with the net assets, which is debited to the Good Will account in order to maintain the equilibrium of debits and credits in the ledger.

The Good Will account may be allowed to remain on the books permanently to show the original cost of the good will, or it may be written off the books gradually against profits until it is closed. It is written off by charging profit and loss and crediting the Good Will account for a certain percentage of its original cost annually at the end of each period. If profits permit, it is usually eliminated from the books in about five years. Good will written off is always a direct charge against profits or surplus. It should never be charged to Expense.

The argument in favor of allowing the Good Will account to remain as a permanent book asset is that if the business continues to be prosperous, the price paid for it was a good investment. It is further argued that its value under these conditions has been maintained and probably increased under the management of the new owner, and to charge it off unfairly reduces the showing of profits for the years in which the Good Will account is written down. The argument on the other side of the question is that the good will of the former owner will gradually be merged into and become a part of the good will being created by the new owner, and that as good will is a realizable asset only in case of a resale of the business, it should gradually be eliminated from the books.

The accountant must abide by the wishes and decision of the management in regard to his treatment of the Good Will account. No one can be deceived by its inclusion in the books and on the Balance Sheet because the account merely represents what was originally paid for good will. Anyone to whom the Balance Sheet is submitted would understand that the good will included among the assets could not be applied to the payment of debts.

Exercise 82

J. A. Locke and R. B. Mann have purchased the business of the Peerless Grocery Company for the sum of $14,000. Each of them invested $7,500 to finance the purchase and to have a cash capital of $1,000 with which to begin business. They will conduct the business as equal partners. The assets and liabilities of the Peerless Grocery Company on the date of the sale to Locke and Mann, after being verified and appraised, were found to be as follows:

Stock in Trade	$3,000.00
Notes Payable	1,000.00
Building Investment	5,000.00
Land Investment	2,800.00
Accounts Payable	500.00
Notes Receivable	300.00
Delivery Equipment	1,200.00
Store Furniture and Fixtures	900.00

1. Draft the entry in journal form for the cash invested by the partners.

2. Draft the journal entry for the purchase of the assets and liabilities of the Peerless Grocery Co.

3. Post the entries to ledger accounts.

4. What was the sum paid for the good will of the Peerless Grocery Company?

Chapter 40—Liabilities

281. The **Current Liabilities** of a trading business are its short-time obligations which will be payable within the near future. Current liabilities include, besides notes and accounts payable, such expense items as accrued salaries, wages, taxes, interest, and similar expenses due but not paid. Current liabilities, generally speaking, are the obligations arising out of current routine transactions which must be liquidated within the terms of credit usually granted on purchases of merchandise and bills for expenses. Current liabilities represent the first claims on current assets. Careful management requires that care be taken at all times to have sufficient current assets available to pay current liabilities as they mature, in order to keep the credit of a concern unimpaired.

Accrued Liabilities

282. During a fiscal period it is not customary to record the liabilities for the payment of expense bills, salaries, wages, interest, and similar expense items, at the time the liabilities are incurred. On the other hand, the custom is to record expenses *only when and as paid*, for the reason that this procedure requires but one entry—a charge to the proper expense account and a credit to Cash. It follows, therefore, that at the time of closing the books, there may be certain liabilities existing for expenses unpaid which do not as yet appear on the books. Such liabilities are referred to as *accrued liabilities*. They must be recorded when the books are closed in order to secure an accurate statement of all expenses incurred during the current period, as well as a complete statement of all existing liabilities. Accrued liabilities are consequently the opposite of accrued assets. Accrued assets consist of income earned but not entered. Accrued liabilities consist of expenses incurred but not entered.

For example, suppose a concern which pays salaries and wages twice a month—on the 10th and 25th—closes its books on December 31. It is apparent that the salaries and wages earned for the remaining six days of December are liabilities as of December 31. It follows that in order to show the total expense at that date, an adjustment of the accounts is necessary in order to include the accrued salaries and wages. Again, suppose that this concern has not yet paid its real estate taxes for the year for which it is closing its books. It is evident that this expense has been incurred; and as the taxes, salaries, and wages have not been paid, they should appear as liabilities if the books are to show all expenses and reflect the true financial condition.

283. Accounting for Accrued Liabilities. Accrued liabilities are set up on the books at the date of closing by inventorying all expenses incurred and unpaid. The proper expense accounts are debited, and the Accrued Liabilities account is credited by an adjusting journal entry. After the books are closed, this entry is reversed under date of the first day of the next fiscal period. This procedure is identical in principle with the handling of accrued assets and deferred debit items.

Assume that there are accrued liabilities for salaries and wages of $200 chargeable to general expense, for taxes of $300 chargeable to taxes and insurance, and for interest on notes payable of $25 at the date of closing. The journal entry required to record them is as follows:

General Expense	200.00	
Taxes and Insurance	300.00	
Interest Expense	25.00	
Accrued Liabilities		525.00

Assuming that there are no other items in the expense accounts, when the foregoing entry is posted these items will appear as follows:

General Expense	Taxes and Insurance	Interest Expense	Accrued Liabilities
200.00		300.00		25.00			525.00

Statements would then be prepared and the ledger closed, which would result in the balances of the expense accounts being carried to the Profit and Loss Summary account. This account would then be closed into the Capital account. The Accrued Liabilities account would remain open and appear as a liability in the Balance Sheet. To simplify the example, let us assume that the assets consisted of cash, $1,000, that the invested capital was $1,000, and that there were no other accounts involved. The accounts would appear as follows, after the closing of the ledger was completed:

General Expense		Taxes and Insurance		Interest Expense	
200.00	200.00	300.00	300.00	25.00	25.00

Cash		Accrued Liabilities		Capital	
1,000.00			525.00	525.00	1,000.00

Observe that the liability for the payment of these accrued expenses is recorded in the Accrued Liabilities account, while their cost is a loss charged to the Capital account when the books are closed. The foregoing journal entry would be reversed at the beginning of the following period, thus:

Accrued Liabilities	525.00	
General Expense		200.00
Taxes and Insurance		300.00
Interest Expense		25.00

The accounts will appear as follows when this entry is posted:

General Expense			Taxes and Insurance			Interest Expense	
200.00	200.00		300.00	300.00		25.00	25.00
	200.00			300.00			25.00

Cash			Accrued Liabilities			Capital	
1,000.00			525.00	525.00		525.00	1,000.00

Observe that the Accrued Liabilities account is now closed and that the unpaid expenses are recorded as credits to their respective accounts. These credits will be canceled by the debits to the accounts when the liabilities are paid, and thus the accounts will be balanced in the new period as far as these items are concerned. In other words, they will show no expense for the accrued liabilities during the new period, because they were included as expenses during the preceding period, as we have seen above.

Now let us assume that on January 10 the salaries, wages, taxes, and interest accounted for as accrued liabilities on December 31 were paid. The accounts would then show the following final results:

General Expense			Taxes and Insurance			Interest Expense	
200.00	200.00		300.00	300.00		25.00	25.00
200.00	200.00		300.00	300.00		25.00	25.00

Cash			Accrued Liabilities			Capital	
1,000.00	525.00		525.00	525.00		525.00	1,000.00

Observe that the expense accounts are now in balance, that the cash assets have been reduced by the amount of cash consumed in paying the expenses, and that the debit balance of the Cash account equals the credit balance of the Capital account.

Accrued liabilities should be listed first among the current liabilities, because the majority of them represent preferred or secured claims. Salaries and wages of employees must be paid before any other creditors are satisfied. Interest on notes, mortgages, and past-due accounts payable must be settled before any sums paid on such debts are applied against the principal. Mortgages are also secured and preferred claims against assets. Notes and accounts payable, including unpaid bills for expense items, are unsecured claims; that is to say, all secured obligations must be satisfied out of the available assets before the remainder, if any, is applied to the settlement of unsecured claims.

Exercise 83

The Oriole Mercantile Company inventoried its accrued liabilities on December 31 as follows:

(a) Interest accrued at the rate of $5\frac{1}{2}\%$ from March 15 on a $6,000 mortgage on its real estate.

(b) Interest accrued at 6% on its three months' note for $3,000 dated October 25 in favor of Harris & Jackson, the note having been issued to cover an account for merchandise purchased.

(c) Salaries and wages accrued from December 20 amounting to $387.50.

(d) Unpaid bills for warehouse supplies and materials amounting to $95.

(e) Unpaid advertising bills amounting to $211.44, chargeable to advertising expense.

1. Draft the journal entry required to record the accrued liabilities on the books, and post to ledger accounts.

2. Transfer the balances of the accounts that would be closed at the end of the period to the Profit and Loss Summary account, and close the Summary account into the Capital account.

3. Draft the journal entry required to adjust the accrued liabilities as of January 1 of the next period, and post to the ledger accounts.

4. Assume that on January 5 all accrued liabilities as of December 31 were paid except the accrued interest. Make the entry required in journal form, and post to the accounts.

5. Assuming there are no charges to it, explain why the Interest Expense account shows a credit balance on January 5.

6. Set up in journal form the entries required for paying the principal and accrued interest when the note and mortgage matured, assuming that the note was paid in full and that $1,000 was paid on the principal of the mortgage.

Fixed Liabilities

284. A mortgage may be placed on property purchased in order to spread the payments for it over a period of years. A mortgage may also be placed on property owned in order to raise capital. Bonds are also issued to raise capital. Mortgage notes are issued to enable small investors to participate in lending money to a concern which borrows by placing a mortgage on its property. Consequently, all the securities referred to are liabilities of the enterprises which issue them. The borrowing concerns are debtors to the holders of their mortgages, mortgage notes, or bonds until they are retired.

The security back of such evidences of indebtedness usually consists of the fixed assets of the borrowing company. Bonds and mortgages consequently are liens on such assets. The indebtedness of a concern secured by a mortgage is referred to as its mortgaged indebtedness; when secured by a bond issue, as its bonded indebtedness. Inasmuch as mortgages, mortgage notes, and bonds are to be paid off and retired over a period of years, they are long-time obligations and are therefore classified as fixed liabilities.

Deferred Credit Items

285. It is customary to record income as it is collected; hence, at the close of a fiscal period the accounts may contain certain items of income collected and credited during the current period *which are yet to be earned*. For instance, if a tenant paid his December and January rent of $200 on December 15, and the books are closed on December 31, it is apparent that one-half of the rent collected is income earned for the current period, and the other half is income to be earned during the succeeding period. The December rent is income *earned and collected*. The January rent is income *collected but not earned*. In other words, it is income *collected in advance*. It follows that if an adjustment of the accounts at the date of closing is not made, the income for the current period will be overstated by $100, and the income for the succeeding period will be understated by the same amount.

Similarly, of the total interest of $30 paid in advance on a note receivable for $2,000 dated November 1, $20 is income for the period ending December 31 and $10 is income for the period beginning January 1. In order to state correctly the income for the current period, it is necessary at the time the books are closed to inventory income collected and credited in advance, and to adjust the accounts so that the succeeding period will receive the proper credit for such income. The adjustment is made by opening the Deferred Credit Items account. This account is credited for all income collected during the current period that is applicable to the succeeding period or periods, the income accounts which were credited for the income during the current period being debited. After the books are closed, the adjusting entry is reversed, with the result that the deferred credit items are closed out and the income collected in advance is credited back to the income accounts for the new period under the date of the first business day.

Accounting for Deferred Credit Items

286. If we take the rent and interest referred to above as examples and eliminate all other items to simplify the illustration, the following entries would have been made when the rent and interest were collected:

Cash	200.00	
Real Estate Income		200.00
Cash	30.00	
Interest Income		30.00

When these entries are posted, the accounts appear as follows:

Cash		Real Estate Income		Interest Income	
200.00			200.00		30.00
30.00					

On December 31, the following adjusting journal entries would be required to defer the income unearned during the current period to the following period:

Real Estate Income	100.00	
Interest Income	10.00	
Deferred Credit Items		110.00

When posted, the foregoing accounts would then appear as follows:

Cash		Real Estate Income		Interest Income		Deferred Credit Items	
200.00		100.00	200.00	10.00	30.00		110.00
30.00							

The Real Estate Income and Interest Income accounts would be closed into the Profit and Loss Summary account and thence into the Capital account when the ledger is closed, with the following effect upon the accounts:

Cash		Real Estate Income		Interest Income	
200.00		100.00	200.00	10.00	30.00
30.00		100.00		20.00	
		200.00	200.00	30.00	30.00

Deferred Credit Items		Capital	
	110.00		120.00

Observe that the real estate income of $100 and the interest income of $20 for the current period now stand credited to the Capital account, and that the unearned income stands as a credit to the Deferred Credit Items account to reflect the liabilities to furnish the use of the rented space for January and the use of the money covered by the note until the note is due.   In other words, such liabilities merely represent obligations to give value received.   On January 1 the foregoing entry adjusting the deferred credit items would be reversed, resulting in the changes in the accounts shown below:

	Deferred Credit Items	110.00
	Real Estate Income	100.00
	Interest Income	10.00

Cash		Real Estate Income		Interest Income	
200.00		100.00	200.00	10.00	30.00
30.00		100.00		20.00	
		200.00	200.00	30.00	30.00
			100.00		10.00

Deferred Credit Items		Capital	
110.00	110.00		120.00

Observe that the Deferred Credit Items account is now closed, and that the income of $110 applicable to the new period is credited to the proper income accounts.   The Deferred Credit Items account thus functions as an inventory account, being opened at the close of a period in order to adjust income collected in advance, and being closed again at the beginning of the next period.

Exercise 84

The Howard Tool Company inventoried its income credited or collected in advance on December 31 as follows:

(a) Interest collected in advance on notes receivable not due until the following period, $45.

(b) Prepaid rentals on leased equipment, the lease to expire on March 1, $100. The total rentals under the lease of $300 were recorded in the Miscellaneous Income account.

(c) On December 29 a printer occupying the fourth floor of the company's building paid his January rent of $150.   The check was deposited on the same date.

1. The credit balances of the accounts before this adjustment were as follows: interest income, $160; miscellaneous income, $300; real estate income, $1,950.

2. Draft the entry required to adjust these transactions as of December 31, and post to ledger accounts. Close out the accounts that would be eliminated in the process of closing the ledger.

3. Draft and post the entry required to adjust the items as of January 1. How much of the income collected represented income for the old period, and how much income for the new period?

Questions

1. What are current liabilities? What accounts represent current liabilities? What are fixed liabilities? What accounts represent fixed liabilities?
2. What are accrued liabilities? What is the purpose of setting them up on the books? Explain the procedure in accounting for them.
3. What liabilities are preferred or secured claims against assets? What liabilities are unsecured claims?

Chapter 41—Income and Profit and Loss Accounts

287. The Income and Profit and Loss accounts of a trading or general mercantile business are usually subdivided into the following principal groups:

> Cost of Goods Sold Group
> Income from Sales Group
> Operating Expense Group
> Deductions from Income Group
> Additions to Income Group

As the principal profit of a trading or mercantile business is derived from the purchase and sale of merchandise, the accounts in which are recorded the income from sales and the cost of goods sold are of primary importance. These accounts may be referred to as the *trading accounts*, because it is from their results that the gross trading profit or the gross trading loss is determined.

288. The elements entering into the cost of goods sold are—

> 1. The initial inventory.
> 2. The purchases during an accounting period.
> 3. The closing inventory.
> 4. Deductions from the cost of purchases.
> 5. Additions to the cost of purchases.

In wholesale and other large mercantile businesses, it is customary to classify in separate accounts the various items which constitute the foregoing elements of cost, the purpose being to have each account show one definite unit of information. The process of analyzing the results from trading operations at the time statements are prepared is thereby simplified; in fact, the analysis is provided for in advance as original entries are made. The accounts usually opened are—

> Purchases
> Purchases Returned
> Purchase Rebates and Allowances
> Purchase Discounts

Purchases Account

289. The basic account in the cost of goods sold group is the Purchases account. It is opened at the beginning of a fiscal period by an adjustment entry in which the inventory of goods carried over from the preceding period is debited to the Purchases account and credited to the Inventory account. The latter account is balanced and closed by this entry.

The Purchases account is also debited for the purchases of stock in trade made during the period as the totals of the purchases book are posted from month to month. The account is credited for the inventory of unsold goods on hand at the close of the fiscal period, this adjustment being necessary in order to have the Purchases account show the invoice cost of goods sold, and to set up the closing inventory as an asset on the books when they are closed for the current period. It will thus be observed that the first three elements of cost—the beginning inventory, the purchases, and the closing inventory—are accounted for in the Purchases account.

It is important that every bill of goods purchased, before being entered in the purchases book, be verified as to actual delivery of the goods charged on the invoice, correctness of unit prices, and correctness of extensions, in order to avoid incorrect charges to the Purchases account. However, the most important factor in keeping the Purchases account correctly is the valuation which is placed on inventories of stock in trade.

Deductions from Cost of Purchases

290. The Purchases account, as kept in Part One, received credit for purchases returned and rebates and allowances on purchases. In most instances, the volume of such items justifies their classification in separate books of original entry and the keeping of separate general ledger accounts for them. Instead of being credited to the Purchases account, they are credited to the "Purchases Returned" and the "Purchase Rebates and Allowances" accounts. While entries to these accounts may be passed through the general journal, it is the better practice to record them in a special journal under the title, "Purchase Returns and Allowances Journal." This journal contains special columns for returns and for rebates and allowances. The accounts of vendors—the parties from whom goods are purchased—are debited daily as entries are made in this book. The totals are posted monthly to the debit of Accounts Payable account and to the credit of Purchases Returned and the Purchase Rebates and Allowances accounts in the general ledger.

Additions to Cost of Purchases

291. As previously stated, the cost of merchandise purchased, as recorded in the Purchases account, is the invoice cost. *Invoice cost* may be defined as the price at which goods are billed at the point of purchase or point of shipment.   To the invoice cost there must be added the expenses incurred for freight, express, postage, and cartage charges paid for transporting goods from the point of shipment or of purchase to the store or warehouse of the buyer.   Duties on imported goods materially increase their cost.   After goods are received, they must be unpacked, sorted, placed in stock, or stored, such handling expenses likewise increasing their cost.   Additional expenses are incurred in filling orders and preparing the goods for shipment.

All these expenses *incurred directly in handling goods*, from the time they are ordered *until they are ready for shipment or delivery to customers*, constitute costs and charges which must be added to invoice cost in determining the prices at which they can be sold at a profit.   In other words, they are additions to cost, or *direct trading expenses*.   Additions to cost are recorded in the Freight and Cartage Inward, Duties and Storage, Warehouse Salaries and Labor, and other accounts under similar titles which indicate that they are merchandising costs of handling goods to be added to invoice cost.

Applying Additions to Cost to Inventories

The following illustration shows the proper form and arrangement of the Cost of Goods Sold section of the Income and Profit and Loss Statement.

Cost of Goods Sold:		
Inventory, January 1, 19—		$ 6,000.00
Purchases during year		50,000.00
Total Invoice Cost of Merchandise		56,000.00
Inventory, December 31, 19—		8,000.00
Total Invoice Cost of Goods Sold		48,000.00
Deductions from Cost:		
Purchases Returned	100.00	
Purchase Rebates and Allowances	200.00	300.00
Net Invoice Cost of Goods Sold		47,700.00
Additions to Cost:		
Freight and Cartage Inward		3,000.00
Duties and Storage		1,000.00
Warehouse Salaries and Labor		6,000.00
Total Cost of Goods Sold		$57,700.00

Exercise 85

At the end of a fiscal year the ledger of Barton-Gillett & Co. showed the following data:

Stock in Trade Inventory, Jan. 1	9,000.00	Purchases Returned	500.00
Purchases during period	84,000.00	Freight and Cartage Inward	3,900.00
Purchase Rebates and Allowances	800.00	Warehouse Salaries and Labor	7,200.00
Duties and Storage	1,400.00	Stock in Trade Inventory, Dec. 31	12,000.00

1. Prepare the Cost of Goods Sold section of the company's Income and Profit and Loss Statement showing the trading costs and expenses for the year.

2. Both inventories as given above were taken at invoice cost. Assuming that the initial inventory had been taken at market prices which averaged 10% above cost, and the closing inventory at market prices which averaged 5% below cost, what would have been the total cost of goods sold?

3. Assuming that the initial inventory had been taken at market prices averaging 10% below cost, and the closing inventory at market prices averaging 5% above cost, what would have been the total cost of goods sold?

4. Assuming that the initial inventory had been taken at market prices averaging 10% below cost, and the closing inventory at market prices averaging 5% below cost, what would have been the total cost of goods sold?

5. Assuming that the market prices were 10% and 5% above cost, respectively, what would have been the total cost of goods sold?

6. What amount in your judgment represents the correct cost of goods sold to be used as the basis of determining gross trading income, it being assumed that normal commodity prices prevail at the time the inventories were taken?

Exercise 86

The accounts of the Potter Dry Goods Company at the end of the year contained the following data:

Merchandise Inventory, Jan. 1	80,000.00	Warehouse Labor	11,000.00
Purchases	160,000.00	Goods Donated at Cost	200.00
Inward Freight and Express	8,500.00	General Warehouse Expense	6,300.00
Purchases Returned	2,100.00	Duties on Imported Goods	5,400.00
Cartage Inward	1,300.00	Storage Expense	400.00
Purchase Rebates and Allowances	700.00	Merchandise Inventory, Dec. 31	30,000.00

1. Prepare the Cost of Goods Sold section of the Income and Profit and Loss Statement.

2. The inventory of January 1 was taken at invoice cost. At the time the goods included in this inventory were purchased, prices were advancing rapidly, but during the current year commodity prices declined. By the end of the year business conditions were so unsettled and the supply of goods so far exceeded the demand that the goods included in the closing inventory could have been replaced, if purchased at that time, for about 60% of the prices at which they were placed in stock. The closing inventory of $30,000 was therefore taken at 60% of the invoice cost. What was the amount of the loss incurred by the drop in commodity prices?

3. What would have been the total cost of the goods sold if the closing inventory had been taken on the basis of invoice cost?

4. If commodity prices had still been advancing at the time the closing inventory was taken, on what basis should this inventory have been valued?

Income from Sales Group

292. In ascertaining income from sales, there are two elements to be considered:

    1. Gross sales.
    2. Deductions from sales.

Sales Account

293. The principal source of income of a trading or mercantile business is the proceeds from sales of merchandise. The amount of the gross sales is the sum of the amounts at which the goods sold during a fiscal period were billed to customers, and is the gross income from sales. This amount is subject to certain deductions for credits allowed to customers and for certain trading expenses which reduce the proceeds of sales. The difference between gross income from sales and the sum of all deductions is the net income from sales.

Deductions from Sales

294. Returned Goods and Rebates and Allowances. The item of goods returned for credit is the first deduction from sales, because the amount of any particular sale is reduced by the selling price of the goods returned. The actual amount of the sale is therefore the difference between the two. Rebates and allowances to customers for defective, damaged, or inferior goods are likewise deductions from gross sales, because they reduce the liability of customers for the payment of goods sold to them. In Part One of the text such items were treated as debits to the Sales account, but in the majority of the larger businesses they occur so frequently as to justify setting up separate accounts for them. They are recorded in the "Sales Returned and Allowances Journal," credits to customers' accounts in this book being posted daily. Returns are entered in one column, and rebates and allowances in another. At the end of each month the totals are posted to the debit of the Sales Returned and the Sales Rebates and Allowances accounts in the general ledger. The total amount credited to customers for such items is posted to the credit of Accounts Receivable account.

295. Freight and Cartage Outward and Delivery Expense. All direct charges for receiving, handling, and storing the goods should be included in the cost of goods sold. *Any additional direct charges for handling goods*, such as delivery expense, cartage from the store or warehouse to freight stations, and freight outward must be excluded from cost, and must be treated *either as deductions from sales or selling expenses.*

If the seller bears the expense of delivering goods, he receives that much less for them, and he must take this fact into consideration in fixing his selling price. The same reasoning applies to outward freight and cartage. It is clear that if these expenses were not incurred by the seller, the proceeds from his sales would be so much greater. The fact that such expenses are direct charges on handling goods after their cost has been fully determined is the *controlling factor* in classifying them as deductions from sales and not as selling expenses. Selling expenses properly consist of the expenses incurred in finding new customers or retaining the patronage of old customers. However, many accountants consider all selling expenses as operating expenses and so classify them on the Statement of Profit and Loss.

296. Sales Discounts. Most wholesale and mercantile concerns allow a term of credit of 30, 60, or 90 days on goods sold on open account. It is customary, however, to offer customers a deduction from the amounts of their bills if they pay within the time usually required to secure delivery of the goods—in most instances a period of 10 days. For example, a customer who orders a bill of goods amounting to $100, terms 30 days, may be offered a discount of 2% on the bill if he pays it within 10 days. In other words, the seller will accept $98 within a period of 10 days in full settlement of his claim of $100 against the customer; otherwise, a payment of $100 will be required to settle the account. The discount is referred to as *merchandise discount*.   It is a sales discount to the seller and a purchase discount to the buyer.   Some wholesalers who sell on a term of credit of 60 days offer a 2% cash discount for payment within 10 days, 1% for payment within 30 days, or net 60 days.   Such terms would be written, 2/10, 1/30, n/60, on the bill rendered for the goods.

Assuming that a customer who has bought goods amounting to $100 has taken advantage of a discount of 2%, what disposition is to be made in the accounts of the seller of the $2 deducted?   The customer has been charged for $100, and Sales account has been credited for the same amount.   The seller receives $98 in cash in full settlement of the account, but he must credit the customer for $100.   The entries to be made on the books of the seller for the sale and for the $98 received are, in journal form—

Customer	100.00	
Sales		100.00
Cash	98.00	
Sales Discount	2.00	
Customer		100.00

The ledger accounts below show the posted items:

Customer		Sales		Cash	
100.00	98.00	2.00	100.00	98.00	
	2.00				

However, instead of debiting the Sales account for discounts allowed to customers, it is the practice to charge them to a separate account under the title "Sales Discount" in order to ascertain monthly and annually the total discounts allowed to customers, which amount is one of the deductions from gross sales in the Income from Sales section of the Income and Profit and Loss Statement.

The illustration below exhibits the proper arrangement of the Income from Sales section of the Income and Profit and Loss Statement.

Income from Sales:		
Gross Sales		92,000.00
Deductions from Sales:		
Returned Goods	1,000.00	
Rebates and Allowances	2,000.00	
Freight and Cartage Outward	3,000.00	
Delivery Expense*	4,000.00	
Sales Discounts Allowed	5,000.00	15,000.00
Net Income from Sales		77,000.00

* Delivery Expense may be considered as a deduction from sales or as a deduction from Gross Profit (as a selling expense).   It is commonly considered as an operating or selling expense.   In the treatment of this item you are to follow the direction of your instructor.

Exercise 87

At the close of a fiscal period the accounts of the Warner Hardware Company contained the following data in connection with the sales of trading merchandise:

Gross Sales	65,300.00	Returned Goods	680.00
Sales Discounts	1,340.00	Delivery Expense	4,316.00
Freight Outward	512.00	Sales Rebates and Allowances	175.00

1. Prepare the Income from Sales section of the company's Statement of Income and Profit and Loss.
2. What was the average percentage of sales discount allowed?
3. If no allowances for freight out or discounts on accounts receivable had been granted, what would have been the net income from sales?

Exercise 88

The trading accounts of the Madison Supply Company at the end of a year showed the following data:

Merchandise Inventory, Jan. 1	26,312.92	Warehouse Salaries and Labor	4,928.00
Sales	118,495.36	Sales Returned	811.65
Purchases Returned	611.30	Duties and Storage	1,828.36
Purchases	72,901.06	Freight and Cartage Out	2,772.91
Freight, Express, and		Sales Rebates and Allowances	322.45
Cartage In	4,312.14	Inventory, Dec. 31	31,428.42
Delivery Expense	5,920.80	Sales Discounts	1,590.96
Purchase Rebates and Allowances	312.92		

1. Determine which of these accounts are debits and which are credits in the trial balance.
2. Prepare a statement of the results of trading operations.
3. What final result will this statement show?

Chapter 42—Operating Expenses

297. Operating Expenses of wholesale and mercantile concerns are deductible from gross trading income in ascertaining the net income from operations. They are usually classified as follows:

> Purchasing Department Expense
> Selling Department Expense
> General Expense
> Administrative Expense

298. General Expenses consist principally of the fixed charges incurred in conducting a business enterprise as a whole. They are not properly chargeable to particular departments or operations, unless they are pro-rated over them in the proper proportions. General expenses consist of rent, heat, and light; telephone and telegraph charges; licenses and fees paid for the privilege of doing business; taxes on stock in trade and other tangible personal property; taxes on real estate and other fixed capital assets; repairs and maintenance of real estate and equipment; depreciation of fixed capital assets; insurance to cover losses from fire, theft, destruction by the elements, etc. These expenses may be recorded in one general Expense account, but for statistical purposes and for the purpose of preparing income tax returns readily, they are classified in separate accounts under such titles as the following:

> Rent, Heat, and Light
> Licenses, Fees, and Taxes
> Real Estate Expense
> Insurance Expense
> Equipment Repairs and Maintenance
> Depreciation
> Sundry General Expense

In case a concern owns the premises in which its business is conducted, personal property taxes on buildings and land are usually recorded in the Real Estate Expense account. In such case, insurance on buildings and immovable fixtures would also be charged to Real Estate Expense, while insurance on furniture, fixtures, and other movable equipment would be charged to the Insurance Expense account.

299. Administrative Expense. Administrative expenses consist of the cost of the general management and administrative direction and control of a business enterprise. They are the expenses incurred in maintaining the executive department of the business. Such expenses are usually recorded in one account, but may be classified under the following headings:

> Officers' Salaries
> Officers' Bonuses and Commissions
> Officers' Traveling Expense
> Legal Expense
> Executive Office Expense

The operating expenses of a mercantile or trading business, therefore, constitute the cost of the capital consumed in maintaining the organization and in promoting its general operations and activities. Certain operating expenses, such as purchasing, selling, and administrative expenses, tend to fluctuate in amount in proportion to the volume of business done. Other operating expenses, consisting largely of those classified as general expenses, accrue and must be paid irrespective of the volume of business transacted and regardless of whether business is brisk or dull.

Depreciation as a Part of Operating Expense

300. Depreciation consists of the gradual decrease in the value of wasting assets, and therefore represents a *loss of invested capital* that takes place continuously in proportion to the degree of wear and tear on physical property and the rapidity with which it tends to go out of style or out of date and become obsolete. It follows, therefore, that in the course of time property which depreciates must be replaced with new or improved equipment that will restore efficiency to the necessary standard or keep pace with modern progress in business.

The number of years during which it is estimated a given physical asset can be used to advantage constitutes its *useful life*. This period largely determines the rate of depreciation to be charged off on it. When the asset wears out or becomes obsolete, a second capital investment approximating the cost of the original property will be required to replace it. The object of accounting for depreciation is therefore to charge it in annually as an operating expense at the estimated rate at which depreciation takes place, so as to retain in the business and accumulate a sufficient sum or reserve of earned profits with which to replace the property when its usefulness is ended. Consequently, at the end of each year an entry should be made charging some operating expense account and crediting Reserve for Depreciation for the depreciation which has taken place during the year. It is the best practice to open a separate Depreciation account; otherwise, depreciation is chargeable to General Expense.

Depreciation is charged off annually as an operating expense to record the cost of the capital consumed through the use of wasting assets. The reserve for depreciation represents an accumulation of capital out of profits against the time when wasting assets will have to be replaced. It has been explained, however, that in preparing the Balance Sheet, reserves for depreciation should be deducted from the balances of capital asset investment accounts in order to show the book value at which the assets are carried on the books.

Exercise 89

White, Burnside & Company conduct a wholesale supply business. There are three partners in the concern—Charles H. White, J. H. Burnside, and L. B. Werner. Mr. White has charge of the buying, and two-thirds of his salary of $3,000 is chargeable to the purchasing department. Mr. Werner has charge of the sales department, and two-thirds of his salary of $3,000 is chargeable to the sales department. Mr. Burnside is the senior partner, and has charge of the general administration, accounting, and finances of the concern. All his salary of $4,000 is chargeable to administrative expense. In addition to these salaries, the operating expenses of the concern for a fiscal period were as follows:

Licenses and fees for doing business	176.00
Traveling expenses on buying trips	472.83
Real estate taxes on building and land	978.62
Salesmen's salaries	2,400.00
Coal for heating	312.50
Insurance on buildings	96.75
Attorneys' fees	300.00
Salesmen's traveling expenses	1,562.91
Electric light bills	78.91
Accountants' fees for auditing books	250.00
Purchasing office expenses	912.20
Sales office expenses	1,309.92
Administrative office expense	1,922.40
Telephone and telegraph charges	185.26
Insurance on the stock in trade and on furniture, fixtures, and equipment	385.20
Depreciation on buildings	495.83
Salesmen's commissions	1,711.44
Auto truck licenses	56.00
Depreciation on delivery equipment	826.30
Store clerks' salaries	2,360.00
Repairs and upkeep of building	116.14
Burglary insurance	60.00
Advertising	925.80
Depreciation on furniture and fixtures	56.22

Open four expense accounts under the titles of Purchasing, Selling, General, and Administrative Expense, and classify the foregoing items properly.

Chapter 43—Additions To Income Group

301. The **additions to income** group includes those accounts in which are recorded the incidental and miscellaneous incomes and profits of a business that are not earned by the regular income-producing operations. As such profits and incomes are earned from sources other than sales of trading merchandise, they are frequently referred to as non-operating incomes and profits. Some of them represent earnings of surplus capital not needed temporarily in financing regular operations; others consist of earnings of capital invested in fixed assets which produce some incidental revenue.

Additions to income are consequently referred to as *capital incomes*. They are sometimes called *secondary incomes*, to distinguish them from the primary income received from sales of goods. They consist of real estate rentals received, interest on notes and accounts receivable, interest received on bank deposits, interest and dividends on securities owned, cash discounts deducted from bills for merchandise purchased, miscellaneous profits from the sale or hire of equipment, and similar items. The sum of all capital incomes is added to the net income from operations in order to ascertain the *net income from operations and all other sources*. It should be noted that if additions to income are added to gross trading income, the total is the gross income and profit from all sources. Additions to income in trading and mercantile businesses are usually accounted for in the following accounts:

> Real Estate Income
> Interest Income
> Interest on Bank Deposits
> Interest on Mortgages Receivable
> Purchases Discounts
> Miscellaneous Profits

Unless it is desired to show in separate ledger accounts the interest received on bank deposits and mortgages receivable, if any, such interest may be credited to the regular Interest Income account kept to receive the credits for interest on notes and accounts receivable and other routine transactions. Any additions to income not provided for in the foregoing classification of accounts should be recorded in the Miscellaneous Profits account, which may be analyzed in the Income Statement to show the source of each profit.

Purchase Discounts as a Capital Income

302. From the standpoint of the seller of goods, the cash discounts which he allows on accounts receivable are *sales discounts*. From the standpoint of the buyer of goods, the cash discounts he deducts on his accounts payable are *purchase discounts*. As sales discounts are treated in this text as a deduction from sales, and not as a capital expense to be included in deductions from income, some explanation is necessary regarding the classification of purchase discounts as an addition to income, or capital earning.

It has been pointed out that in every case sales discounts cannot be considered expenses incurred in securing early collections of accounts receivable because many concerns have sufficient capital invested to carry customers' accounts for the full term of credit, but nevertheless are compelled to allow cash discounts for competitive reasons. Sales discounts therefore *may or may not be* expenses of financing. However, as it is optional with customers whether they will discount their bills or take advantage of the full term of credit, *it is always true* that if the seller allows cash discounts he receives so much less for his goods, regardless of his financial position. Consequently, after taking all factors into consideration, it seems to be the better practice to consider sales discounts as deductions from sales.

In the case of purchase discounts, however, the taking of the discount is a matter to be decided by the buyer. His ability to discount bills is almost entirely determined by whether he has the ready cash to take advantage of discounts or has sufficient credit to enable him to borrow funds with which to discount his bills. If he borrows money to do so, the interest he pays is chargeable as an *expense of securing working capital*. It therefore seems logical to treat the discount received by applying the money borrowed to the payment of bills of merchandise as a *capital income* to offset the capital expense for interest. If discounts on purchases are taken, the savings are always made possible by the favorable condition of the buyer's finances. For these reasons the consensus of opinion among accountants is that purchase discounts are *earnings of capital* and not deductions from the cost of purchases. As in the case of sales discounts, however, the conditions obtaining in any particular business and the wishes of its management must be the deciding factors as to the manner in which they are classified in the Income and Profit and Loss Statement.

Exercise 90

At the end of the year the accounts of Vernon & Lang showed the following incomes in addition to the net income from operations:

Real estate rentals received	1,500.00
Rentals received from hiring out an automobile truck not needed from time to time	165.00
Interest on past-due accounts receivable	38.95
Cash discounts deducted on accounts payable	785.42
Interest on notes receivable	78.46
An automobile delivery truck, which cost $1,200, and on which $800 had previously been charged off for depreciation, was sold during the period for $500.	
Interest received on daily balances of cash in bank	138.36

From the foregoing data prepare the Additions to Income section of the Income and Profit and Loss Statement.

Deductions from Income Group

303. The **deductions from income** group includes those accounts in which are recorded the financing and incidental expenses of a business which cannot be properly charged against the regular income-producing operations as operating expenses. This group also includes miscellaneous losses which are incurred from sources other than losses on trading operations. Deductions from income consist of interest on notes and accounts payable, interest on mortgages payable, losses from bad debts and uncollectible accounts, miscellaneous losses on investments and on the sale of capital assets, and similar items. Generally speaking, deductions from income consist of *capital expenses* incurred in securing sufficient funds with which to operate successfully, as well as non-operating losses. They are usually classified in the following accounts:

> Interest Expense
> Interest on Mortgaged Debt
> Bad Debt Losses
> Miscellaneous Losses

Unless it is desired to record in a separate account the interest paid on the fixed liabilities, interest on mortgages may be charged to the regular Interest Expense account.

304. Bad Debt Losses and Reserves for Bad Debts. Nearly all concerns that sell goods on credit incur losses on uncollectible accounts. For this reason it is quite generally the practice to set up an annual reserve for bad debts in the same manner in which reserves for depreciation are created. A certain percentage of the total accounts receivable due from customers at the time books are closed—approximating from ½% to 2% according to past experience—is charged against the Profit and Loss account and credited to the Reserve for Bad Debts account. Then, as accounts are determined to be uncollectible, they are charged to the Reserve account, the debtors' accounts being credited and closed out. When the Balance Sheet is prepared, the balance of the Reserve for Bad Debts account is deducted from the balance of the Accounts Receivable account to show the amount that is expected to be collected from customers.

The creation of a reserve for bad debts thus *withholds from distribution* to the owners *a certain amount of profits* which are retained in the working capital of a concern with which to meet future losses from bad accounts as they are incurred.

Exercise 91

The capital expenses and miscellaneous losses of Gardner, King & Company for a fiscal period are as follows:

Interest on past-due accounts payable	26.12
Uncollectible accounts receivable charged off during the period	235.42
Interest on mortgage payable	360.00
A typewriter which cost $105, on which depreciation for five years at the rate of 12½% was charged off, was traded in on a new machine, the allowance for the old machine being $20.	
Interest on notes payable	176.48

Prepare the Deductions from Income section of the Income and Profit and Loss Statement.

Chapter 44—Procedure for Adjusting Accounts, Preparing Statements, and Closing Books

305. Preliminary Trial Balance. The trial balance of the Empire Wholesale Company for the year ending December 31 shown on page 270 was taken from the general ledger after all entries and totals in the books of original entry had been posted.

306. No **adjusting entries** for accruals, depreciation, and other adjustments are reflected in the preliminary trial balance. After it is taken, the accounts included are examined to determine what adjustments are necessary. The adjusting entries are then made in the general journal and after they are posted, a final trial balance is taken. The entries required to adjust properly the accounts of the Empire Wholesale Company are illustrated and explained in the paragraphs following. In an actual set of books these entries would of course include proper explanations.

307. The following entry is made to charge off the annual **depreciation** on fixed capital assets:

Depreciation	1,292.73	
Reserve for Building Depreciation		326.00
Reserve for Office Equipment Depreciation		48.63
Reserve for Store Equipment Depreciation		180.60
Reserve for Delivery Equipment Depreciation		737.50

The building in which the business is conducted is depreciated at the rate of 2% of the debit balance shown by the Building Investment account on December 31, the estimated life of the building being fifty years. The Office Furniture and Equipment account is depreciated 4%, its estimated life being averaged over twenty-five years; the Store Fixtures and Equipment account is depreciated 5% on the basis of an average life of twenty years; and the Delivery Equipment, consisting of an automobile truck purchased during the current year, is depreciated at the rate of 25%, based on a life of four years.

308. The original cost of the firm's **good will** was $5,000. The partners decided at the time the business was purchased to write off the good will at the rate of $500 annually, if profits were sufficient to do so. The following entry charges the good will written off against the profits for the year, as all final profit and loss items are closed out through the Profit and Loss Summary account.

Profit and Loss Summary	500.00	
Good Will Account		500.00

Empire Wholesale Company
Preliminary Trial Balance, December 31, 19—

Cash	10171 50	
Accounts Receivable	12448 51	
Advances to Employees	300 —	
Notes Receivable	3082 54	
Trade Acceptances Receivable	900 —	
Mortgage Receivable	2400 —	
American Millinery Co. Stock Investment	1000 —	
Government Bonds	2000 —	
Land Investment	5200 —	
Delivery Equipment	2950 —	
Building Investment	16300 —	
Reserve for Depreciation of Building		960 —
Office Furniture and Fixtures	1215 80	
Reserve for Depreciation of Office Furniture and Fixtures		262 30
Store Fixtures and Equipment	3611 90	
Reserve for Depreciation of Store Fixtures and Equipment		854 30
Good Will	2000 —	
Accounts Payable		7342 37
Notes Payable		2625 —
Trade Acceptances Payable		1890 —
Mortgage Payable		11000 —
F. B. Greene, Partner		30000 —
A. M. Browning, Partner		10000 —
F. B. Greene, Drawing	4200 —	
A. M. Browning, Drawing	2500 —	
Sales		108704 43
Sales Rebates and Allowances	248 76	
Sales Returned	843 90	
Sales Discounts	1329 47	
Freight Out	309 18	
Shipping Materials and Supplies	1591 20	
Purchases	79736 21	
Purchases Returned		476 14
Purchasing Expense	396 28	
Purchase Rebates and Allowances		126 28
Freight and Cartage In	1965 86	
Duties and Storage	1325 40	
Warehouse Salaries and Labor	3892 50	
Interest on Mortgaged Debt	455 70	
Interest on Bank Deposits		262 43
Real Estate Income		1050 —
Interest Expense	216 28	
Interest Income		185 62
Selling Expense	6322 48	
Delivery Expense	3285 90	
General Expense	2846 73	
Purchase Discounts		922 44
Administrative Expense	1626 41	
Interest on Mortgage Receivable		41 82
Bad Debt Losses	214 20	
Miscellaneous Losses	76 42	
Miscellaneous Profits		260 —
	176963 13	176963 13

309. Included in the balances shown by the Notes Receivable and Accounts Receivable accounts are a note for $100 which is five months past due and open accounts amounting to $235.48, the collection of which is doubtful. The partners are not yet ready to charge them off as bad debts because they may succeed in making partial collections. The following entry is made to segregate the doubtful items from the current Notes and Accounts Receivable accounts.

Doubtful Assets	335.48	
Notes Receivable		100.00
Accounts Receivable		235.48

310. Mr. Greene is the senior partner, having sold a one-fourth interest in the business to Mr. Browning at the time the partnership was formed. Mr. Greene has charge of the firm's finances, supervises the accounting, passes on credits, and looks after the administrative affairs of the business. His salary of $3,000 a year is chargeable to administrative expense.

Mr. Browning does all the buying and directs the selling. He has full charge of the merchandising operations of the concern, which require about 80% of his time; therefore, 40% of his salary of $4,000 a year is chargeable to purchasing expense, 40% to selling expense, and 20% to administrative expense.

Instead of drawing a regular monthly salary, the partners follow the plan of drawing the sums they require from time to time, which are charged to their Personal accounts. At the close of each year they credit their Personal accounts for their annual salaries, and then close the balances of the Personal accounts into their Capital accounts. The proper entries for the current period are the following:

Administrative Expense	3,800.00	
Purchasing Expense	1,600.00	
Selling Expense	1,600.00	
F. B. Greene, Drawing		3,000.00
A. M. Browning, Drawing		4,000.00
F. B. Greene, Partner	1,200.00	
F. B. Greene, Drawing		1,200.00
A. M. Browning, Drawing	1,500.00	
A. M. Browning, Partner		1,500.00

311. The inventory of trading merchandise on hand at the close of the period is $18,241.18, the required adjusting entry for which is—

Merchandise Inventory	18,241.18	
Purchases		18,241.18

312. The delivery equipment owned by the concern is employed in hauling incoming goods and in delivering outgoing shipments to local customers or to freight stations.   During the year the salaries of the truck driver and of his helper and the other expenses of operating the truck are charged to the Delivery Expense account as paid.   The management estimates that 30% of the cost of operating the truck is incurred in hauling goods purchased, and that 70% is incurred in delivering goods sold.   The truck makes many more trips and longer hauls in delivering goods than in carting incoming goods from freight stations to the store; hence, the division of the expense on the basis of 30% and 70%.   The following entry properly distributes the cost of operating the truck.

Freight and Cartage Inward	985.77	
Delivery Expense		985.77

313. There is interest accrued on notes receivable of $28.24, and interest accrued on the mortgage receivable of $102.18.

One-half year's interest at the rate of $4\frac{1}{2}\%$ per annum has accrued but has not been collected on the Government bonds owned by the concern, and a 7% dividend on the American Millinery stock had been declared but was not received.

To avoid opening separate accounts to record the income from these sources, the interest on the Government bonds is credited to the regular Interest account, and the dividend on the stock is credited to Miscellaneous Profits, the following being the proper entry:

Accrued Assets	245.42	
Interest Income		28.24
Interest on Mortgage Receivable		102.18
Interest Income		45.00
Miscellaneous Profits		70.00

314. The interest accrued on the mortgage payable amounts to $264.30, the necessary adjusting entry being—

Interest on Mortgaged Debt	264.30	
Accrued Liabilities		264.30

315. Inventories of materials and supplies on hand in the various departments of the business show the following results: shipping supplies, $211.60; sales department, $85; purchasing department, $110; administrative office, $125; and new auto truck tires on hand, $72.60.   The following adjusting entry is required.

Deferred Debit Items	604.20	
Shipping Materials and Supplies		211.60
Selling Expense		85.00
Purchasing Expense		110.00
Administrative Expense		125.00
Delivery Expense		72.60

From time to time during the year premiums on insurance policies covering building, furniture and fixtures, stock in trade, and delivery equipment were paid, amounting to $542.50. The cost of this insurance was charged to the General Expense account as operating expense. The unexpired premium value of the insurance in force at the end of the year was $178.50. The entry to adjust is—

| Deferred Debit Items | 178.50 | |
| General Expense | | 178.50 |

316. The tenant who occupies the third floor of the concern's building pays his rent quarterly in advance, the payments beginning on December 1 of each year. At the time the books were closed he had prepaid his January and February rent, amounting to $150, which required the following adjusting entry:

| Real Estate Income | 150.00 | |
| Deferred Credit Items | | 150.00 |

You should remember that no adjustment of accounts as described above is required during a fiscal period, as monthly trial balances are taken. Such adjustments are made only at the close of a fiscal period so that profits and losses and the true financial condition may be ascertained.

317. Final Trial Balance. After all the adjusting entries required at the close of a period are made and posted, a second, or *final*, trial balance is taken, which is used as the basis for preparing the annual statements.

Chapter 45—Problems

Exercise 92

1. On a double sheet of ledger paper open the accounts included in the preliminary trial balance which begins on page 270, and debit or credit the accounts with the balances given in the trial balance, rearranging the accounts as they will appear in the statements. The schedule of accounts on pages 163 and 164 gives the proper classification and arrangement of accounts. Allow six lines for each account.

2. Prepare a Work Sheet of ten columns, entering in the adjustment column all the adjusting entries shown in the text following the preliminary trial balance.

3. Then prepare the final trial balance from the ledger accounts as they now stand. It should agree with the following trial balance.

4. Prepare the Income and Profit and Loss Statement and the Balance Sheet, after making an examination of the statements shown on the following pages to become familiar with their form and arrangement.

Empire Wholesale Company
Final Trial Balance, December 31, 19—

Cash	10171 50	
Accounts Receivable	12213 03	
Advances to Employees	300 —	
Notes Receivable	2982 54	
Trade Acceptances Receivable	900 —	
Mortgages Receivable	2400 —	
Merchandise Inventory	18241 18	
Accrued Assets	245 42	
American Millinery Co. Stock Investment	1000 —	
Government Bonds	2000 —	
Land Investment	5200 —	
Building Investment	16300 —	
Reserve for Depreciation of Building		1286 —
Office Furniture and Fixtures	1215 80	
Reserve for Depreciation of Office Furniture and Fixtures		310 93
Store Fixtures and Equipment	3611 90	
Reserve for Depreciation of Store Fixtures and Equipment		1034 90
Delivery Equipment	2950 —	
Reserve for Depreciation of Delivery Equipment		737 50
Deferred Debit Items	782 70	
Doubtful Assets	335 48	
Good Will	1500 —	
Accounts Payable		7342 37
Accrued Liabilities		264 30

Notes Payable			2625 —
Trade Acceptances Payable			1890 —
Deferred Credit Items			150 —
Mortgages Payable			11000 —
F. B. Greene, Partner			28800 —
A. M. Browning, Partner			11500 —
Sales			108704 43
Sales Rebates and Allowances	248 76		
Sales Returned	843 90		
Sales Discounts	1329 47		
Freight Out	309 18		
Shipping Materials and Supplies	1379 60		
Purchases	61495 03		
Purchases Returned			476 14
Purchase Rebates and Allowances			126 28
Purchasing Expense	1886 28		
Freight and Cartage In	2951 63		
Duties and Storage	1325 40		
Warehouse Salaries and Labor	3892 50		
Selling Expense	7837 48		
Delivery Expense	2227 53		
General Expense	2668 23		
Administrative Expense	5301 41		
Depreciation	1292 73		
Real Estate Income			900 —
Interest Income			258 86
Interest on Bank Deposits			262 43
Interest on Mortgages Receivable			144 —
Purchase Discounts			922 44
Miscellaneous Profits			330 —
Interest Expense	216 28		
Interest on Mortgages Payable	720 —		
Bad Debt Losses	214 20		
Miscellaneous Losses	76 42		
Profit and Loss Summary	500 —		
	179065 58		179065 58

Empire Wholesale Company
Profit and Loss Statement for year ending December 31, 19—

Income from Sales:			
Gross Sales		108704 43	
Deductions from Sales:			
Sales Returned	843.90		
Sales Rebates and Allowances	248.76		
Freight Out on Sales	309.18		
Delivery Expense	2227.53		
Sales Discounts	1329.47	4958 84	
Net Income from Sales:			103745 59

Cost of Goods Sold			
Total Invoice Cost of Goods Sold		61495 03	
Deductions from Cost:			
Purchases Returned	476.14		
Purchase Rebates and Allowances	126.28	602 42	
Net Invoice Cost of Goods Sold		60892 61	
Additions to Cost:			
Freight and Cartage Inward		2951 63	
Duties and Storage		1325 40	
Warehouse Salaries and Labor		3892 50	
Total Cost of Goods Sold			69062 14
Gross Trading Income			34683 45
Operating Expenses:			
Purchasing Expense		1886 28	
Selling Expense		7837 48	
Shipping Materials and Supplies		1379 60	
General Expense		2668 23	
Administrative Expense		5301 41	
Depreciation of Capital Assets		1292 73	20365 73
Net Income from Operations			14317 72
Additions to Income.			
Real Estate Income		900 —	
Interest Income		258 86	
Interest on Bank Deposits		262 43	
Interest on Mortgage Receivable		144 —	
Purchase Discounts		922 44	
Miscellaneous Profits		330 —	2817 73
Net Income from Operations and All Other Sources			17135 45
Deductions from Income:			
Interest Expense		216 28	
Interest on Mortgaged Debt		720 —	
Bad Debt Losses		214 20	
Miscellaneous Losses		76 42	
Good Will written off		500 —	1726 90
Net Profit for the Year			15408 55

Empire Wholesale Company
Balance Sheet, December 31, 19—

Assets		
Current Assets:		
Cash in Bank	10171 50	
Merchandise Inventory	18241 18	
Notes Receivable	2982 54	
Trade Acceptances Receivable	900 —	
American Millinery Co. Stock	1000 —	
Government Bonds	2000 —	
Accounts Receivable	12213 03	
Advances to Employees	300 —	

Accrued Assets:			
Interest Accrued on Notes Receivable	28.24		
Interest Accrued on Mortgage Receivable	102.18		
Interest Accrued on Government Bonds	45.00		
Accrued Dividends on Stock Owned	70.00	245 42	
Total Current Assets			48053 67
Fixed Assets:			
Building	16300.00		
Less—Reserve for Depreciation	1286.00	15014 —	
Land		5200 —	
Office Furniture and Equipment	1215.80		
Less—Reserve for Depreciation	310.93	904 87	
Store Fixtures and Equipment	3611.90		
Less—Reserve for Depreciation	1034.90	2577 —	
Delivery Equipment	2950.00		
Less—Reserve for Depreciation	737.50	2212 50	
Mortgage Receivable		2400 —	
Total Fixed Capital Assets			28308 37
Deferred Debit Items:			
Materials and Supplies on hand		604 20	
Prepaid Insurance Premiums		178 50	
Total Deferred Debit Items			782 70
Other Assets:			
Doubtful Notes and Accounts Receivable		335 48	
Good Will		1500 —	
Total Miscellaneous Assets			1835 48
Total Assets			78980 22
Liabilities			
Current Liabilities:			
Accrued Liabilities:			
Interest Accrued on Mortgaged Debt	264.30		
Notes Payable	2625.00		
Trade Acceptances Payable	1890.00		
Accounts Payable	7342.37		
Total Current Liabilities		12121 67	
Fixed Liabilities:			
Mortgage Payable		11000 —	
Deferred Credit Items:			
Rent Collected in Advance		150 —	
Total Liabilities			23271 67
Net Assets			55708 55

Capital

F. B. Greene's Capital Account Jan. 1, 19—	30000.00		
Deduct Net Withdrawals during year	1200.00		
	28800.00		
Add 75% of Net Profit for year	11556.41		
F. B. Greene's Net Capital Dec. 31, 19—		40356 41	
A. M. Browning's Capital Account Jan. 1, 19—	10000.00		
Add Salary not withdrawn	1500.00		
Add 25% of Net Profit for year	3852.14		
A. M. Browning's Net Capital Dec. 31, 19—		15352 14	
Total Capital Investment of Partners December 31, 19—			55708 55

Exercise 93

1. Prepare and post the entries required to close the ledger of the Empire Wholesale Company as of December 31. Credit each partner's Capital account with his share of the net profit.

2. After closing the ledger, prepare and post the adjusting entries required to open the books as of January 1 in the next fiscal period. Take a post-closing trial balance.

Exercise 94

The trial balance on page 279 was taken from the ledger of the Fisher, Bates & Carr Company before any adjusting entries were made. The necessary adjustments are given below.

(a) The interest accrued on notes receivable and past-due accounts receivable amounts to $48.56.

(b) The firm pays salaries and wages of employees on the 10th and 25th of the month. The accrued salaries as of December 31 for general office employees are $22.50; sales department employees, $78; and warehouse employees, $36.

(c) The delivery equipment should be depreciated at the rate of 25% of the full cost as charged to the Investment account.

(d) The furniture and fixtures are depreciated at the rate of 4%.

(e) Each partner is to be credited in his Personal account for interest for one year at 6% on the credit balance of his Capital account as of January 1. There have been no charges or credits to the partners' Capital accounts during the year.

(f) The inventory of stock in trade on hand at the close of the period is $16,285.40.

(g) The net profit or loss is to be closed into the partners' Capital accounts in proportion to their capital investments at the beginning of the year.

1. Open the ledger, prepare a Work Sheet, prepare and post the adjusting entries required, take a final trial balance, and prepare statements.

2. Prepare and post the necessary closing entries and the entries required to open the accounts at the beginning of the next period.

Fisher, Bates & Carr Company
Preliminary Trial Balance, December 31, 19—

Cash	8317 24	
Accounts Receivable	12628 92	
Notes Receivable	3876 81	
Stock and Bond Investments	3000 —	
Furniture and Fixtures	3728 50	
Reserve for Depreciation cf Furniture and Fixtures		985 53
Delivery Equipment	3156 84	
Reserve for Depreciation of Delivery Equipment		1289 21
Shipping Materials and Supplies	2135 47	
Accounts Payable		4576 90
Notes Payable		2716 83
Trade Acceptances Payable		2691 45
Martin Fisher, Partner		4946 18
L. M. Carr, Partner		9892 36
C. C. Bates, Partner		14838 54
Martin Fisher, Personal		285 —
C. C. Bates, Personal	540 —	
Sales		116519 18
Sales Rebates and Allowances	396 40	
Sales Discounts	1109 19	
Sales Returned	1026 19	
Purchases	81985 43	
Freight and Cartage In	3846 78	
Purchasing Expenses (salaries, etc.)	763 28	
Purchases Returned		502 90
Purchase Rebates and Allowances		765 20
Freight and Cartage Out	1367 20	
Delivery Expense	2758 40	
Salesmen's Salaries and Commissions	4562 28	
Salesmen's Traveling Expenses	1897 23	
Advertising	3276 95	
Duties and Storage	3286 70	
General and Administrative Expenses	1875 40	
Sample Goods	527 40	
Warehouse Salaries and Labor	2776 95	
Purchase Discounts		1205 30
Interest Expense	478 68	
Interest Income		128 16
Bad Debt Losses	628 30	
Sundry Selling Expense	596 20	
Partners' Salaries	10800 —	
	161342 74	161342 74

Exercise 95

The trial balance of Foster-Hughes & Company given below was submitted by the company's bookkeeper to Mr. Foster at the close of business, December 31.

The bookkeeper, a young man who has had only about a year's experience, then prepared a Work Sheet and statements from this trial balance. His statements included an inventory of trading merchandise

Foster-Hughes & Company
Trial Balance, December 31, 19—

Cash	7360 70	
Accounts Receivable	14385 90	
Advances to Employees	150 —	
Notes Receivable	2284 80	
Trade Acceptances Receivable	1368 22	
Real Estate Investment	15685 28	
Furniture and Fixtures	2108 12	
Reserve for Depreciation of Furniture and Fixtures		502 12
Good Will	3000 —	
Accounts Payable		5218 36
Notes Payable		2108 30
Trade Acceptances Payable		560 18
Mortgage Payable		6000 —
H. A. Foster, Capital		16808 18
G. B. Hughes, Capital		8404 09
Sales		74853 16
Sales Rebates and Allowances	648 84	
Sales Returned	211 82	
Sales Discounts	925 42	
Freight Out	528 13	
Shipping Materials	1925 40	
Purchases	46278 19	
Purchase Rebates and Allowances		395 40
Purchases Returned		209 72
Purchasing Expenses	2109 43	
Freight In	3619 22	
Warehouse Labor	2926 82	
Selling Expenses	4926 18	
Delivery Expense	1209 25	
General Expense	3242 18	
Bad Debts	328 42	
Purchase Discounts		781 26
Real Estate Income		360 —
Interest Income		139 22
Real Estate Expense	911 45	
Interest Expense	206 22	
	116339 99	116339 99

of $9,374.28, this inventory having been taken by the store and warehouse employees under the general supervision of Mr. Hughes.

1. Prepare statements to agree with those prepared by the bookkeeper.

The ledger was not closed pending the examination of the accounts by the firm of accountants employed by Foster-Hughes & Company to make out the company's annual income tax return. When the bookkeeper's statements were submitted to Mr. Foster, he asked whether all accruals had been taken into consideration. When informed that they had not been, he sent for the accountant who usually verifies their annual statements. After examining the accounts, the accountant discovered that the following adjustments had not been made, and also recommended the changes mentioned below.

(a) The firm's real estate, consisting of a store building and lot, was purchased on May 1 preceding. The prices fixed on the building and lot at the time of the purchase were $11,600 and $3,200, respectively. Of the remaining $885.28 charged to the Real Estate account, $658.78 consisted of expenses for examining the title, recording the deed, and other charges incurred in connection with the purchase, and $226.50 represented charges for small repairs made from time to time after the building was occupied, which properly should not have been treated as capital expenditures. At the same time, the accountant found that a contractor's bill of $428.60 for carpenter work and painting covering alterations and improvements made before the company moved into the building was charged to the Real Estate Expense account. Taking these facts into consideration, the accountant opened separate accounts for the building and land and made the proper adjustment of all accounts involved.

(b) As no depreciation had been taken into account, he set up a depreciation charge at the rate of $2\frac{1}{2}\%$ for two-thirds of a year on the full purchase price of the building when it was ready for occupancy, and wrote off depreciation on the furniture and fixtures at the rate of 5% per annum.

(c) He accrued the interest on the mortgage payable from May 1 to December 31, a period of eight months, at 6%. The interest accrued on notes payable amounted to $11.42. The Interest Income and Interest Expense accounts only are kept.

(d) On examination of notes and accounts receivable, the accountant found that the interest accrued amounted to $34.28 on past-due accounts and $16.73 on notes.

(e) It was found that several bills for expense items had been received but had not been entered because they had not been paid. When classified, these bills showed the following charges: delivery expense, $109.18; general expense, $46.35; selling expense, $308.11; and purchasing expense, $98.43.

(f) The firm employs a transfer company to haul its incoming and outgoing goods, the monthly bills for which are charged to Delivery Expense account. In past years the hauling expenses were apportioned on the basis of 40% to purchases and 60% to sales.

(g) In verifying the prices used in calculating the merchandise inventory of $9,374.28, the accountant found that one lot of goods, consisting of 482 yards, was inventoried at the selling price of 89¢ instead of at the cost price of 52¢ a yard. He also found that on December 30 the Purchases account had been charged for a bill of goods amounting to $588.62, purchased for cash, but as the shipment had not been received, the goods were not included in the inventory. He therefore made the proper adjustment of the amount in the inventory.

(h) The partners have decided to withdraw $3,000 of the net profit, of which Mr. Foster is to receive $2,000 and Mr. Hughes $1,000. When the books are closed, these amounts are to be credited to their Personal accounts subject to withdrawal.

2. Prepare a Work Sheet in accordance with the changes recommended by the accountant.

3. Draft the journal entries required for these adjustments, and then prepare a final trial balance to show the status of the accounts after being adjusted.

4. Prepare statements which will exhibit the correct net profit and financial condition of the business.

5. Prepare the closing entries and the adjusting entries to be made at the opening of business on January 1 in the next period.

Appendix A

Corporation Accounting

318. A Corporation was defined by Chief Justice Marshall as "an artificial being, invisible, intangible, and existing only in contemplation of law." A corporation is sometimes termed an "artificial person."

319. *Corporations are necessary* to provide a convenient means of combining the funds which a number of individuals may have for investment, in order to supply the capital required to conduct and carry on large commercial and industrial enterprises without requiring those who contribute this capital, whether in large or in small amounts, to assume the responsibilities and liabilities of the ordinary partner; consequently, laws have been enacted by the legislatures of the various states creating for corporations a separate legal existence, and extending to stockholders certain privileges and exemptions from liability, and other advantages which cannot be secured in the ordinary partnership relation. Corporations, as a rule, may be formed for any legitimate purpose.

320. *Corporations are created* in two ways—by *special charter* and by *general statute.* When created by charter, a special act must be passed for each corporation, which is known as its *charter.* This charter defines its powers and privileges. When created by general statute all that is necessary is to comply with the provisions of the statute, which defines its powers and privileges. Nearly all corporations are now created by general statute, and very few by special charter.

321. *The method of procedure* in forming a corporation under a general statute is simple. The required number of individuals (not less than two and usually not less than five) join in a written instrument known as "Articles of Incorporation," which, when properly acknowledged before some competent officer, is submitted to the judge of a court for his examination as to whether or not it conforms to the law creating it. When properly approved and certified by him, it becomes a *Certificate of Incorporation,* the act under which the corporation is formed being its charter. After this certificate is properly recorded, the corporation is formed; and when by-laws are adopted and the board of directors and officers are elected, the corporation is ready to proceed in conducting the business for which it was created.

Note: The legal part of the formation of a corporation should invariably be entrusted to an attorney.

Certificate of Incorporation

of

THE ACE CORPORATION

Pursuant to Article II of the
Stock Corporation Law

We, the undersigned, for the purpose of forming a corporation, pursuant to Article II of the Stock Corporation Law of the State of New York, certify:

FIRST: The name of the corporation shall be THE ACE CORPORATION.

SECOND: The purposes for which it shall be formed are: _____
_____ The manufacture and sale of automobile heaters _____

THIRD: The total number of shares that may be issued is 2000 all of which are to be $ 10 _____ par value.

The capital of the corporation shall be $ 20,000 .

FOURTH: The shares shall consist of 2000 shares, all of which shall be common stock.

FIFTH: The office of the corporation shall be located in the County of Westchester , City of White Plains .

SIXTH: The duration of the corporation shall be perpetual.

SEVENTH: The number of directors shall be 5 , and said directors need not be shareholders of the corporation.

EIGHTH: The names and post office addresses of the directors until the first annual meeting of the stockholders are (minimum of three):

Names	Post Office Addresses
William J. Summers	406 South St., Yonkers, N. Y.
Henry F. Pratt	261 Madison Ave., New York City
Frank W. Kirk	118 Jackson St., White Plains, N. Y.
George H. Harris	18 Franklin St., White Plains, N. Y.
Charles A. Hunter	410 Lane St., White Plains, N. Y.

NINTH: The name and post office address of each subscriber of this certificate of incorporation and a statement of the number of shares which each agrees to take in the corporation are as follows:

Names	Shares	Post Office Addresses
William J. Summers	600	406 South St., Yonkers, N. Y.
Henry F. Pratt	400	261 Madison Ave., New York City
Frank W. Kirk	500	118 Jackson St., White Plains, N. Y.
George H. Harris	300	18 Franklin St., White Plains, N. Y.
Charles A. Hunter	200	410 Lane St., White Plains, N. Y.

TENTH: The Secretary of State is hereby designated as the agent of the corporation, on whom process in any action or proceeding against it may be served. A copy of the process may be mailed to the corporation in care of
William J. Summers, 406 South St., Yonkers, N. Y.

ELEVENTH: All the subscribers to this certificate are of full age; at least two-thirds of them are citizens of the United States; at least one of the persons named as directors is a citizen of the United States and a resident of the State of New York; and at least one of the subscribers is a resident of the State of New York.

IN WITNESS WHEREOF, we have hereunto made and subscribed this certificate in triplicate this ___10th___ day of __September__, 19

W. J. Summers

Henry F. Pratt

Frank W. Kirk

George H. Harris

Charles A. Hunter

STATE OF NEW YORK}
County of Westchester } ss:

On this ___10th___ day of __September__, 19 , before me personally came __William J. Summers, Henry F. Pratt, Frank W. Kirk,__ __George H. Harris, and Charles A. Hunter__ to me known and known to me to be the individuals described in and who executed the foregoing instrument; and they duly and severally acknowledged to me that they executed the same.

George New

Notary Public
Westchester County No. 315
Commission expires April 5, 19—

Illustration 77
CERTIFICATE OF INCORPORATION

322. Terms and definitions.   There are certain terms and definitions used in connection with corporations with which you should be familiar.   Some of them are described here.

323. The capital stock is the amount of stock authorized by the charter or certificate of incorporation, at its par value.   *The paid-in capital* is the amount paid on the subscribed shares of stock by the stockholders.

324. Treasury stock is stock of a corporation which has been previously issued to stockholders, and is later purchased from the funds of the corporation or is secured by donation or gift.   Unissued shares of the authorized capital stock must not be considered as treasury stock. Treasury stock does not participate in dividends.

325. The stockholders of a corporation are the individuals who own the property of the corporation.   Each stockholder's interest is measured by the number and value of the shares he holds.

326. A stock certificate is a document issued by the corporation to each stockholder, certifying that he is the owner of a certain specified number of shares of the capital stock of a specified par value.

Illustration 78
Stock Certificate

327. The board of directors is elected by the stockholders and represents them. It is vested with the management and direction of all the affairs of the corporation through its officers, who are generally elected from among its own number. These officers are usually a president, a vice-president, a secretary, and a treasurer, whose duties are defined in the by-laws.

328. The president is the chief executive officer, who presides at the meetings of the board and ordinarily exercises the authority of the board when it is not in session.

329. The secretary keeps the official records of the corporation. He is custodian of and is responsible for the charter and seal of the corporation, as well as for the minute book and the various other books containing the records relating to the stockholders of the corporation. The most important of these books are:

(a) *The minute book*, in which are recorded the proceedings of all the meetings of the stockholders and of the board of directors. This record should be most complete, as the officers must look to it for the necessary authority to conduct the affairs of their respective offices. In case of litigation it is taken as *prima facie* evidence for the acts of the board of directors and of the officers. It should contain the by-laws of the corporation. The minutes of each meeting should be signed by the secretary and also by the president.

(b) *The stock certificate book* is a book of printed certificates, with stubs, which are filled out and issued to the stockholders.

(c) *The transfer book*, or journal, receives entries for all transfers of stock from one stockholder to another, and from it the proper entries are made in the different accounts in the stock ledger. Entries for *the original certificates* issued may be entered in this book also, and posted from it to the stock ledger. When this procedure is followed, the amount of the original stock issued should be charged to Capital Stock Issued account in the stock ledger, which would then show a debit balance equal to the credit balance shown by the Capital Stock account in the general ledger, as well as the sum of the credits to the various stockholders' accounts in the stock ledger. The stock ledger is thus made self-balancing.

(d) *The stock ledger* contains the accounts with the various stockholders, and shows the number and the par value of the shares of stock owned by each. It is a subordinate ledger, of which the Capital Stock account in the general ledger is the controlling account. It receives its entries from the stock certificate book and from the transfer book. From the stock book, each stockholder is credited for the number of shares and the par value of the stock issued to him. From the transfer book, he is debited for the number of shares and the par value of stock transferred by him to others. The balance shown by each account is the par value of the stock owned by the stockholder.

(e) *The dividend book* is kept to show the dividends declared and paid to each stockholder. A dividend is a certain percentage declared on the capital stock to be paid from the surplus earnings of the company.

330. The treasurer is the financial officer of the corporation. He is usually the custodian of and is responsible for all the funds of the corporation. The ordinary books of account in which is recorded the general business of the company are kept in his office. It should be remembered that the books of the secretary and those of the treasurer are distinct and separate, although the duties of one, either in whole or in part, may be and frequently are performed by the other, to meet the requirements of a particular business or as required by the board of directors or by the by-laws.

Some Differences Between Partnerships and Corporations

331. Formation. *A partnership* is an association of two or more persons for the purpose of conducting a business and sharing in the profits and losses accruing, with all the powers and privileges under the law that each partner enjoys as an individual. *A corporation* is an association of individuals authorized by law to act as a single person, with powers and privileges restricted to those definitely set forth in its special charter or in the general corporation statute under which it is formed.

332. How formed. A partnership is formed by an agreement between two or more persons to contribute capital, ability, or service, or all of them, for a certain purpose. The associated partners are known as a *firm*. A corporation is formed by the association of two or more persons under a special charter or under a certificate of incorporation issued by some officer of the state, in accordance with the general or special law under which it is created, and is usually designated as a *company*.

333. Liability. In a partnership each partner is liable *for all the debts of the firm*. In a corporation each stockholder is liable only for such an amount as is defined by law, which is usually the amount of his stock, but always in proportion to his share in the capital stock of the corporation.

334. Continuation. A partnership continues until the expiration of the time agreed upon for dissolution, or until the death or legal disability of one of the partners. A corporation continues until the expiration of its charter, which may be perpetual. The death or disability of a stockholder does not affect a corporation.

335. Powers. A partnership has no restrictions that the individuals composing it do not have. It may engage in any line of business, so long as it is legal. A corporation is restricted to the performance of only such acts as are necessary to conduct the particular business or accomplish the particular purpose for which it was created.

336. By whom conducted. The affairs of a partnership are conducted by the members of the firm, or such of them or their agents as are so authorized by the agreement between the partners. The affairs of a corporation are transacted only through the officers elected by the stockholders, or their legal representatives, as authorized and defined by the charter and by-laws. The officers act as agents of the corporation.

Corporation Accounts

337. The accounts of a corporation are in no way different from those of a firm or an individual proprietor so far as they relate to the routine transactions of the business conducted, but there are a number of accounts made necessary by the requirements of corporate ownership which are found only in connection with corporation accounting. These accounts relate to the investments of the stockholders and to the distribution of profits.

338. Capital Stock account. This account, in a way, corresponds to the Capital account of a proprietor or partner. It is an ownership account and shows the par value of the stock owned by the stockholders; but it is not affected by the gains or losses of the business, which are shown in undivided profits, surplus, and other similar accounts, or by the purchase and sale of the stock among the stockholders.

(*a*) The Capital Stock account is *credited* for the par value of the stock issued, up to the amount of the authorized stock.

(*b*) It is *debited*, when the capital stock is reduced, for the amount of shares retired and canceled, at their par value.

(*c*) *The balance* shows the amount of stock of the corporation, at its par value, in the hands of its stockholders. That balance should equal the sum of the balances shown by the accounts with the various stockholders in the stock ledger. If treasury stock is held, its par value must be added to the sum of the balances in the stock ledger to equal the balance of the Capital Stock account. Capital stock represents a *secondary liability* of the corporation.

Note: Capital Stock account should be credited only for the actual stock issued, and not for the total authorized capital stock unless all of it has been issued.

339. Treasury Stock account. This account shows the amount of the capital stock of the corporation previously issued to stockholders, which has been secured from them by purchase, gift, or donation.

(*a*) It is *debited* for the *cost* of all treasury stock purchased by the corporation or for the *market value* of stock received by gift or donation.

(*b*) It is *credited*, when treasury stock is disposed of, for the *cost* of the stock if purchased, or for the *market value* of the stock, if received by gift or donation. If sold for more or less than the price charged in the account, Surplus account should be debited or credited for the difference between that price and the selling price.

If the stock is retired and canceled, credit the account for the amount for which it was debited when the stock was received, and debit or credit Surplus account with the difference between that amount and the par value of the stock retired, debiting Capital Stock account for the par value of the stock retired and canceled.

(*c*) *The balance* shows either the cost or the market value of the treasury stock on hand, which is a resource.

Note: Treasury stock does not participate in dividends declared, and in many states the purchase of its own stock by corporations, as treasury stock or otherwise, is forbidden.

340. Subscription account. This account is opened to show the par value of stock which has been subscribed but not issued. It is credited at par value for the amount of stock subscribed and not issued at that time; it is debited for such stock when finally issued. The balance, if any, shows the par value of stock subscribed but not issued.

Accounts Debited and Credited in Connection with Transactions Relating to the Stockholders of a Corporation

341. In disposing of the transactions relating to stockholders in the books of a corporation, the names of the accounts to be debited and credited are given, following each proposition stated:

(*a*) When stock is subscribed and immediately paid for:

Cash, Dr.   *For par value of the stock sold.*
    Capital Stock, Cr.

(*b*) When stock is subscribed and not all paid for at one time:

Subscriber, Dr.   For total amount of stock subscribed, at par
   Subscription account, Cr.   value.

(*c*) When part of the subscription price is paid when stock is subscribed, or when part is paid later:

Cash, Dr.   For the amount paid in cash or otherwise.
   To Subscriber, Cr.

(*d*) When subscribed stock has been paid for in full and the stock issued:

Subscription account, Dr.   For the amount of stock issued, at par value.
   Capital Stock account, Cr.

(*e*) When stock is subscribed and payment made by cash, notes, and property—that is, if A, B, and C each subscribed for twenty shares of the D Company stock, par value $2000—A pays cash, B pays half cash and the balance by note at thirty days, and C deeds to the company land appraised at $2000:

Cash, Dr.	$2000		For amount of stock issued and paid for, at
Capital Stock, Cr.		$2000	par value, by A.
Cash, Dr.	1000		For amount of stock issued and paid for, at
Notes Receivable, Dr.	1000		par value, by B—one-half cash and one-
Capital Stock, Cr.		2000	half note.
Land, or Real Estate, or Cost of Property, Dr.	2000		For amount of stock issued and paid for, at
Capital Stock, Cr.		2000	par value, by C, in land.

In like manner, if the stock was paid for by a patent right, machinery, services, or other value, a corresponding account, under an appropriate title that would clearly set forth the nature of the transaction, should be debited, such as Patent Rights account, Machinery account, Cost of Property account, etc.

(*f*) E. F. Brand, C. W. Worth, and R. A. Drew are partners. They decide to incorporate their business, each taking stock for his interest in the old concern. If the business is to be recorded in the old books, the entry to adjust is:

E. F. Brand, Dr.   Each for the amount of his net capital in the
C. W. Worth, Dr.   firm, for which he has received stock in the
R. A. Drew, Dr.   new company, at par.
   Capital Stock, Cr.

If they desire to open a new set of books, the accounts shown by the Balance Sheet would be debited and credited for the amounts shown therein, in connection with the entry shown above.

If stock was sold to additional stockholders, the entry would in every way be similar to those given in previous examples under like conditions.

(g) A. F. Charles and R. C. Wood are partners, each with a net capital of $25,000 shown in their Capital accounts.   They decide to incorporate with a capital stock of $100,000, of which they are to receive $75,000 par value in payment of their interest in the former business, represented by their Capital accounts, the $25,000 being for good will.   The remaining $25,000 was disposed of to outsiders, at par value.   The entry to adjust is:

A. F. Charles, Capital, Dr...............	$25,000	To close Capital account
R. C. Wood, Capital, Dr...............	25,000	To close Capital account
Good Will, Dr........................	25,000	To open
Cash, Dr..........................	25,000	To transfer to new books
Capital Stock, Cr.................	$100,000	

Cost of Property is a term that is used to designate the difference between the current assets and liabilities of a business or property purchased and the purchase price.   Oftentimes, when it is desired to state the assets purchased, at their cost, on the books of the company, it is necessary to set up an account called Reserve for Capital Investment.   This reserve is sometimes referred to as Capital Reserve.

(h) When both common and preferred stock are issued to stockholders, the total amount equals the capital stock of the company, although separate accounts are opened for each; for instance, in Example (g), if the capital stock of $100,000 was divided into $50,000 preferred stock, $50,000 of common stock, instead of capital stock being credited, preferred stock would be credited $50,000, and common stock $50,000.

(i) When stock is sold at a discount—that is, if A. L. Frank and W. T. King purchase ten shares of stock, par value $100, at $75 a share, and if the shares are paid for in cash, the entry is:

Cash, Dr...........................	$1,500	
Discount on Stock Sold, Dr..............	500	
Capital Stock, Cr..................	$2,000	

(j) In the foregoing transaction, if one-half is to be paid in cash, the entry is:

A. L. Frank, Dr........................	$750	
W. T. King, Dr........................	750	
Discount on Stock Sold, Dr..............	500	
Subscription account, Cr..............	$2,000	

As the stock is paid for, Cash is debited and A. L. Frank and W. T. King are credited.   When each has paid $750 for the stock and it is issued, the entry to adjust is:

Subscription account, Dr..................	$2,000	For the par value of the stock issued.
Capital Stock, Cr..................	$2,000	

Alternative Method of Handling Capital Stock Transactions

342. Opening Entries. The preceding illustrations show a simple method of opening corporation books. Some accountants, however, prefer that the opening entries indicate fully the various steps involved in the selling of the capital stock and its issuance. To accomplish this purpose, it is necessary to set up one additional account called *Unissued Capital Stock*, and change the name of the account called Subscription to *Capital Stock Subscribed*.

Example: The J. G. Adams Company was incorporated on June 1 with an authorized Capital Stock of $100,000; June 5, received subscriptions to $75,000; June 10, subscribers paid in $50,000, of which $20,000 represented paid-up subscriptions. The opening entries are as follows:

June 1, 19—

Unissued Capital Stock	100000 —	
Capital Stock		100000 —
To record the 1,000 shares authorized by the charter		
5		
Subscribers	75000 —	
Capital Stock Subscribed		75000 —
To record the subscriptions to 750 shares of stock		
10		
Cash	50000 —	
Subscribers		50000 —
To record the payment by subscribers for stock subscribed		
10		
Capital Stock Subscribed	20000 —	
Unissued Capital Stock		20000 —
To record issue of stock to subscribers		

Appendix B

Accounting Aspects of the Federal Social Security Act

Purpose of the Act. The Federal "Social Security Act" provides among other things for unemployment insurance and old-age pensions. The Act is supported by a threefold system of payroll taxes.

The purpose of the Act is stated in the opening paragraph:

"An Act to provide for the general welfare by establishing a system of Federal old-age benefits, and by enabling the several States to make more adequate provision for aged persons, blind persons, dependent and crippled children, maternal and child welfare, public health, and the administration of their unemployment compensation laws; to establish a Social Security Board; to raise revenue; and for other purposes."

The law is a series of related measures intended to alleviate the principal causes of insecurity in our economic life by making provision for the following: (1) Old-age security, (2) unemployment compensation, (3) aid to dependent children, (4) public health measures, and (5) aid to the blind.

The purpose of this discussion is to explain the accounting aspects of those phases of the Act which have to do primarily with old-age benefits and unemployment compensation.

Social Security. The Federal Social Security Act imposes an excise tax on employers for the following purposes:

(1) Old-age pensions.
(2) Unemployment compensation.

The first excise tax is imposed equally on the employer and the employee, and is applicable to the entire payroll up to and including annual amounts of $3,000. The second excise tax is imposed on the employer, and is applicable to the total payroll, which includes all amounts paid as wages, salaries, bonuses, and commissions. Certain classes of employers and employees described in the Act are not subject to the taxes imposed by it.

Old-age Benefits. Under the Federal Social Security Act two systems are set up for aiding the aged. One is designed to help States give immediate assistance to aged individuals on the basis of immediate need; the other provides for future annuities for persons over 65, the amount depending on their wage experience.

Under the first system the law provides that the Federal Government shall aid the States in providing old-age pensions to men and women over 65 years of age who are dependent on the public for support; for this purpose the Federal Government matches the expenditures of the States. The maximum amount payable by the Federal Government is $15 per person per month.

Under the second system the law provides a plan of Federal old-age benefits computed on a reserve basis and providing for old-age security. Under this system old-age benefits are payable to every individual who has reached 65 years of age and who has fulfilled certain qualifications. Such benefits are based on wages received in any employment or in any service performed within the United States, Alaska, and Hawaii. The law does not apply to persons engaged in the following vocations: (1) Agricultural labor; (2) domestic service in a private home; (3) casual labor not in the course of the employer's trade or business; (4) service performed as an officer or member of the crew of a vessel documented under the laws of the United States or of any foreign country; (5) employees of the United States; (6) employees of a state or political subdivision; and (7) employees of certain charitable, religious, scientific, literary, or educational institutions.

Under this system old-age benefits are not payable until after January, 1942. In order to qualify for payments, a person must meet the following conditions:

(1) Be at least 65 years of age;

(2) Receive, after December 31, 1936, and before the age of 65, salary or wages amounting to not less than $2,000; and

(3) Be paid wages on some day in each of the five years after December 31, 1936, and before the age of 65.

If an employee has made contributions to the old-age pension fund and dies before the age of 65, the law provides for payments of certain sums to his estate.

The cost of the old-age benefit provisions of the law is met by two kinds of taxes; namely, (1) an income tax on employees and (2) an excise tax on employers. Both kinds of taxes are based on wages paid to employees. All employers are liable, without regard to the number of their employees, both for the income tax on employees and the excise tax on employers. Taxes were first payable as of December 31, 1936.

These taxes are based on earnings up to $3,000 per annum, beginning January 1, 1937. The schedule of the taxes is as follows:

Years	Employer's Tax	Employee's Tax	Total
1937, 1938, 1939	1%	1%	2%
1940, 1941, 1942	1½%	1½%	3%
1943, 1944, 1945	2%	2%	4%
1946, 1947, 1948	2½%	2½%	5%
1949 and thereafter	3%	3%	6%

Under the Act the employer must deduct the employee's tax from the wages paid to the employee. At the time of making the deduction, employers must notify employees in writing as to the exact amount of the tax deducted from their wages. Such notice must be given to the employees every time payment is made to them.

Unemployment Compensation. The Social Security Act provides for grants to the States for the administration of unemployment compensation laws. The law sets up certain standard requirements which must be incorporated in the State law in order that the State may secure the administrative appropriation specified in the Act.

To provide for this unemployment compensation, a uniform tax is imposed on all employers of eight or more persons. This number may be modified by the State law.

The tax is based on the employer's payroll, and the total amount of all salaries and wages paid is subject to this tax, regardless of the sum paid. The first tax payable was 1% of the employer's payroll for the year 1936. For 1937 the rate was 2%, and for 1938 and thereafter it is 3%. The employer may pay the tax in quarterly installments if he desires to do so.

The taxpayer may credit against the Federal tax, the amount of contributions paid by him into an unemployment insurance fund under a State unemployment insurance law. The total credit allowed, however, may not exceed 90% of the Federal tax.

Administration. The Act creates a Social Security Board to administer certain of the provisions relating to unemployment insurance and old-age pensions. The Board has charge of the approval of State plans under the provisions relating to grants to States for old-age assistance and for unemployment compensation administration; the certification of persons entitled to old-age pensions; and the determination and approval of grants to the States for aid to the blind. The Board is authorized to make such rules and regulations as may be necessary.

The Secretary of the Treasury has charge of the payment of old-age benefits, the collection of taxes (through the Bureau of Internal Revenue), and the payment of appropriations and grants to the States when approved by either the Social Security Board, the Secretary of Labor, or the Surgeon-General of the Public Health Service. Rules and regulations necessary for the administration of these provisions may be promulgated from time to time by the Secretary of the Treasury.

Accounts Required.   In order to provide the necessary information required by the Social Security Law, it seems desirable to keep the following accounts:

(a) Old-Age Benefit Tax.
(b) Unemployment Compensation Tax.
(c) Federal Old-Age Benefit Tax Payable
(d) Federal Unemployment Compensation Tax Payable.
(e) State Unemployment Compensation Tax Payable.

Illustrative Entries.   The Plymouth Company reports a payroll on January 31, 1938, as follows: Officers' Salaries, $400; Office Salaries, $400; Salesmen's Salaries, $200.

If no employee has earned more than $3,000 for the current year, the taxes would be computed as follows:

(a) *Old-Age Benefits.*   The tax imposed on the employer is 1% of $1,000, or $10; the tax levied on the employee is also 1% of payroll, or $10.
(b) *Unemployment Compensation.*   This tax is imposed on the employer for the total payroll, regardless of the amount earned. The rate for 1938 is 3% of the payroll, or $30.

The following journal was prepared on the assumption that the State has passed an Unemployment Compensation Law. In States in which no such law is in force, the entire tax is payable to the Federal Government.

January 31, 1938		
Office Salaries	400 —	
Officers' Salaries	400 —	
Salesmen's Salaries	200 —	
Payroll		1,000 —
To record total payroll for January		
O A B Excise Tax	10 —	
Payroll (Employees' Tax)	10 —	
O A B Tax Payable		20 —
To record taxes and set up liability		
Payroll	990 —	
Cash		990 —
To record payment of payroll		
U C Excise Tax	30 —	
Federal U C Excise Tax Payable 10%		3 —
State U C Excise Tax Payable 90%		27 —
To record taxes and set up liability		

Where a payroll record with proper distributive columns is kept, the entries could be made as follows:

Office Salaries		400 —	
Officers' Salaries		400 —	
Salesmen's Salaries		200 —	
O A B Excise Tax		10 —	
O A B Tax Payable			20 —
Cash			990 —
To record Total payroll for January			
U C Excise Tax		30 —	
Federal U C Tax Payable 10%			3 —
State U C Tax Payable 90%			27 —
To record U C Taxes and set up liability			

After posting this entry, the amount of the liability for the excise tax and the deductions from employees' salaries will be shown in one liability account as "O A B Tax Payable."

The liability for the Unemployment Compensation tax of 3% of the payroll will be recorded in two accounts. The amount due the Federal Government is called "Federal U. C. Tax Payable," and the amount due the State is called "State U. C. Tax Payable."

Payroll Record. No particular form is prescribed for keeping the records; but in order to avoid confusion and reduce the work required in preparing the returns, each employer should be careful to use only forms that will give him complete information. Such forms will include the account number, name and address of each employee, the amount owed him, the amount deducted from his salary or wages, and the amount paid him. If the state law requires the employer to make deductions from the wages of employees for a State tax, an additional column will be required to record the amount due the State. A simple form is illustrated below.

Payroll for Period Ending   193

Employee Acct. No.	Name of Employee	Salary or Wages	State Unemp. Ins. Tax	Federal Old-age Ben. Tax	Net Amount	Check No.

Index

299